Food Matters

Food Matters

A BEDFORD SPOTLIGHT READER

Holly Bauer
University of California, San Diego

Bedford/St. Martin's

Boston | New York

For Bedford/St. Martin's

Publisher for Composition: Leasa Burton
Executive Editor: John E. Sullivan III
Publishing Services Coordinator: Elizabeth M. Schaaf
Production Supervisor: Steven Dowling
Marketing Manager: Emily Rowin
Editorial Assistant: Rachel Greenhaus
Project Management: Westchester Publishing Services
Senior Art Director: Anna Palchik
Text Design: Castle Design
Cover Design: Billy Boardman
Cover Photo: Corn © MIXA/Getty
Composition: Westchester Publishing Services
Printing and Binding: RR Donnelley and Sons

President, Bedford/St. Martin's: Denise B. Wydra
Editorial Director, English and Music: Karen S. Henry
Director of Marketing: Karen R. Soeltz
Production Director: Susan W. Brown
Director of Rights and Permissions: Hilary Newman

Manufactured in the United States of America.

8 7 6 5

f

For information, write: Bedford/St. Martin's, 75 Arlington Street, Boston, MA 02116 (617-399-4000)

ISBN 978-1-4576-6096-2

About the Bedford Spotlight Reader Series

The Bedford Spotlight Reader Series is a new line of single-theme readers, each featuring Bedford's trademark care and quality. The readers in the series collect thoughtfully chosen readings sufficient for an entire writing course — about thirty-five selections — to allow instructors to provide carefully developed, high-quality instruction at an affordable price. Bedford Spotlight Readers are designed to help students make inquiries from multiple perspectives, opening up topics such as money, food, sustainability, and gender to critical analysis. An Editorial Board, made up of a dozen compositionists at schools focusing on specific themes, has assisted in the development of the series.

Spotlight Readers offer plenty of material for a composition course while keeping the price low. Combine a Spotlight Reader with a handbook or rhetoric and save 20 percent off the combined price. Or package your Spotlight Reader with *Critical Reading and Writing: A Bedford Spotlight Rhetoric*, a brief rhetoric covering the essentials of critical reading, the writing process, and research, for free (a $10 value).

Each volume in the series offers multiple perspectives on the topic and its effects on individuals and society. Chapters are built around central questions such as "What Determines What We Eat?" and "What Rituals Shape Our Gender?" and so offer numerous entry points for inquiry and discussion. High-interest readings, chosen for their suitability in the classroom, provide a mix of genres and disciplines, as well as accessible and challenging selections to allow instructors to tailor their approach to each classroom. Each chapter thus brings to light related — even surprising — questions and ideas.

A rich editorial apparatus provides a sound pedagogical foundation. A general introduction, chapter introductions, and headnotes provide context. Following each selection, writing prompts provide avenues of inquiry tuned to different levels of engagement, from reading comprehension ("Understanding the Text"), to critical analysis ("Reflection and Response"), to the kind of integrative analysis appropriate to the research paper ("Making Connections"). A Web site for the series offers support for teaching: **bedfordstmartins.com/spotlight**.

Food matters to everyone. What we eat, where it comes from, and why our food choices matter are important and increasingly visible issues in our public life. The ongoing debates about food that surround us present a real opportunity for writers; the complexities, nuances, and difficulties around the issues make food a compelling writing subject. This is surely a large part of the reason why so many professional writers focus on food. It is also a good reason for a writing course to center on what food is and why it matters. Food offers real and engaging opportunities for students to weigh in on the issues and to learn about academic writing while doing so.

The idea for this book came from my own food-focused writing course. My course was popular with students because they could see many ways to connect their own experiences and lives to the larger academic questions posed by the writing course. A course that centers on a theme like food provides a real writing opportunity: everyone has a lot of experiences with food and something at stake in the present and future food supply. There are many ways to join the conversation. Students can examine food from a variety of angles and write about it from a variety of perspectives — personal, academic, journalistic, historical, cultural, and scientific. Students can read and write personal narratives, political pieces, and academic arguments. They can analyze, explain, argue, and advocate. While it goes without saying that everyone eats food, many people do not think much about the broader implication of their food choices or the political and socioeconomic structures that help determine what they eat. Because there are not easy answers or obviously right ways to think about food, the topic offers legitimate — and interesting — contested terrain for students to explore. Thinking and writing about food helps students learn to care about ideas; ideally, they will link their own experiences with food to larger academic questions that they can explore in writing.

After all, the course in which you will use this reader is not primarily about food; food is simply the occasion for engaging in the many practices that will help make your students successful college students: careful reading, critical thinking, textual analysis, argumentation, and academic writing. This book offers meaningful ways to practice inquiry and engage with ideas. This reader's focus on food will allow you and your students to delve into the topic on various levels — personal, political, social, academic, and scientific. The book includes academic essays, journalistic accounts, personal narratives, blogs, memoirs, and arguments of various sorts. It also includes photographs from around the world and images of the federal nutrition guidelines. A range of disciplinary viewpoints are represented — science, history, social sciences, philosophy. The texts come from a variety of sources — newspapers, magazines, academic journals, government recommendations, online forums and blogs, and chapters from books. In selecting texts, I have taken care to represent a range of viewpoints, many of which are in conversation with each other. I hope that this variety of tenable and legitimate perspectives, grouped carefully to respond to the questions that frame each chapter, will help your students to weigh the evidence, consider their values and beliefs, and think through what really matters to them when they write their narratives, analyze the various authors' positions, and construct their own arguments. The inquiry-based nature of the questions that introduce each chapter, along with the headnotes that introduce the readings and the questions that follow them, will spark productive discussion and critical engagement.

Food is a pertinent contemporary topic. We all eat to stay alive, and we all have a stake in the present and future food supply — whether we care to think about it or not. This reader provides real opportunities for students to engage with and write about the multidimensional controversies and debates surrounding food. My writing courses on food have been successful in engaging students in meaningful writing activities. I hope you and your students find this material as engaging as I do.

Acknowledgments

Many people helped and supported me in the creation of this book. First, I'd like to acknowledge the students in the courses I have taught that have focused on food; these students have offered insights and ideas that have helped me understand why our food choices matter in new ways. These students have also helped me think through how to best select materials and teach a writing course that focuses on food. I also would like to thank the Warren College Writing Program instructors at UC San Diego with whom I first taught a course on food: Amanda Brovold, Ben Chapin, Vidit Desai, and Veronica Pear. We developed our course through negotiation, making careful and deliberate choices about what to include. Our lively discussions were often on my mind as I selected texts for this book. Also important to me were the conversations about teaching writing that I have had with my UC San Diego colleagues Madeleine Picciotto and Carrie Wastal.

I also would like to thank these friends with whom I chat (and learn) about food: Sam Przywitowski, Melissa Leasure, Brian Keyser, and Eugene Ahn. In their own ways, each has nourished me with thoughts, suggestions, images, recipes, ideas, and arguments that have helped me better understand the subject of food and select texts for this book.

I am also grateful to all the reviewers who provided thoughtful and detailed feedback during the book's development process: Kristina Allende, Mount St. Antonio College; Chidsey Dickson, Lynchburg College; Bill Doyle, University of Tampa; Bonnie Erwin, Wittenberg University; Ken Gillam, Missouri State University; Laura Hicks, University of Tennessee; Veronica House, University of Colorado at Boulder; Matt Paproth, Georgia Gwinnett College; Jennifer Parrott, Bucknell University; and Jennie Vaughn, Georgia State University. Thanks also to the Bedford Spotlight Series Editorial Board: Craig Bartholomaus, Metropolitan Community College, Penn Valley; Laurie Cella, Shippensburg University; Robert Cummings, University of Mississippi; Lynée Lewis Gaillet, Georgia State University; Karen Gardiner, University of Alabama; Christine Howell, Metropolitan Community College, Penn Valley; Samantha Looker, University of Wisconsin, Oshkosh; Derek Malone-France, George Washington University; Stephanie Odom, University of Texas at Austin; Megan O'Neill, Stetson University; Michelle Sidler, Auburn University; and Carrie Wastal, University of California, San Diego.

I also must acknowledge all of the wonderful people I have met at Bedford/St. Martins. Amy Shefferd, sales representative, and Lauren Arrant, humanities specialist, have provided immeasurable support. I also would like to thank Leasa Burton, publisher for composition and business and technical writing, and John Sullivan, executive editor, for encouraging me to take on this project (even when I hesitated) and for seeing me through the process. This project would not have been possible without Denise Wydra, president of Bedford/St. Martin's; Barbara Hernandez, permissions researcher; Elizabeth Schaaf, production editor; and Rachel Childs, editorial assistant. My biggest shout-out goes to Sophia Snyder, editor extraordinaire. Sophia and I have talked food and shared articles and links about food for more than a year now; she is still the first person I think of contacting when I read something interesting about food. Mostly, though, I appreciate her keen editor's eye; every single suggestion she made improved this book, and I am a better writer for having worked with her.

Last, my family deserves special recognition — especially my mother, Gayle Bauer, who taught me to value cooking, shopping for produce, and healthy eating; my late father, Walter Bauer, who used to squeeze orange juice for us every single morning and who made certain dishes (beef Wellington!) over and over again until he perfected them; and my husband, Wade Seeley, and children, Kai and Stella, who might not always be ready to help me grow and harvest the kale but who always drink it down in a breakfast smoothie. I am thankful for our rich food life and our ability to reflect on that life in conversation and in writing. I also thank them for the patience they offered when I spent large chunks of time on this project instead of with them (and our sometimes neglected vegetable garden).

Holly Bauer

You Get More Choices

B edford/St. Martin's offers resources and format choices that help you and your students get even more out of the book and your course. To learn more about or order any of the following products, contact your Bedford/St. Martin's sales representative, e-mail sales support (sales_support@bfwpub.com), or visit the Web site at **bedfordstmartins .com/spotlight/catalog**.

Choose the Flexible *Bedford e-Portfolio*

Students can collect, select, and reflect on their coursework and personalize and share their *e-portfolio* for any audience. Instructors can provide as much or as little structure as they see fit. Rubrics and learning outcomes can be aligned to student work, so instructors and programs can gather reliable and useful assessment data. Every *Bedford e-Portfolio* comes pre-loaded with *Portfolio Keeping* and *Portfolio Teaching*, by Nedra Reynolds and Elizabeth Davis. *Bedford e-Portfolio* can be purchased separately or packaged with the book at a significant discount. An activation code is required. To order *Bedford e-Portfolio* with the print book, use ISBN 978-1-4576-8018-2. Visit **bedfordstmartins.com/eportfolio**.

Watch Peer Review Work

Eli Review lets instructors scaffold their assignments in a clearer, more effective way for students — making peer review more visible and teachable. *Eli Review* can be purchased separately or packaged with the book at a significant discount. An activation code is required. To order *Eli Review* with the print book, use ISBN 978-1-4576-8014-4. Visit **bedfordstmartins.com/eli**.

Select Value Packages

Add value to your course by packaging one of the following resources with *Food Matters* at a significant discount. To learn more about package options, contact your Bedford/St. Martin's sales representative or visit **bedfordstmartins.com/spotlight/catalog**.

- *Critical Reading and Writing: A Bedford Spotlight Rhetoric,* **by Jeff Ousborne**, provides a brief overview of the critical reading, writing, and research process — for free when packaged (a $10 value). To order *Critical Reading and Writing* packaged with *Food Matters*, use ISBN 978-1-4576-8300-8.

- *EasyWriter,* **Fifth Edition, by Andrea Lunsford**, distills Andrea Lunsford's teaching and research into the essentials that today's writers need to make good choices in any rhetorical situation. To order *EasyWriter* packaged with *Food Matters,* use ISBN 978-1-4576-8321-3.

- *A Pocket Style Manual,* **Sixth Edition, by Diana Hacker and Nancy Sommers**, is a straightforward, inexpensive quick reference, with content flexible enough to suit the needs of writers in the humanities, social sciences, sciences, health professions, business, fine arts, education, and beyond. To order *A Pocket Style Manual* with *Food Matters,* use ISBN 978-1-4576-8322-0.

- *LearningCurve for Readers and Writers*, Bedford/St. Martin's adaptive quizzing program, quickly learns what students already know and helps them practice what they don't yet understand. Game-like quizzing motivates students to engage with their course, and reporting tools help teachers discern their students' needs. An activation code is required. To order LearningCurve packaged with *Food Matters,* use ISBN 978-1-4576-8017-5. For details, visit **bedfordstmartins.com /englishlearningcurve**.

- *Portfolio Keeping,* **Third Edition, by Nedra Reynolds and Elizabeth Davis**, provides all the information students need to use the portfolio method successfully in a writing course. *Portfolio Teaching,* a companion guide for instructors, provides the practical information instructors and writing program administrators need to use the portfolio method successfully in a writing course. To order *Portfolio Keeping* packaged with *Food Matters,* use ISBN 978-1-4576-8011-3.

Try *Re:Writing 2* for Fun

What's the fun of teaching writing if you can't try something new? The best collection of free writing resources on the Web, *Re:Writing 2* gives you and your students even more ways to think, watch, practice, and learn about writing concepts. Listen to Nancy Sommers on using a teacher's comments to revise. Try a logic puzzle. Consult our resources for writing centers. All free for the fun of trying it. Visit **bedfordstmartins.com/rewriting**.

Instructor Resources

You have a lot to do in your course. Bedford/St. Martin's wants to make it easy for you to find the support you need — and to get it quickly.

- **TeachingCentral** (bedfordstmartins.com/teachingcentral) offers the entire list of Bedford/St. Martin's print and online professional resources in one place. You'll find landmark reference works, sourcebooks on pedagogical issues, award-winning collections, and practical advice for the classroom — all free for instructors.

- *Bits* (bedfordbits.com) collects creative ideas for teaching a range of composition topics in an easily searchable blog format. A community of teachers — leading scholars, authors, and editors — discuss revision, research, grammar and style, technology, peer review, and much more.

- **Bedford Coursepacks** (bedfordstmartins.com/coursepacks) allow you to easily download digital materials from Bedford/ St. Martin's for your course for the most common course management systems — Blackboard, Angel, Desire2Learn, Canvas, Moodle, or Sakai.

Contents

Michael Pollan, *Eat Food: Food Defined*   9
"Only when we participate in a short food chain are we reminded every week that we are indeed part of a food chain and dependent for our health on its people and soils and integrity — on its health."

Eric Schlosser, *Why the Fries Taste Good*   20
"The distinction between artificial and natural flavors can be somewhat arbitrary and absurd, based more on how the flavor has been made than on what it actually contains."

Jill McCorkle, *Her Chee-to Heart*   31
"There's something about unnatural food colors that has always attracted me."

Camille Kingsolver, *Taking Local on the Road*   37
"It still surprises a girl like me . . . that so many young adults couldn't guess where their food comes from, or when it's in season where they live."

Lily Wong, *Eating the Hyphen*   40
"I'm not sure why I often think that to be a Chinese American means that you relish authentic Chinese food . . . but I do."

Amy Cyrex Sins, *Doberge Cake after Katrina*   45
"Even though our home was under water, and coated with mold and mud, I mourned the loss of my recipe collection."

Chapter 4 What Does It Mean to Eat Ethically? 163

"Hunger is not caused by a scarcity of food but by a scarcity of democracy."

"The reality is that the issues within our food system are rooted in historical racial and economic injustice."

"A farm built as a high-rise, with different crops or livestock layered on every floor, could conceivably allow large-scale food production right into the middle of any space-starved urban setting."

Food Matters

A BEDFORD SPOTLIGHT READER

Introduction for Students

When we sit down to write, we need something to write about, something that will stimulate our thinking and interest others, too. All writers need a topic — journalists, historians, professional writers, poets, textbook authors like myself, and students like you. This book, *Food Matters,* aims to provide you with a topic: the subject of food. It offers reading and writing assignments that ask you to consider a range of questions about what you eat, how you make food choices, what they say about you and your culture, and why they matter. The book invites you to explore what others have written about food and provides a variety of writing opportunities for students with varied interests and backgrounds.

While the subject is food, the real purpose of this book is to provide you with a set of texts that provoke critical inquiry and lead to productive writing opportunities. To write well at the college level, you need to practice critical reading and critical thinking; you need to learn to analyze and evaluate the ideas you are asked to write about. Food is a great topic for engaging in a range of interesting, complex, thought-provoking issues — and thus for practicing critical reading, thinking, and writing. This book asks you to consider a range of issues, debates, problems, and questions about food. These are matters about which I hope you will care deeply — and thus about which you will have something to say, and, more important, *something to write.*

Why Food?

Do you eat breakfast? Is it from a box, your garden, or the corner coffee shop? Do you sit down with your family to eat? Or do you eat in your car, on the bus, or walking to work or school? Have you ever thought about where your food comes from? When you buy food, do you select what is cheapest, healthiest, or most ethically produced? Do you care if it is organic or conventionally grown? Does it matter if it was produced in your area or on the other side of the globe? Do you think about whether it was picked or packaged or processed by workers who were compensated fairly? What is food anyway? Is it a product of nature? Is it a product of food science? Does it matter? What does it mean to *eat food*? Do you eat for health, for sustenance, for pleasure, or something else? Where does your food come from? Do you know? Do you care? Is eating supposed to be pleasurable? social? for survival? How should we decide what to eat? On what should our decisions be based — our sense of what is healthy, what is fast and easy, the organic food movement, the slow food movement, federal health guidelines, concern for the environment, animal rights, labor rights, or other ethical considerations?

These questions probably would not have been posed this way until recently. But an increasing number of authors and movements have propelled the topic of food to the forefront. News headlines, blogs, TV shows, documentaries, books, and advertisements bombard us with talk about food. What we eat, where it comes from, and why our food choices are important are issues that are increasingly visible in U.S. political, social, and cultural life. We are surrounded by writing about food, and the more we read about food and think through the lists of considerations, the more complex and confusing it gets.

As a student joining this conversation, you might start to wonder, as some prominent writers have, if much of what we eat can even be called food anymore. Or you might think that certain critics are too particular and their critiques are overblown. These complexities and difficulties are what make *food* such a viable writing subject. And the answers to the questions I have posed here are not necessarily easy or obvious. There is a reason so many people are writing about food, and there are lots of fruitful ways for students like you to join the conversation.

The confusion and controversy I describe — and the ongoing debates about food that accompany it — are a real opportunity for writers. I imagine that this is why so many professional writers focus on food, and I am certain that this is why writing about food is such a great opportunity for students like you to practice critical reading, thinking, and writing. In fact, it is because there are no easy answers and obviously right ways to think about food that the topic offers legitimate — and interesting — contested terrain for you to explore. There are many ways for you to join the conversation, and providing ways for you to consider, analyze, and write about real issues and controversies is the purpose of this book.

Reading, Thinking, Writing

While this book focuses on food and asks you to contemplate difficult questions, it does not advocate a particular ethical stance or political point of view. Instead, the book offers a range of tenable and legitimate positions and invites you to weigh the evidence, consider your values and beliefs, and think through what really matters to you as you construct narratives and arguments about food. After all, the course in which you will use this reader is not primarily about food. It is a writing course. Food is simply the occasion for writing.

When you sit down to write, how do you decide what to do? The authors in this book demonstrate the importance of considering the purpose and audience for which they are writing, the idea or emotion or position that they are trying to put forward or communicate, and the argument they want to make. How they write about their ideas — the form and structure their writings take — are at least partially determined by what they want to say. I encourage you to compare the genres included here and how the writers use rhetorical strategies that help them say what they want to say. I have chosen pieces that take a range of forms — essays, blogs, magazine articles, academic arguments, book excerpts, speeches, and images. Not only do the pieces offer a variety of viewpoints on food, they also offer a range of models for writing and taking a stand on a particular issue or problem.

One unique quality of this reader is that its focus on a theme allows you to delve into the topic of food on various levels — personal, political, social, academic, and scientific. As you develop a base of knowledge about the topic, a sense of the key issues, and an understanding of the values and beliefs that motivate and inform various perspectives, you will become a kind of expert; this will allow you an opportunity to write about the issues in meaningful and legitimate ways. I hope your engagement with these texts will lead you to feel that it is worth your while to figure out where you stand in relation to the narratives, arguments, and materials offered here. This book invites you to join the scholarly conversation and to position yourself in relation to real issues, ongoing problems, and contested positions.

Organization of the Book

Food Matters provides a sense of the contemporary conversations and debates about how to define food, what food is for, what determines what we eat, what constitutes eating ethically, and what the future of food looks like. Each chapter poses a question and includes a set of carefully chosen selections that speak to the question by defining key terms, providing context, or taking a position. While each chapter includes selections you can use to explore the chapter's guiding question, you might find that these are artificial divisions, as many of the selections could be responses to the lead questions of other chapters, too. I encourage you to make connections between and among them as you go.

Each chapter begins with an introduction that summarizes the themes and issues that are central to that chapter, and poses some questions to think about as you read. Headnotes for each piece introduce the author and contextualize the selection. Following the readings, three sets of questions ask you to demonstrate your understanding of the text, to respond to and reflect on it, and to make connections between the readings and conduct research. Effective responses to these questions will also take into account how your own values, beliefs, and experiences contribute to your understanding of the issues and the positions you take on them.

The book is organized around five questions for you to explore. These questions are intended as starting points for inquiry and are certainly not exhaustive in scope or topic. The first chapter, "What Is Food?," asks us to examine something that may at first seem obvious — what makes something count as "food." Scientists, philosophers, essayists, and activists complicate simple definitions and encourage us to think about what our definitions of food say about our culture, values, and identities.

The second chapter, "What Is the Purpose of Food?," explores the reasons we eat and the varied purposes food serves in our lives — purposes that extend beyond nutrition to culture, politics, environment, and pleasure. The selections explore the complex ways food nourishes us, and in so doing they tie the purpose of food to historical, cultural, spiritual, and political matters.

The third chapter, "What Determines What We Eat?," examines the complex mix of laws, social realities, health guidelines, patents, and trade agreements that help determine what we eat. While in one sense *we* determine what we eat, the selections in this chapter ask us to look at the many larger forces at work that direct what food choices are available, where, and for whom.

The fourth chapter, "What Does It Mean to Eat Ethically?," turns to an exploration of the role of ethics in determining what we eat and why our food choices matter. While acknowledging the larger political, social, cultural, and economic forces that affect food choices, the selections in this chapter ask us to consider what it means to declare that eating is necessarily a moral act.

The fifth and last chapter, "What Is the Future of Food?," identifies problems and possibilities that will influence the future of food. The readings indicate that this future will be no less complex than the present and that food production and consumption will continue to evolve as other aspects of society, culture, business, politics, and the environment change. The chapter returns to themes of previous chapters and asks us to think critically about the scope and variety of influences that will impact our food choices in the future.

While each chapter focuses on a specific aspect of food, the chapters also include a range of genres and approaches to the topic. Academic essays, journalistic accounts, personal narratives, blogs, memoirs, images, and arguments are included. A range of disciplinary viewpoints are represented — science, history, social sciences, philosophy. The texts come from a variety of sources — newspapers, magazines, academic journals, government recommendations, online forums, blogs, and chapters of books. The selections represent a range of viewpoints, which are in conversation with one another. While the questions are meant to be starting points for thinking, discussing, and writing, they are certainly not exhaustive. Thus, you might choose to pursue other fruitful connections and potential occasions for writing that this collection suggests.

Writing That Matters

A course that centers on a theme provides a real writing opportunity for you. You can examine a topic from a variety of angles and write about it from a variety of perspectives — personal, cultural, political, academic, journalistic, and ethical. Working with this book, you will read and write personal narratives, political pieces, and academic arguments. One benefit of spending a significant amount of time studying one topic is that doing so yields more substantial writing opportunities. Writing about food is a great way to stimulate your thinking about how your own experiences, values, and positions are related to larger scientific, cultural, academic, and ethical questions. While it goes without saying that everyone eats food, many people do not think much about the broader implications of their food choices. We wake up and eat breakfast, or we order a sandwich in a deli. But we do not always think or know much about where our food comes from, how it was produced, how it affects the environment, or who harvested our vegetables or raised the livestock. Food matters to all of us, and we make food choices that affect the world around us whether we are aware of this or not.

We all need to eat to stay alive (or live to eat), and we all have a stake in the present and future food supply. This book gives you opportunities to examine, analyze, and write about the major arguments in the myriad controversies and debates surrounding food. This is good practice for the other kinds of writing you will do in college, work, and life. I hope you will find this to be an engaging and productive way to practice and develop your writing skills.

 **1** | What Is Food?

Strictly speaking, food is defined as edible and nutritious substances that we consume in order to live and grow. But food can be much more than this. The many ways we define food — what we emphasize and what we ignore — say something important about our health, values, culture, identities, even our psychology. Is food a product of nature? Is it a product of science? We eat and drink many things that we probably categorize as food but are produced in labs and no longer resemble their plant and animal sources. Where does our food come from? Do we know, and do we care? What makes food "real"? What makes food "good"? And are those the same things?

The readings in this chapter ask us to consider these questions and more. Taken together, these readings complicate the definition of what food "really" is. Michael Pollan provides a set of rules on how to define food, which he differentiates from "foodish products." Eric Schlosser looks at the flavoring industry and how it affects the "authenticity" of our dining experiences. The very manufactured flavors and artificially produced "foodish products" that Pollan and Schlosser criticize are what Jill McCorkle loves most about food. Her vivid memories of her life as a junk-food junkie indicate that there might be more to authentic eating than the freshness, quality, and origin of what we eat.

In describing their own food experiences, Camille Kingsolver, Lily Wong, and Amy Cyrex Sins demonstrate that what makes food "good" or "authentic" is deeply individual and personal. For Kingsolver, good food is fresh, locally grown, and home cooked. For Wong and Sins, it is tied to aspects of their cultural identities and traditions. Such personal stories complicate the view of food as nutrition and draw attention to the myriad ways food might be said to sustain us.

Finally, Jordan Shapiro seems to suggest that defining food inevitably requires us to consider how our food defines us. Shapiro encourages us to recognize that we come from the same environment and are made of the same matter as our food. We are, very literally, what we eat. As you read this chapter, think about the various ways we define food and what our definitions of food say about who we are.

Eat Food: Food Defined

Michael Pollan

Best known for his engaging writing about food and his ability to tell complex stories that weave together politics, culture, nutrition, ethics, and history, Michael Pollan is an award-winning author, *New York Times Magazine* writer, and professor of journalism at University of California, Berkeley. He has written numerous articles and books, including four *New York Times* best sellers: *Food Rules: An Eater's Manual* (2010); *In Defense of Food: An Eater's Manifesto* (2008); *The Omnivore's Dilemma: A Natural History of Four Meals* (2006); and *The Botany of Desire: A Plant's-Eye View of the World* (2001). This selection comes from *In Defense of Food: An Eater's Manifesto*, a book in which Pollan works to define just what should count as food. He argues that "food" must be differentiated from "foodish products" and makes a case for how to define the difference.

The first time I heard the advice to "just eat food" it was in a speech by Joan Gussow, and it completely baffled me. Of course you should eat food — what else is there to eat? But Gussow, who grows much of her own food on a flood-prone finger of land jutting into the Hudson River, refuses to dignify most of the products for sale in the supermarket with that title. "In the thirty-four years I've been in the field of nutrition," she said in the same speech, "I have watched real food disappear from large areas of the supermarket and from much of the rest of the eating world." Taking food's place on the shelves has been an unending stream of foodlike substitutes, some seventeen thousand new ones every year — "products constructed largely around commerce and hope, supported by frighteningly little actual knowledge." Ordinary food is still out there, however, still being grown and even occasionally sold in the supermarket, and this ordinary food is what we should eat.

But given our current state of confusion and given the thousands of products calling themselves food, this is more easily said than done. So consider these related rules of thumb. Each proposes a different sort of map to the contemporary food landscape, but all should take you to more or less the same place.

• **DON'T EAT ANYTHING YOUR GREAT GRANDMOTHER WOULDN'T RECOGNIZE AS FOOD.** Why your great grandmother? Because at this point your mother and possibly even your grandmother is as confused as the rest of us; to be safe we need to go back at least a couple generations, to a time before the advent of most modern foods. So depending on your

age (and your grandmother), you may need to go back to your great-
or even great-great grandmother. Some nutritionists recommend
going back even further. John Yudkin, a British nutritionist whose
early alarms about the dangers of refined carbohydrates were over-
looked in the 1960s and 1970s, once advised, "Just don't eat anything
your Neolithic° ancestors wouldn't have recognized and you'll be ok."

What would shopping this way mean in the supermarket? Well,
imagine your great grandmother at your side as you roll down the
aisles. You're standing together in front of the dairy case. She picks
up a package of Go-Gurt Portable Yogurt tubes — and has no idea what
this could possibly be. Is it a food or a toothpaste? And how, exactly, do
you introduce it into your body? You could tell her it's just yogurt in a
squirtable form, yet if she read the ingredients label she would have
every reason to doubt that that was in fact the case. Sure, there's some
yogurt in there, but there are also a dozen other things that aren't remotely yogurtlike, ingredients she would probably fail to recognize
as foods of any kind, including high-fructose corn syrup, modified
corn starch, kosher gelatin, carrageenan, tri-calcium phosphate, natural and artificial flavors, vitamins, and so forth. (And there's a whole
other list of ingredients for the "berry bubblegum bash" flavoring,
containing everything but berries or bubblegum.) How did yogurt,
which in your great grandmother's day consisted simply of milk in-
oculated with a bacterial culture, ever get to be so complicated? Is a
product like Go-Gurt Portable Yogurt still a whole food? A food of any
kind? Or is it just a food product?

There are in fact hundreds of foodish products in the supermarket 5
that your ancestors simply wouldn't recognize as food: breakfast cereal bars transected by bright white veins representing, but in reality
having nothing to do with, milk; "protein waters" and "nondairy
creamer"; cheeselike foodstuffs equally innocent of any bovine° contribution; cakelike cylinders (with creamlike fillings) called Twinkies
that never grow stale. Don't eat anything incapable of rotting is another personal policy you might consider adopting.

There are many reasons to avoid eating such complicated food
products beyond the various chemical additives and corn and soy de-
rivatives they contain. One of the problems with the products of food
science is that, as Joan Gussow has pointed out, they lie to your body;
their artificial colors and flavors and synthetic sweeteners and novel

Neolithic: Of or relating to the period of human history about 10,000 years ago, when
humans began to develop agriculture and polished stone tools.
bovine: Relating to cows.

fats confound the senses we rely on to assess new foods and prepare our bodies to deal with them. Foods that lie leave us with little choice but to eat by the numbers, consulting labels rather than our senses.

It's true that foods have long been processed in order to preserve them, as when we pickle or ferment or smoke, but industrial processing aims to do much more than extend shelf life. Today foods are processed in ways specifically designed to sell us more food by pushing our evolutionary buttons—our inborn preferences for sweetness and fat and salt. These qualities are difficult to find in nature but cheap and easy for the food scientist to deploy, with the result that processing induces us to consume much more of these ecological rarities than is good for us. "Tastes great, less filling!" could be the motto for most processed foods, which are far more energy dense than most whole foods: They contain much less water, fiber, and micronutrients, and generally much more sugar and fat, making them at the same time, to coin a marketing slogan, "More fattening, less nutritious!"

The great grandma rule will help keep many of these products out of your cart. But not all of them. Because thanks to the FDA's° willingness, post-1973, to let food makers freely alter the identity of "traditional foods that everyone knows" without having to call them imitations, your great grandmother could easily be fooled into thinking that that loaf of bread or wedge of cheese is in fact a loaf of bread or a wedge of cheese. This is why we need a slightly more detailed personal policy to capture these imitation foods; to wit:

• AVOID FOOD PRODUCTS CONTAINING INGREDIENTS THAT ARE A) UNFAMILIAR, B) UNPRONOUNCEABLE, C) MORE THAN FIVE IN NUMBER, OR THAT INCLUDE D) HIGH-FRUCTOSE CORN SYRUP. None of these characteristics, not even the last one, is necessarily harmful in and of itself, but all of them are reliable markers for foods that have been highly processed to the point where they may no longer be what they purport to be. They have crossed over from foods to food products.

Consider a loaf of bread, one of the "traditional foods that every- 10 one knows" specifically singled out for protection in the 1938 imitation rule. As your grandmother could tell you, bread is traditionally made using a remarkably small number of familiar ingredients: flour, yeast, water, and a pinch of salt will do it. But industrial bread—even industrial whole-grain bread—has become a far more complicated product of modern food science (not to mention commerce and hope).

FDA: United States Food and Drug Administration, the federal agency that (among other mandates) is responsible for regulating and supervising food safety.

Here's the complete ingredients list for Sara Lee's Soft & Smooth Whole Grain White Bread. (Wait a minute — isn't "Whole Grain White Bread" a contradiction in terms? Evidently not anymore.)

Enriched bleached flour [wheat flour, malted barley flour, niacin, iron, thiamin mononitrate (vitamin B₁), riboflavin (vitamin B₂), folic acid], water, whole grains [whole wheat flour, brown rice flour (rice flour, rice bran)], high fructose corn syrup [hello!], whey, wheat gluten, yeast, cellulose. Contains 2% or less of each of the following: honey, calcium sulfate, vegetable oil (soybean and/or cottonseed oils), salt, butter (cream, salt), dough conditioners (may contain one or more of the following: mono- and diglycerides, ethoxylated mono- and diglycerides, ascorbic acid, enzymes, azodicarbonamide), guar gum, calcium propionate (preservative), distilled vinegar, yeast nutrients (monocalcium phosphate, calcium sulfate, ammonium sulfate), corn starch, natural flavor, beta-carotene (color), vitamin D₃, soy lecithin, soy flour.

There are many things you could say about this intricate loaf of "bread," but note first that even if it managed to slip by your great grandmother (because it is a loaf of bread, or at least is called one and strongly resembles one), the product fails every test proposed under rule number two: It's got unfamiliar ingredients (monoglycerides I've heard of before, but ethoxylated monoglycerides?); unpronounceable ingredients (try "azodicarbonamide"); it exceeds the maximum of five ingredients (by roughly thirty-six); and it contains high-fructose corn syrup. Sorry, Sara Lee, but your Soft & Smooth Whole Grain White Bread is not food and if not for the indulgence of the FDA could not even be labeled "bread."

Sara Lee's Soft & Smooth Whole Grain White Bread could serve as a monument to the age of nutritionism. It embodies the latest nutritional wisdom from science and government (which in its most recent food pyramid recommends that at least half our consumption of grain come from whole grains) but leavens that wisdom with the commercial recognition that American eaters (and American children in particular) have come to prefer their wheat highly refined — which is to say, cottony soft, snowy white, and exceptionally sweet on the tongue. In its marketing materials, Sara Lee treats this clash of interests as some sort of Gordian knot° — it speaks in terms of an ambitious quest to build a "no compromise" loaf — which only the most sophisticated food science could possibly cut.

Gordian knot: In legend, a knot impossible to untangle. Alexander the Great "untied" the knot by cutting it with his sword.

And so it has, with the invention of whole-grain white bread. Because the small percentage of whole grains in the bread would render it that much less sweet than, say, all-white Wonder Bread — which scarcely waits to be chewed before transforming itself into glucose — the food scientists have added high-fructose corn syrup and honey to make up the difference; to overcome the problematic heft and toothsomeness of a real whole-grain bread, they've deployed "dough conditioners," including guar gum and the aforementioned azodicarbonamide, to simulate the texture of supermarket white bread. By incorporating certain varieties of albino wheat, they've managed to maintain that deathly but apparently appealing Wonder Bread pallor.

> Only when we participate in a short food chain are we reminded every week that we are indeed part of a food chain and dependent for our health on its peoples and soils and integrity—on its health.

Who would have thought Wonder Bread would ever become an ideal of aesthetic and gustatory perfection to which bakers would actually aspire — Sara Lee's Mona Lisa?

Very often food science's efforts to make traditional foods more nu- 15 tritious make them much more complicated, but not necessarily any better for you. To make dairy products low fat, it's not enough to remove the fat. You then have to go to great lengths to preserve the body or creamy texture by working in all kinds of food additives. In the case of low-fat or skim milk, that usually means adding powdered milk. But powdered milk contains oxidized cholesterol, which scientists believe is much worse for your arteries than ordinary cholesterol, so food makers sometimes compensate by adding antioxidants, further complicating what had been a simple one-ingredient whole food. Also, removing the fat makes it that much harder for your body to absorb the fat-soluble vitamins that are one of the reasons to drink milk in the first place.

All this heroic and occasionally counterproductive food science has been undertaken in the name of our health — so that Sara Lee can add to its plastic wrapper the magic words "good source of whole grain" or a food company can ballyhoo the even more magic words "low fat." Which brings us to a related food policy that may at first sound counterintuitive to a health-conscious eater:

• **AVOID FOOD PRODUCTS THAT MAKE HEALTH CLAIMS.** For a food product to make health claims on its package it must first *have* a package, so right off the bat it's more likely to be a processed than a whole food.

Generally speaking, it is only the big food companies that have the wherewithal to secure FDA-approved health claims for their products and then trumpet them to the world. Recently, however, some of the tonier fruits and nuts have begun boasting about their health-enhancing properties, and there will surely be more as each crop council scrounges together the money to commission its own scientific study. Because all plants contain antioxidants, all these studies are guaranteed to find *some*thing on which to base a health oriented marketing campaign.

But for the most part it is the products of food science that make the boldest health claims, and these are often founded on incomplete and often erroneous science — the dubious fruits of nutritionism. Don't forget that trans-fat-rich margarine, one of the first industrial foods to claim it was healthier than the traditional food it replaced, turned out to give people heart attacks. Since that debacle, the FDA, under tremendous pressure from industry, has made it only easier for food companies to make increasingly doubtful health claims, such as the one Frito-Lay now puts on some of its chips — that eating them is somehow good for your heart. If you bother to read the health claims closely (as food marketers make sure consumers seldom do), you will find that there is often considerably less to them than meets the eye.

Consider a recent "qualified" health claim approved by the FDA for (don't laugh) corn oil. ("Qualified" is a whole new category of health claim, introduced in 2002 at the behest of industry.) Corn oil, you may recall, is particularly high in the omega-6 fatty acids we're already consuming far too many of.

> Very limited and preliminary scientific evidence suggests that eating about one tablespoon (16 grams) of corn oil daily may reduce the risk of heart disease due to the unsaturated fat content in corn oil.

The tablespoon is a particularly rich touch, conjuring images of moms administering medicine, or perhaps cod-liver oil, to their children. But what the FDA gives with one hand, it takes away with the other. Here's the small-print "qualification" of this already notably diffident health claim:

> [The] FDA concludes that there is little scientific evidence supporting this claim.

And then to make matters still more perplexing:

> To achieve this possible benefit, corn oil is to replace a similar amount of saturated fat and not increase the total number of calories you eat in a day.

This little masterpiece of pseudoscientific bureaucratese was extracted from the FDA by the manufacturer of Mazola corn oil. It would appear that "qualified" is an official FDA euphemism for "all but meaningless." Though someone might have let the consumer in on this game: The FDA's own research indicates that consumers have no idea what to make of qualified health claims (how would they?), and its rules allow companies to promote the claims pretty much any way they want — they can use really big type for the claim, for example, and then print the disclaimers in teeny-tiny type. No doubt we can look forward to a qualified health claim for high-fructose corn syrup, a tablespoon of which probably does contribute to your health — as long as it replaces a comparable amount of, say, poison in your diet and doesn't increase the total number of calories you eat in a day.

When corn oil and chips and sugary breakfast cereals can all boast being good for your heart, health claims have become hopelessly corrupt. The American Heart Association currently bestows (for a fee) its heart-healthy seal of approval on Lucky Charms, Cocoa Puffs, and Trix cereals, Yoo-hoo lite chocolate drink, and Healthy Choice's Premium Caramel Swirl Ice Cream Sandwich — this at a time when scientists are coming to recognize that dietary sugar probably plays a more important role in heart disease than dietary fat. Meanwhile, the genuinely heart-healthy whole foods in the produce section, lacking the financial and political clout of the packaged goods a few aisles over, are mute. But don't take the silence of the yams as a sign that they have nothing valuable to say about health.

Bogus health claims and food science have made supermarkets particularly treacherous places to shop for real food, which suggests two further rules:

• **SHOP THE PERIPHERIES OF THE SUPERMARKET AND STAY OUT OF THE** 25 **MIDDLE.** Most supermarkets are laid out the same way: Processed food products dominate the center aisles of the store while the cases of ostensibly fresh food — dairy, produce, meat, and fish — line the walls. If you keep to the edges of the store you'll be that much more likely to wind up with real food in your shopping cart. The strategy is not foolproof, however, because things like high-fructose corn syrup have slipped into the dairy case under cover of Go-Gurt and such. So consider a more radical strategy:

• **GET OUT OF THE SUPERMARKET WHENEVER POSSIBLE.** You won't find *any* high-fructose corn syrup at the farmers' market. You also won't find any elaborately processed food products, any packages with long lists of unpronounceable ingredients or dubious health claims, nothing microwavable, and, perhaps best of all, no old food from far away. What you *will* find are fresh whole foods picked at the peak of their taste and nutritional quality — precisely the kind your great grandmother, or even your Neolithic ancestors, would easily have recognized as food.

Indeed, the surest way to escape the Western diet is simply to depart the realms it rules: the supermarket, the convenience store, and the fast-food outlet. It is hard to eat badly from the farmers' market, from a CSA box (community-supported agriculture, an increasingly popular scheme in which you subscribe to a farm and receive a weekly box of produce), or from your garden. The number of farmers' markets has more than doubled in the last ten years, to more than four thousand, making it one of the fastest-growing segments of the food marketplace. It is true that most farmers' markets operate only seasonally, and you won't find everything you need there. But buying as much as you can from the farmers' market, or directly from the farm when that's an option, is a simple act with a host of profound consequences for your health as well as for the health of the food chain you've now joined.

When you eat from the farmers' market, you automatically eat food that is in season, which is usually when it is most nutritious. Eating in season also tends to diversify your diet — because you can't buy strawberries or broccoli or potatoes twelve months of the year, you'll find yourself experimenting with other foods when they come into the market. The CSA box does an even better job of forcing you out of your dietary rut because you'll find things in your weekly allotment that you would never buy on your own. Whether it's a rutabaga or an unfamiliar winter squash, the CSA box's contents invariably send you to your cookbooks to figure out what in the world to do with them. Cooking is one of the most important health consequences of buying food from local farmers; for one thing, when you cook at home you seldom find yourself reaching for the ethoxylated diglycerides or high-fructose corn syrup. . . .

To shop at a farmers' market or sign up with a CSA is to join a short food chain, and that has several implications for your health. Local produce is typically picked ripe and is fresher than supermarket produce, and for those reasons it should be tastier and more nutritious. As for supermarket organic produce, it too is likely to have come from far away — from the industrial organic farms of California or, increasingly, China.[1] And while it's true that the organic

---

[1] One recent study found that the average item of organic produce in the supermarket had actually traveled farther from the farm than the average item of conventional produce. [Pollan's note.]

label guarantees that no synthetic pesticides or fertilizers have been used to produce the food, many, if not most, of the small farms that supply farmers' markets are organic in everything but name. To survive in the farmers' market or CSA economy, a farm will need to be highly diversified, and a diversified farm usually has little need for pesticides; it's the big monocultures that can't survive without them.[2]

If you're concerned about chemicals in your produce, you can sim- 30 ply ask the farmer at the market how he or she deals with pests and fertility and begin the sort of conversation between producers and consumers that, in the end, is the best guarantee of quality in your food. So many of the problems of the industrial food chain stem from its length and complexity. A wall of ignorance intervenes between consumers and producers, and that wall fosters a certain careless- ness on both sides. Farmers can lose sight of the fact that they're growing food for actual eaters rather than for middlemen, and con- sumers can easily forget that growing good food takes care and hard work. In a long food chain, the story and identity of the food (Who grew it? Where and how was it grown?) disappear into the undiffer- entiated stream of commodities, so that the only information com- municated between consumers and producers is a price. In a short food chain, eaters can make their needs and desires known to the farmer, and farmers can impress on eaters the distinctions between ordinary and exceptional food, and the many reasons why excep- tional food is worth what it costs. Food reclaims its story, and some of its nobility, when the person who grew it hands it to you. So here's a subclause to the get-out-of-the-supermarket rule: *Shake the hand that feeds you.*

As soon as you do, accountability becomes once again a matter of relationships instead of regulation or labeling or legal liability. Food safety didn't become a national or global problem until the indus- trialization of the food chain attenuated° the relationships between food producers and eaters. That was the story Upton Sinclair told about the Beef Trust in 1906, and it's the story unfolding in China today, where the rapid industrialization of the food system is lead- ing to alarming breakdowns in food safety and integrity. Regulation

---

attenuated: Made smaller, thinner, or weaker.

[2]Wendell Berry put the problem of monoculture with admirable brevity and clarity in his essay "The Pleasures of Eating": "But as scale increases, diversity declines; as diversity declines, so does health; as health declines, the dependence on drugs and chemicals necessarily increases." [Pollan's note.]

is an imperfect substitute for the accountability, and trust, built into a market in which food producers meet the gaze of eaters and vice versa. Only when we participate in a short food chain are we reminded every week that we are indeed part of a food chain and dependent for our health on its peoples and soils and integrity — on its health.

"Eating is an agricultural act," Wendell Berry famously wrote, by which he meant that we are not just passive consumers of food but cocreators of the systems that feed us. Depending on how we spend them, our food dollars can either go to support a food industry devoted to quantity and convenience and "value" or they can nourish a food chain organized around *values* — values like quality and health. Yes, shopping this way takes more money and effort, but as soon as you begin to treat that expenditure not just as shopping but also as a kind of vote — a vote for health in the largest sense — food no longer seems like the smartest place to economize.

Understanding the Text

1. What is the "industrial food chain"?
2. What are "foodish products"? What reasons does Pollan offer for avoiding "foodish products"?
3. What are the differences between processed and whole foods? Why does this distinction matter to Pollan?

Reflection and Response

4. What does the advice to "just eat food" mean to you?
5. Does Pollan think we can trust food labels? Explain.
6. Select a packaged or processed food product that you like to eat, and examine the ingredients. Would Pollan classify your item as "food"? Why or why not? Do you classify it as "food"? Explain.
7. How would following Pollan's advice change your eating patterns? How might you benefit? What would you give up?

Making Connections

8. How might Pollan evaluate the Food Pyramid and Food Plate developed by the United States Department of Agriculture (p. 112)? Locate textual evidence to support your case.
9. Pollan quotes Wendell Berry, author of "The Pleasures of Eating" (p. 64), in the last paragraph of this selection. What ideals do Pollan and Berry share? What selections in this book complicate these ideals? How?

10. Prince Charles of Wales ("On the Future of Food," p. 222) argues that the future of food will depend on our ability to recognize the complex interrelationships among food production, health, sustainability, and the global food supply. What would Prince Charles of Wales say about Pollan's rules? What role might they play in promoting Prince Charles's agenda?

Why the Fries Taste Good

Eric Schlosser

Eric Schlosser is an award-winning journalist best known for his exhaustive research on the fast food industry and his best-selling book *Fast Food Nation* (2001), which began as a two-part article in *Rolling Stone*. Schlosser began his writing career as a fiction writer, then turned to nonfiction and became a correspondent for the *Atlantic Monthly*, where he is still a contributor. More recently, he appeared in the documentary *Food, Inc.*, which draws on his searing critiques of the food industry to demonstrate their potential to damage our health and the environment. In this essay, excerpted from *Fast Food Nation*, Schlosser discusses how McDonald's flavors its fries as an example of larger industry flavoring practices. He offers an in-depth look at the flavor industry and how it differentiates "natural" and "artificial" flavorings.

The taste of McDonald's french fries has long been praised by customers, competitors, and even food critics. James Beard loved McDonald's fries. Their distinctive taste does not stem from the type of potatoes that McDonald's buys, the technology that processes them, or the restaurant equipment that fries them. Other chains buy their french fries from the same large processing companies, use Russet Burbanks, and have similar fryers in their restaurant kitchens. The taste of a fast food fry is largely determined by the cooking oil. For decades, McDonald's cooked its french fries in a mixture of about 7 percent cottonseed oil and 93 percent beef tallow. The mix gave the fries their unique flavor — and more saturated beef fat per ounce than a McDonald's hamburger.

Amid a barrage of criticism over the amount of cholesterol in their fries, McDonald's switched to pure vegetable oil in 1990. The switch presented the company with an enormous challenge: how to make fries that subtly taste like beef without cooking them in tallow. A look at the ingredients now used in the preparation of McDonald's french fries suggests how the problem was solved. At the end of the list is a seemingly innocuous, yet oddly mysterious phrase: "natural flavor." That ingredient helps to explain not only why the fries taste so good, but also why most fast food — indeed, most of the food Americans eat today — tastes the way it does.

Open your refrigerator, your freezer, your kitchen cupboards, and look at the labels on your food. You'll find "natural flavor" or "artificial flavor" in just about every list of ingredients. The similarities between these two broad categories of flavor are far more significant than their differences. Both are man-made additives that give most processed food its taste. The initial purchase of a food item may be driven by its packaging or appearance, but subsequent purchases are determined mainly by its taste. About 90 percent of the money that Americans spend on food is used to buy processed food. But the canning, freezing, and dehydrating techniques used to process food destroy most of its flavor. Since the end of World War II, a vast industry has arisen in the United States to make processed food palatable. Without this flavor industry, today's fast food industry could not exist. The names of the leading American fast food chains and their best-selling menu items have become famous worldwide, embedded in our popular culture. Few people, however, can name the companies that manufacture fast food's taste.

The flavor industry is highly secretive. Its leading companies will not divulge the precise formulas of flavor compounds or the identities of clients. The secrecy is deemed essential for protecting the reputation of beloved brands. The fast food chains, understandably, would like the public to believe that the flavors of their food somehow originate in their restaurant kitchens, not in distant factories run by other firms.

The New Jersey Turnpike runs through the heart of the flavor 5 industry, an industrial corridor dotted with refineries and chemical plants. International Flavors & Fragrances (IFF), the world's largest flavor company, has a manufacturing facility off Exit 8A in Dayton, New Jersey; Givaudan, the world's second-largest flavor company, has a plant in East Hanover. Haarmann & Reimer, the largest German flavor company, has a plant in Teterboro, as does Takasago, the largest Japanese flavor company. Flavor Dynamics has a plant in South Plainfield; Frutarom is in North Bergen; Elan Chemical is in Newark. Dozens of companies manufacture flavors in New Jersey industrial parks between Teaneck and South Brunswick. Indeed, the area produces about two-thirds of the flavor additives sold in the United States.

The IFF plant in Dayton is a huge pale blue building with a modern office complex attached to the front. It sits in an industrial park, not far from a BASF plastics factory, a Jolly French Toast factory, and a plant that manufactures Liz Claiborne cosmetics. Dozens of tractor-trailers were parked at the IFF loading dock the afternoon I visited, and a thin cloud of steam floated from the chimney. Before entering the plant, I signed a nondisclosure form, promising not to reveal the brand names of products that contain IFF flavors. The place reminded me of Willy Wonka's chocolate factory. Wonderful smells drifted through the hallways, men and women in neat white lab coats cheerfully went about their work, and hundreds of little glass bottles sat on laboratory tables and shelves. The bottles contained powerful but fragile flavor chemicals, shielded from light by the brown glass and the round plastic caps shut tight. The long chemical names on the little white labels were as mystifying to me as medieval Latin. They were the odd-sounding names of things that would be mixed and poured and turned into new substances, like magic potions.

I was not invited to see the manufacturing areas of the IFF plant, where it was thought I might discover trade secrets. Instead, I toured various laboratories and pilot kitchens, where the flavors of well-established brands are tested or adjusted, and where whole new flavors are created. IFF's snack and savory lab is responsible for the flavor of potato chips, corn chips, breads, crackers, breakfast cereals, and pet food. The confectionery lab devises the flavor for ice cream, cookies, candies, toothpastes, mouthwashes, and antacids. Everywhere I looked, I saw famous, widely advertised products sitting on laboratory desks and tables. The beverage lab is full of brightly colored liquids in clear bottles. It comes up with the flavor for popular soft drinks, sport drinks, bottled teas, and wine coolers, for all-natural juice drinks, organic soy drinks, beers, and malt liquors. In one pilot kitchen I saw a dapper chemist, a middle-aged man with an elegant tie beneath his lab coat, carefully preparing a batch of cookies with white frosting and pink-and-white sprinkles. In another pilot kitchen I saw a pizza oven, a grill, a milk-shake machine, and a french fryer identical to those I'd seen behind the counter at countless fast food restaurants.

In addition to being the world's largest flavor company, IFF manufactures the smell of six of the ten best-selling fine perfumes in the United States. It makes the smell of Estée Lauder's Beautiful, Clinique's Happy, Ralph Lauren's Polo, and Calvin Klein's Eternity. It also makes the smell of household products such as deodorant, dishwashing detergent, bath soap, shampoo, furniture polish, and floor wax. All of these aromas are made through the same basic process: the manipulation of volatile chemicals to create a particular smell. The basic science behind the scent of your shaving cream is the same as that governing the flavor of your TV dinner.

The aroma of a food can be responsible for as much as 90 percent of its flavor. Scientists now believe that human beings acquired the sense of taste as a way to avoid being poisoned. Edible plants generally taste sweet; deadly ones, bitter. Taste is supposed to help us differentiate food that's good for us from food that's not. The taste buds on our tongues can detect the presence of half a dozen or so basic tastes, including: sweet, sour, bitter, salty, astringent, and umami (a taste discovered by Japanese researchers, a rich and full sense of deliciousness triggered by amino acids in foods such as shellfish, mushrooms, potatoes, and seaweed). Taste buds offer a relatively limited means of detection, however, compared to the human olfactory system, which can perceive thousands of different chemical aromas. Indeed "flavor" is primarily the smell of gases being released by the chemicals you've just put in your mouth.

The act of drinking, sucking, or chewing a substance releases its 10 volatile gases. They flow out of the mouth and up the nostrils, or up the passageway in the back of the mouth, to a thin layer of nerve cells called the olfactory epithelium, located at the base of the nose, right between the eyes. The brain combines the complex smell signals from the epithelium with the simple taste signals from the tongue, assigns a flavor to what's in your mouth, and decides if it's something you want to eat.

Babies like sweet tastes and reject bitter ones; we know this because scientists have rubbed various flavors inside the mouths of infants and then recorded their facial reactions. A person's food preferences, like his or her personality, are formed during the first few years of life, through a process of socialization. Toddlers can learn to enjoy hot and spicy food, bland health food, or fast food, depending upon what the people around them eat. The human sense of smell is still not fully understood and can be greatly affected by psychological factors and expectations. The color of a food can determine the perception of its taste. The mind filters out the overwhelming majority of chemical aromas that surround us, focusing intently on some, ignoring others. People can grow accustomed to bad smells or good smells; they stop noticing what once seemed overpowering. Aroma and memory are somehow inextricably linked. A smell can suddenly evoke a long-forgotten moment. The flavors of childhood foods seem to leave an indelible mark, and adults often return to them, without always knowing why. These "comfort foods" become a source of pleasure and reassurance, a fact that fast food chains work hard to promote. Childhood memories of Happy Meals can translate into frequent adult visits to McDonald's, like those of the chain's "heavy users," the customers who eat there four or five times a week.

The human craving for flavor has been a largely unacknowledged and unexamined force in history. Royal empires have been built, unexplored lands have been traversed, great religions and philosophies have been forever changed by the spice trade. In 1492 Christopher Columbus set sail to find seasoning. Today the influence of flavor in the world marketplace is no less decisive. The rise and fall of corporate empires — of soft drink companies, snack food companies, and fast food chains — is frequently determined by how their products taste.

The flavor industry emerged in the mid-nineteenth century, as processed foods began to be manufactured on a large scale. Recognizing the need for flavor additives, the early food processors turned to perfume companies that had years of experience working with essential oils and volatile aromas. The great perfume houses of England, France, and the Netherlands produced many of the first flavor compounds. In the early part of the twentieth century, Germany's powerful chemical industry assumed the technological lead in flavor production. Legend has it that a German scientist discovered methyl anthranilate, one of the first artificial flavors, by accident while mixing chemicals in his laboratory. Suddenly the lab was filled with the sweet smell of grapes. Methyl anthranilate later became the chief flavoring compound of grape Kool-Aid. After World War II, much of the perfume industry shifted from Europe to the United States, settling in New York City near the garment district and the fashion houses. The flavor industry came with it, subsequently moving to New Jersey to gain more plant capacity. Man-made flavor additives were used mainly in baked goods, candies, and sodas until the 1950s, when sales of processed food began to soar. The invention of gas chromatographs and mass spectrometers — machines capable of detecting volatile gases at low levels — vastly increased the number of flavors that could be synthesized. By the mid-1960s the American flavor industry was churning out compounds to supply the taste of Pop Tarts, Bac-Os, Tab, Tang, Filet-O-Fish sandwiches, and literally thousands of other new foods.

The American flavor industry now has annual revenues of about $1.4 billion. Approximately ten thousand new processed food products are introduced every year in the United States. Almost all of them require flavor additives. And about nine out of every ten of these new food products fail. The latest flavor innovations and corporate realignments are heralded in publications such as *Food Chemical News, Food Engineering, Chemical Market Reporter,* and *Food Product Design.* The growth of IFF has mirrored that of the flavor industry as a whole. IFF was formed in 1958, through the merger of two small companies. Its annual revenues have grown almost fifteenfold since the early 1970s, and it now has manufacturing facilities in twenty countries.

The quality that people seek most of all in a food, its flavor, is usu- 15 ally present in a quantity too infinitesimal to be measured by any traditional culinary terms such as ounces or teaspoons. Today's sophisticated spectrometers, gas chromatographs, and headspace vapor analyzers provide a detailed map of a food's flavor components, detecting chemical aromas in amounts as low as one part per billion. The human nose, however, is still more sensitive than any machine yet invented. A nose can detect aromas present in quantities of a few parts per trillion — an amount equivalent to 0.000000000003 percent. Complex aromas, like those of coffee or roasted meat, may be composed of volatile gases from nearly a thousand different chemicals. The smell of a strawberry arises from the interaction of at least 350 different chemicals that are present in minute amounts. The chemical that provides the dominant flavor of bell pepper can be tasted in amounts as low as .02 parts per billion; one drop is sufficient to add flavor to five average size swimming pools. The flavor additive usually comes last, or second to last, in a processed food's list of ingredients (chemicals that add color are frequently used in even smaller amounts). As a result, the flavor of a processed food often costs less than its packaging. Soft drinks contain a larger proportion of flavor additives than most products. The flavor in a twelve-ounce can of Coke costs about half a cent.

The Food and Drug Administration does not require flavor companies to disclose the ingredients of their additives, so long as all the chemicals are considered by the agency to be GRAS (Generally Regarded As Safe). This lack of public disclosure enables the companies to maintain the secrecy of their formulas. It also hides the fact that flavor compounds sometimes contain more ingredients than the foods being given their taste. The ubiquitous phrase "artificial strawberry flavor" gives little hint of the chemical wizardry and manufacturing skill that can make a highly processed food taste like a strawberry.

A typical artificial strawberry flavor, like the kind found in a Burger King strawberry milk shake, contains the following ingredients: amyl acetate, amyl butyrate, amyl valerate, anethol, anisyl formate, benzyl acetate, benzyl isobutyrate, butyric acid, cinnamyl isobutyrate, cinnamyl valerate, cognac essential oil, diacetyl, dipropyl ketone, ethyl acetate, ethyl amylketone, ethyl butyrate, ethyl cinnamate, ethyl heptanoate, ethyl heptylate, ethyl lactate, ethyl methylphenylglycidate, ethyl nitrate, ethyl propionate, ethyl valerate, heliotropin, hydroxyphrenyl 2-butanone (10 percent solution in alcohol), α-ionone, isobutyl anthranilate, isobutyl butyrate, lemon essential oil, maltol, 4-methylacetophenone, methyl anthranilate, methyl benzoate, methyl cinnamate, methyl heptine carbonate, methyl naphthyl ketone, methyl salicylate, mint essential oil, neroli essential oil, nerolin, neryl isobutyrate, orris butter, phenethyl alcohol, rose, rum ether, γ-undecalactone, vanillin, and solvent.

Although flavors usually arise from a mixture of many different volatile chemicals, a single compound often supplies the dominant aroma. Smelled alone, that chemical provides an unmistakable sense of the food. Ethyl-2-methyl butyrate, for example, smells just like an apple. Today's highly processed foods offer a blank palette: whatever chemicals you add to them will give them specific tastes. Adding methyl-2-peridylketone makes something taste like popcorn. Adding ethyl-3-hydroxybutanoate makes it taste like marshmallow. The possibilities are now almost limitless. Without affecting the appearance or nutritional value, processed foods could even be made with aroma chemicals such as hexanal (the smell of freshly cut grass) or 3-methyl butanoic acid (the smell of body odor).

> The distinction between artificial and natural flavors can be somewhat arbitrary and absurd, based more on how the flavor has been made than on what it actually contains.

The 1960s were the heyday of artificial flavors. The synthetic versions of flavor compounds were not subtle, but they did not need to be, given the nature of most processed food. For the past twenty years food processors have tried hard to use only "natural flavors" in their products. According to the FDA, these must be derived entirely from natural sources — from herbs, spices, fruits, vegetables, beef, chicken, yeast, bark, roots, etc. Consumers prefer to see natural flavors on a label, out of a belief that they are healthier. The distinction between artificial and natural flavors can be somewhat arbitrary and absurd, based more on how the flavor has been made than on what it actually contains. "A natural flavor," says Terry Acree, a professor of food science technology at Cornell University, "is a flavor that's been derived with an out-of-date technology." Natural flavors and artificial flavors sometimes contain exactly the same chemicals, produced through different methods. Amyl acetate, for example, provides the dominant note of banana flavor. When you distill it from bananas with a solvent, amyl acetate is a natural flavor. When you produce it by mixing vinegar with amyl alcohol, adding sulfuric acid as a catalyst, amyl acetate is an artificial flavor.

Either way it smells and tastes the same. The phrase "natural flavor" is now listed among the ingredients of everything from Stonyfield Farm Organic Strawberry Yogurt to Taco Bell Hot Taco Sauce.

A natural flavor is not necessarily healthier or purer than an 20 artificial one. When almond flavor (benzaldehyde) is derived from natural sources, such as peach and apricot pits, it contains traces of hydrogen cyanide, a deadly poison. Benzaldehyde derived through a different process — by mixing oil of clove and the banana flavor, amyl acetate — does not contain any cyanide. Nevertheless, it is legally considered an artificial flavor and sells at a much lower price. Natural and artificial flavors are now manufactured at the same chemical plants, places that few people would associate with Mother Nature. Calling any of these flavors "natural" requires a flexible attitude toward the English language and a fair amount of irony.

The small and elite group of scientists who create most of the flavor in most of the food now consumed in the United States are called "flavorists." They draw upon a number of disciplines in their work: biology, psychology, physiology, and organic chemistry. A flavorist is a chemist with a trained nose and a poetic sensibility. Flavors are created by blending scores of different chemicals in tiny amounts, a process governed by scientific principles but demanding a fair amount of art. In an age when delicate aromas, subtle flavors, and microwave ovens do not easily coexist, the job of the flavorist is to conjure illusions about processed food and, in the words of one flavor company's literature, to ensure "consumer likeability." The flavorists with whom I spoke were charming, cosmopolitan, and ironic. They were also discreet, in keeping with the dictates of their trade. They were the sort of scientist who not only enjoyed fine wine, but could also tell you the chemicals that gave each vintage its unique aroma. One flavorist compared his work to composing music. A well-made flavor compound will have a "top note," followed by a "dry-down," and a "leveling-off," with different chemicals responsible for each stage. The taste of a food can be radically altered by minute changes in the flavoring mix. "A little odor goes a long way," one flavorist said.

In order to give a processed food the proper taste, a flavorist must always consider the food's "mouthfeel" — the unique combination of textures and chemical interactions that affects how the flavor is perceived. The mouthfeel can be adjusted through the use of various fats, gums, starches, emulsifiers, and stabilizers. The aroma chemicals of a food can be precisely analyzed, but mouthfeel is much harder to measure. How does one quantify a french fry's crispness? Food technologists are now conducting basic research in rheology, a branch of physics that examines the flow and deformation of materials. A number of companies sell sophisticated devices that attempt to measure mouthfeel. The Universal TA-XT2 Texture Analyzer, produced by the Texture Technologies Corporation, performs calculations based on data derived from twenty-five separate probes. It is essentially a mechanical mouth. It gauges the most important rheological properties of a food — the bounce, creep, breaking point, density, crunchiness, chewiness, gumminess, lumpiness, rubberiness, springiness, slipperiness, smoothness, softness, wetness, juiciness, spreadability, spring-back, and tackiness.

Some of the most important advances in flavor manufacturing are now occurring in the field of biotechnology. Complex flavors are being made through fermentation, enzyme reactions, fungal cultures, and tissue cultures. All of the flavors being created through these methods — including the ones being synthesized by funguses — are considered natural flavors by the FDA. The new enzyme-based processes are responsible for extremely lifelike dairy flavors. One company now offers not just butter flavor, but also fresh creamy butter, cheesy butter, milky butter, savory melted butter, and super-concentrated butter flavor, in liquid or powder form. The development of new fermentation techniques, as well as new techniques for heating mixtures of sugar and amino acids, have led to the creation of much more realistic meat flavors. The McDonald's Corporation will not reveal the exact origin of the natural flavor added to its french fries. In response to inquiries from *Vegetarian Journal*, however, McDonald's did acknowledge that its fries derive some of their characteristic flavor from "animal products."

Other popular fast foods derive their flavor from unexpected sources. Wendy's Grilled Chicken Sandwich, for example, contains beef extracts. Burger King's BK Broiler Chicken Breast Patty contains "natural smoke flavor." A firm called Red Arrow Products Company specializes in smoke flavor, which is added to barbecue sauces and processed meats. Red Arrow manufactures natural smoke flavor by charring sawdust and capturing the aroma chemicals released into the air. The smoke is captured in water and then bottled, so that other companies can sell food which seems to have been cooked over a fire.

In a meeting room at IFF, Brian Grainger let me sample some of 25 the company's flavors. It was an unusual taste test; there wasn't any food to taste. Grainger is a senior flavorist at IFF, a soft-spoken chemist with graying hair, an English accent, and a fondness for understatement. He could easily be mistaken for a British diplomat or the owner of a West End brasserie with two Michelin stars. Like many in the flavor industry, he has an Old World, old-fashioned sensibility which seems out of step with our brand-conscious, egocentric age. When I suggested that IFF should put its own logo on the products that contain its flavors — instead of allowing other brands to enjoy the consumer loyalty and affection inspired by those flavors — Grainger politely disagreed, assuring me such a thing would never be done. In the absence of public credit or acclaim, the small and secretive fraternity of flavor chemists praises one another's work. Grainger can often tell, by analyzing the flavor formula of a product, which of his counterparts at a rival firm devised it. And he enjoys walking down supermarket aisles, looking at the many products that contain his flavors, even if no one else knows it.

Grainger had brought a dozen small glass bottles from the lab. After he opened each bottle, I dipped a fragrance testing filter into it. The filters were long white strips of paper designed to absorb aroma chemicals without producing off-notes. Before placing the strips of paper before my nose, I closed my eyes. Then I inhaled deeply, and one food after another was conjured from the glass bottles. I smelled fresh cherries, black olives, sautéed onions, and shrimp. Grainger's most remarkable creation took me by surprise. After closing my eyes, I suddenly smelled a grilled hamburger. The aroma was uncanny, almost miraculous. It smelled like someone in the room was flipping burgers on a hot grill. But when I opened my eyes, there was just a narrow strip of white paper and a smiling flavorist.

Understanding the Text

1. How are "artificial" and "natural" flavors similar? How are they different?
2. How does Schlosser describe the process through which food flavors are made?
3. According to Schlosser, what role does "taste" play in our health?

Reflection and Response

4. Why does Schlosser conclude that the distinction between artificial and natural flavors is often "arbitrary and absurd"? Do you agree or disagree? Explain.
5. Why is the production of flavors so secretive? What are the potential benefits of the secrecy to consumers? What are the potential drawbacks?
6. Does Schlosser's article make you think about french fries, fast food, or processed food flavors differently? Will his at-times searing critique change how you eat? Explain.

Making Connections

7. Why is the flavor industry so important? What role does the flavor industry play in what Michael Pollan calls the "industrial food chain" ("Eat Food: Food Defined," p. 9)? Using your campus library resources, locate two external sources to help support your response.

8. Compare Schlosser's description of the flavor industry to Donald L. Barlett and James B. Steele's description of Monsanto and the patented seed industry ("Monsanto's Harvest of Fear," p. 131). What commonalities exist? What differences do you see? How do these industries affect consumers?

Her Chee-to Heart

Jill McCorkle

Jill McCorkle is an award-winning novelist, essayist, and short story writer who has published many collections and novels, most recently *Life after Life*. Several of her stories have been chosen for inclusion in *Best American Short Stories* collections. She teaches creative writing in the MFA Program at North Carolina State University and is a faculty member of the Bennington College Writing Seminars. In this essay, published in the collection *We Are What We Ate* (1998), McCorkle offers vivid memories of life as a "junk-food junkie."

If I could have a perfect day of eating, this would be it: I'd begin with pancakes and sausage patties drenched in Log Cabin syrup. Then I'd visit my grandmother's kitchen, where my sister and I used to watch ravenously as Gramma made her famous pound cake (a real pound cake — a pound of butter, a pound of sugar, egg after egg after egg swirled in Swans Down cake flour). We'd each slurp batter off the mixer whisks and then split what was left in the red-and-white Pyrex bowl. My grandmother also made chicken and pastry (her pastry was more like dumplings) and homemade biscuits (the secret ingredient is lard), which might be dipped in redeye gravy or covered in butter and Karo syrup (doughboys) and eaten as dessert. She made homemade apple pies (the fruit part of our diet) fried in Crisco and filled with sugar.

If I couldn't have homemade food, then I would settle for what could be bought. A foot-long hot dog at the B&R Drive-In, for example; french fries limp with grease and salt from the bowling alley; a barbecue sandwich (Carolina style — chopped fine and spiced up with hot sauce); a triple-chocolate milk shake from Tastee-Freez. Banana splits and hot-fudge sundaes. Maybe a frozen Zero candy bar or a Milky Way, a Little Debbie snack cake and a moon pie, too.

I am a junk-food junkie and always have been. My college roommate and my husband both blame me for their slides into high-fat, preservative-filled meals, like the frozen Mexican TV dinners that my roommate and I ate all the way through college, or the microwavable burritos I now stash at the back of my freezer for desperate moments (desperate meaning a craving for Tex-Mex or a need to drive a nail and not being able to find a hammer). Forget meals, anyway; the truly good treats for a junk-food junkie get served up in between: colorful Ben & Jerry's pints, natural in an ethical way (the money goes to good places, at least) that makes me feel healthy; names — Chubby

Hubby, Chunky Monkey, Wavy Gravy — that make me laugh. Good Humor is what it's all about and has been since childhood: kids trained to respond to the ringing of a bell, to chase alongside trucks in neighborhood streets like so many pups for a Nutty Buddy. Ice cream is near the top of any junk-food junkie's list to be sure, but I haven't even begun to mention the Chee-tos, the Pecan Sandies.

There's something about unnatural food colors that has always attracted me. What tastes or looks better than the frosting on grocery-store-bakery birthday cakes? Hot pink or blue roses that melt in your mouth. The fluorescent brilliance of a crunchy Chee-to. Not too long ago my children (ages four and seven) were eating at a friend's. They were served a lovely meal of home-made macaroni and cheese, white, the way something without any additives and preservatives should be. I was on the other side of the room, helpless to defend myself when I heard my daughter say, "But my mom's macaroni and cheese is bright orange." Well? What can I say? I also love that fuchsia-colored sweet-and-sour sauce that you often find on Chinese food buffets.

> There's something about unnatural food colors that has always attracted me. What tastes or looks better than the frosting on grocery-store-bakery birthday cakes?

At the last big dinner party we had, my husband bought Yodels to 5 throw out on the dessert table along with a fresh-fruit concoction, which had taken me forever to cut up, and little cheesecakes. At the end of the night, there was not a Yodel in sight, but very few people had openly indulged. These scrumptious lunch-box treats (creme-filled chocolate rolls, 140 calories and 8 grams of fat each, which means, of course, that they are good) had instead been slyly tucked away into pockets and purses for the ride home. Yodels, Twinkies, Hostess Snoballs. They make people nostalgic for elementary school, those wonderful years when we were advised to eat beef and pork. Children thriving on sloppy joes and Saturday T-bones. Pork chops with applesauce. Sausage gravy over homemade biscuits. A good green vegetable in the South, where I grew up, was a green-bean casserole in which the beans were camouflaged in Campbell's cream of mushroom soup and canned fried onion rings. All the recipes in my favorite cookbooks begin with Campbell's cream-of-something soup.

I was enamored of a boy named Michael in the first grade who licked Kool-Aid powder from his palm whenever the teacher wasn't looking. He moved away before the end of the year, and yet thirty-one years later, I still remember him with a fond mixture of repulsion at the sticky red saliva that graced his notebook paper and admiration for the open ease with which he indulged his habit. I loved Pixy Stix straws, which, let's face it, were nothing more than dry Kool-Aid mix poured right into your mouth. Sweetarts. Jawbreakers. Firecrackers. Mary Janes. Any item that I was told was *very* bad for my teeth.

Maybe it's an oral-gratification thing. I'm sure that's why I smoked for fifteen years. When I quit nine years ago, I rediscovered my taste buds. I found flavors I had forgotten all about: Sugar Babies and Raisinets, that thick mashed-potato gravy that is the *real* secret ingredient at Kentucky Fried Chicken. I found flavors I had never had before, such as cheese blintzes and latkes smothered in sour cream. I found that wonderful, all-natural, fortified cereal Quaker 100% Natural Oats Honey and Raisins. I need oral participation, oral gratification. Despite what they will tell you on television, a little stick of Juicy Fruit is not going to get you there if you've been lighting up for years. But M&M's? Junior Mints? Those diablo-style peanuts thoroughly doused with cayenne pepper? Now, that's chewing satisfaction. A Coke (or diet Coke for the figure-minded; Jolt cola for the desperate-to-start-the-day-minded) chaser.

I could do a taste test. I can recognize all the sodas. The soda wanna-bes. I drink a good two to three cups of coffee when I get up, and by the time I drive the kids to school, I've switched over to diet Coke. People say, "Doesn't it keep you awake?" I wish! During one of my pregnancies I lost all taste for Coke. I couldn't believe it. I'd been drinking Coke for as long as I could remember. It was so sad; filling myself up on Hawaiian Punch (which is very good in its own right), Pop-Tarts, and ice cream, ice cream, ice cream. But I missed the Coke cans rolling around under the seat of my car. I missed the whoosh and zap of buying a Coke from a vending machine. And one day, like magic, it returned, this desire, like an old love resurfacing.

There are ways a junk-food junkie can feel less guilty about all this food, if indeed you ever do feel guilty. Did I mention caffeine? It's like air — essential for full enjoyment. And it burns calories. If that doesn't work, there are always things like the NordicTrack where I hang my clothes at the end of the day and the Suzanne Somers Thighmaster I keep in my closet for decoration.

Besides, I consider myself a purist; I don't like substitute things — like these new clear sodas. Who cares? I went into the all-natural health-food grocery store not long ago only to discover that there are a lot of things in this world that are foreign to me. The produce section had products you might find growing in a neglected basement. There were name brands I'd never heard of; certainly they don't buy airtime on television. There were cereals without colored marshmallows or prizes in the box. They boasted of having no sugar (as if this were good). It did not take me long to get back to the familiar aisles of the Super Stop & Shop, the red-and-white Campbell's soup labels, the chip-and-cookie aisle (nothing there sweetened with fruit juice or carob imitating chocolate), and the candy bars at the checkout.

One of my fondest junk-food memories is of a rare snow day in Lumberton, North Carolina, when I was in the sixth grade, a wonderful age at which, though I liked boys, they were not nearly as exciting as the ice cream store nearby that served up an oversize cone called a Kitchen Sink. But that day, I sat with a couple of friends in the back of the Kwik-Pik (the South's version of the convenience store) and ate raw chocolate-chip-cookie dough while drinking Eagle Brand sweetened condensed milk straight from the can. My friends and I waddled home feeling sick but warmly nourished, our stomachs coated and glowing with sugar. I mean, really, there is no cake or cookie on earth that tastes as good as dough or batter.

My favorite food in the eighth grade was Slim Jim sausages. For the uninformed, these are the miniature pepperoni sticks usually found near the register of convenience stores, where you might also find the beef jerky and pickled eggs. When I was growing up, there was usually a big jar of pickled pig's feet too, but this was not a treat that ever caught my eye. No, I lived on Slim Jims, spicy and chewy. I kept them with me at all times, getting a good chew while at cheerleading practices. They reminded me of being an even younger kid and getting a little bit of raw, salty country ham from my grandmother and chewing it all day like a piece of gum. (Sorry, Juicy Fruit; failed again.)

My husband, a doctor whose specialty is infectious diseases, is certain that I have been host to many parasites. Maybe, but what I'm certain that I have been host to are the junk-food parasites who refuse to admit that they indulge, but they do. Just put out a bowl of pistachios and check out the red fingertips leaving; chips, M&M's. Ah, M&M's. It was a sad day long ago when they retired the red ones. I had spent years being entertained by a pack; segregate and then integrate, close your eyes and guess which color. I was thrilled when the red ones returned, and now blue! Lovely blue M&M's. I love the pastel ones at Easter, along with those Cadbury eggs, and my own personal favorite: malted Easter eggs. These are actually Whoppers (malted-milk balls) covered in a speckled candy shell. Sometimes they are called robin eggs and sometimes simply malteds, but a Whopper is a Whopper is a Whopper. I like to bite one in half and then suck in. When the air is pulled out of a Whopper, what's left is more like a Milk Dud.

Of course there is also the Whopper from Burger King. Once, after a Friday night high-school football game, I sat down at a table with a bag of food that looked similar to those of all the guys on the team. I had a Whopper with everything, large fries, an apple pie, and a chocolate shake. Our cheerleading adviser told me that I wouldn't always be able to do that.

Thank God I didn't know she was right. It would have ruined the 15 next four years as I continued to down cream-filled Krispy Kreme doughnuts and my own special high-protein omelette that was filled with mayonnaise and cheese. I loved Funyuns, too, except that nobody wanted to sit next to me on the bus when I ate them.

After all these years, I've made some adjustments. I now buy Hebrew National for things like hot dogs and bologna. I figure the kosher laws probably serve me well in this particular purchase, and try as I might to dissuade them, my children love bologna with an absolute passion. They can smell the reject turkey substitute from fifty paces. They don't like *real* mac and cheese. They like the microwave kind. My niece (at age four) once invited me into her playhouse for lunch. She said, "Would you like a diet Coke while I cook lunch in the microwave?" So maybe it's a family thing. Maybe it's the potassium benzoate.

I would love a diet Coke and a cream horn right about now. Some salt-and-vinegar chips. Onion dip and Ruffles. S'mores. I like to get in bed to read with a stash of something close by. I have found that I am especially drawn to things with a high polyglycerol-ester-of-fatty-acids content. It makes me feel *happy*. I think maybe this is the key to a true junk-food junkie's heart: happiness. Just as Proust bit into his little madeleine and had a flood of memories, I bite into my Devil Dog, my Ring-Ding, Twinkie, Ho-Ho, Yodel. I bite into my Hostess Snoball and retreat to a world where the only worry is what to ask your mother to put in your lunch box the next day or which pieces of candy you will select at the Kwik-Pik on your way home from school. Ahead of you are the wasteland years: a pack of cigarettes, some Clearasil pads, a tube of Blistex, and breath spray. But for now, reach back to those purer, those sugar-filled, melt-in-your-mouth, forever-a-kid years. Who cares if there is a little polysorbate 60 and some diglycerides, some carrageenan, some Red 40 and Blue 1, some agar-agar? I have a dream that somewhere out there in the grown-up, low-fat world there is a boy named Michael licking his lips and getting all the fumaric acid that he can.

Understanding the Text

1. What is a "junk-food junkie"?

2. What role does food play in McCorkle's life? Consider how food affects both her self-perception and her relationships with others.

Reflection and Response

3. Does McCorkle's diet fascinate or horrify you? Explain your reaction.

4. Do you think her eating habits are normal in our society? Why or why not?

5. Why do you think she wrote this essay? What do you think she hopes her readers will learn from her stories about food?

Making Connections

6. What attitudes or values do Michael Pollan ("Eat Food: Food Defined," p. 9) and McCorkle share? What would Pollan praise about McCorkle's relationship with food? What would he question?

7. Consider Eric Schlosser's description of the flavor industry ("Why the Fries Taste Good," p. 20). What role does the flavor industry play in McCorkle's diet?

8. Think about what Dhruv Khullar ("Why Shame Won't Stop Obesity," p. 127) and Masanobu Fukuoka ("Living by Bread Alone," p. 87) have to say about the role eating plays in our lives. How would they each analyze McCorkle's attitudes about food?

9. Make a list of what you have eaten in the last two days. In light of the views of Michael Pollan, Eric Schlosser, and Jill McCorkle, evaluate your diet.

Taking Local on the Road

Camille Kingsolver

Camille Kingsolver's family devoted a year to eating only food produced on their family farm or in their local area. In this essay, published in the book-length memoir *Animal, Vegetable, Miracle* (2007) about the year and mostly written by her mother, the author Barbara Kingsolver (see "You Can't Run Away on Harvest Day," p. 184), Camille talks about going to college and adjusting to eating there after growing up in a family devoted to eating locally and growing and preparing its own food. Camille graduated from Duke University in 2009 and continues to be an advocate for the local-food movement. She is especially interested in finding ways to reach out to young adults who are trying to make good food choices in a world that makes it difficult to do so. She lives in North Carolina where she grows her own vegetable garden.

I have a confession to make. Five months into my family's year of devoted local eating, I moved out. Not because the hours of canning tomatoes in early August drove me insane or because I was overcome by insatiable cravings for tropical fruit. I just went to college. It was a challenging life, getting through chemistry and calculus while adjusting to a whole new place, and the limited dining options I had as a student living on campus didn't help. I suppose I could have hoed up a personal vegetable patch on the quad or filled my dorm room with potted tomato and zucchini plants, but then people would *really* have made fun of me for being from Appalachia. Instead, I ate lettuce and cucumbers in January just like all the other kids.

Living away from home, talking with my family over the phone, gave me some perspective. Not having fresh produce at my disposal made me realize how good it is. I also noticed that how I think about food is pretty unusual among my peers. When I perused the salad bar at my dining hall most evenings, grimly surveying the mealy, pinkish tomatoes and paperlike iceberg lettuce, I could pick out what probably came from South America or New Zealand. I always kept this information to myself (because who really cares when there are basketball games and frat parties to talk about?), but I couldn't help noticing it.

I suppose my generation is farther removed from food production than any other, just one more step down the path of the American food industry. More than our parents, we rely on foods that come out of shiny wrappers instead of peels or skins. It still surprises a girl like

It still surprises a girl like me, who actually lives on a real farm with *real animals* and stuff growing out of the *ground*, that so many young adults couldn't guess where their food comes from, or when it's in season where they live.

me, who actually lives on a real farm with *real animals* and stuff growing out of the *ground*, that so many young adults couldn't guess where their food comes from, or when it's in season where they live. It's not that my rising generation is unintelligent or unworldly — my classmates are some of the smartest, most cultured people I know. But information about food and farming is not very available. Most of the people I know have never seen a working farm, or had any reason to do so. Living among people my age from various cities across the United States made me realize I actually know a lot about food production, and I don't take that for granted.

I also won't forget to appreciate how much better local food tastes. Next to getting a good night's sleep on a comfortable mattress, cooking good food became my main motivation for coming home from school to visit. Of course seeing my family was nice, but priorities are priorities, right? It was great after weeks of dorm life to eat eggs with deep golden yolks, and greens that still had their flavor and crunch. I loved being able to look at a table full of food and know where every vegetable was grown, where the meat lived when it was still a breathing animal.

During my first year of college I found two campus eateries that 5 use organic, locally grown produce in their meals, and one that consistently uses free-range meat. For the most part, these vendors did not widely advertise the fact that they were participating in the local food economy. I only found out because I cared, and then tried to buy most of my food from those places.

My generation, I know, has the reputation of sticking iPods in our ears and declining to care about what might happen in ten years, or even next week. We can't yet afford hybrid vehicles or solar homes. But we do care about a lot of things, including what we eat. Food is something real. Living on the land that has grown my food gives me a sense of security I'm lucky to have. Feeling safe isn't so easy for people my age, who face odious threats like global warming, overpopulation, and chemical warfare in our future. But even as the world runs out of fuel and the ice caps melt, I will know the real sources of my sustenance. My college education may or may not land me a good job down the road, but my farm education will serve me. The choices I make now about my food will influence the rest of my life. If a lot of us felt this way, and started thinking carefully about our consumption habits just one meal at a time, we could affect the future of our planet. No matter how grave the predictions I hear about the future, for my peers and me, that's a fact that gives me hope.

Understanding the Text

1. What does it mean to "eat local"? Why did Kingsolver's family make the commitment to eat only locally grown food for one year?

2. How did Kingsolver's diet change when she moved away from home to attend college?

Reflection and Response

3. Kingsolver observes that her generation "is farther removed from food production than any other." On what does she base this observation? Do you agree? Would you draw a similar conclusion about your generation? Why or why not?

4. What aspects of growing and preparing her own food does Kingsolver value? Consider how she presents her values (explicitly *and* implicitly) in the text. Compare her food values to your own.

Making Connections

5. How is Kingsolver's connection to food similar to Jill McCorkle's ("Her Chee-to Heart," p. 31)? How is it different?

6. What do we learn about "flavor" from Kingsolver? How does it compare with what we learn from Eric Schlosser ("Why the Fries Taste Good," p. 20)?

7. Research options for local or organic food on your campus or in your community. What options exist? Is participation in the local food economy valued? How?

Eating the Hyphen

Lily Wong

Lily Wong wrote this essay in a class she took on food and society when she was an undergraduate student at Williams College. After earning a bachelor's degree in history and Asian studies there, she has dabbled in food writing, taught English in Hong Kong, and worked in a museum conducting research and planning exhibits. This essay first appeared in *Gastronomica: The Journal of Food and Culture*, an academic journal that uses food as a source of knowledge about culture; it has been selected for inclusion in *Best Food Writing 2013*. Wong loves food and cooking, and thinking and writing about food continue to intrigue her. Here she describes her love of dumplings eaten with a fork, a knife, a pair of chopsticks, and ketchup to illustrate the important relationship between food and identity.

Fork? check. Knife? check. Chopsticks? Check. It may seem odd to have all three of these eating utensils side by side for the consumption of a single meal, but for me, there's just no other way. Oh, and ketchup, that's key. Definitely need to have the ketchup, pre-shaken to avoid an awkward first squirt of pale red water. There's no place for that on my plate, not when I'm eating dumplings. Yes, that is what I said: I need a fork, a knife, a pair of chopsticks, and ketchup before I eat my dumplings.

Now I've just looked up "dumpling" on the online *Oxford English Dictionary* and discovered that it is "a kind of pudding consisting of a mass of paste or dough, more or less globular in form, either plain and boiled, or enclosing fruit and boiled or baked." I am definitely not talking about whatever unappetizing-sounding food that dumpling is supposed to be. I'm talking about Chinese dumplings, pot stickers, Peking ravioli, *jiaozi*, whatever you want to call them. Do you know what I mean yet? Maybe you've gotten a vague idea, but let me explain, because I am *very* picky about my dumplings.

To begin with, the skin has to be thick. I mean really thick. Thick and chewy and starchy and the bottom should be a bit burnt and dark golden brown from the pan-frying. Have you ever had *gyoza*, the Japanese dumplings? Yes, those thin, almost translucent skins just won't do it for me. Hands-down, no question, until my dying day, I will vouch that the skin is the make-or-break feature of a dumpling. Bad skin equals bad dumpling. Those boiled dumplings that are also a type of Chinese dumplings? The skin is too thin, too soggy, and frankly, rather flavorless. If I had to call it names, I'd say it was limp and weak and characterless. The thick-skinned dumplings that I know and love absorb more of the meaty-flavored goodness inside the dumplings. Also, because they are pan-fried (a key aspect of delicious dumplings), the bottom gets its own texture — a slightly charred crispiness to add that perfect smidgen of crunch. So, if you were to eat just the skin of the dumpling, it would be simultaneously chewy and crispy, with a bit of savory meat flavor mixed in with a burnt taste off the bottom — a wonderfulness that the words of the English language are hard-pressed to capture.

But what about the filling? To me, it's a bit peripheral. The dumplings I'm talking about have a standard pork filling with "Chinese vegetables." I've never been entirely sure what these elusively named Chinese vegetables actually are, but I imagine that they are some combination of leeks and Chinese cabbage. They're not too salty and they don't have cilantro. These dumplings also have enough savory broth secretly sequestered inside the skin so that when you cut them open, you get some oil spatterings, pretty much all over your clothes, plate, and table. That's the sign of a good, moist, and juicy meat section.

I should mention before you envision me slaving away in a 5 kitchen to create the perfect dumpling that the ones I like come out of the freezer. In plastic bags of fifty each. Imported to my house from Boston's Chinatown. It's strange, considering that most days I like the homegrown version of foods more than the store-bought version, but these are the exception. Even though I know they're hand made by a small company, so you get that same small-batch feel as if you made them at home, they're still store-bought and frozen rather than fresh.

But enough about finding the right dumplings; you're probably still confused as to why it's so imperative that I have a fork, knife, chopsticks, and ketchup. Here is your step-by-step guide to an entirely new dumpling eating experience.

1. On a large white plate, place six or seven dumplings (or more if you're particularly ravenous) and add some broccoli or beans for color and nutrition.

2. Squirt a glop of ketchup in one of the empty white spaces on your plate (as in not touching the broccoli or the dumplings). This is where it's key that the ketchup has been shaken a bit, otherwise that red ketchup juice runs all over your plate ruining everything.

3. Take that fork and knife on the side and cut each dumpling in half width-wise. Make sure to cut completely through the skin and meat.

4. Take the backside of your fork and push down on the top of each dumpling half until the meat abruptly pops out in a pool of brothy juice.

5. Once you've finished systematically cutting and squishing, you'll have lots of skins and meat pieces separated and you can put that knife and fork away. Grab the chopsticks.

6. Pick up a piece of the meat (just the meat now, no trying to get some skin in on this too) and dip it into the ketchup. Eat and repeat. If at any point you want to indulge in that steamed broccoli, it's a good idea. You wouldn't want to leave it all to the end. But don't dip it in ketchup. That's weird.

7. Now this is the best part. Use your chopsticks to one-by-one eat every last half dumpling's worth of skin. Savor every part because this is what it's all really been about. No ketchup or meat to obscure the flavor and chewiness, just pure starchy goodness.

And that's how it goes. Every single time. Confused? So was I the first time I really sat down to think about how I eat dumplings. It sounds a little like a grand mutilation of how a dumpling should be eaten for it to be "authentic" (using only chopsticks and with the dumpling left whole and dipped in black vinegar, no ketchup in sight). And I have unabashedly criticized and ridiculed Americanized Chinese food for being fake and something of a disgrace to "authentic" Chinese food. Yet here I am, still eating my dumplings with ketchup and a fork, unceremoniously and quite literally butchering my dumplings before I eat them. My grandmother meanwhile takes small bites out of whole dumplings, careful not to lose any of that broth from inside (with a face only three-quarters filled with disgust as I rush from the table to grab my ketchup from the fridge).

Bottled up in this entirely strange ritual is my status as a Chinese American. It is unclear to me where I ever came up with the idea that dumplings should be cut in half, or that the meat would taste better with ketchup (particularly since this is literally the only time that I use ketchup). Perhaps this combination has something to do with the fact that since both my parents grew up in the States, we've embraced many American traditions while abandoning or significantly modifying many Chinese ones. But even so, I have always embraced my Chinese culture and heritage. It gives me something larger to cling to when I'm feeling ostracized by American culture for looking "different." The suburb I grew up in is mostly white, but it's not as if I didn't have Chinese people around me; after all, there was always Chinatown. But Chinatown was full of people who spoke the language — whether Cantonese or Mandarin — who somehow just seemed so much more Chinese than I ever could be. And perhaps that's true. Maybe that's why I feel so gosh-darned American when I eat my dumplings with ketchup while holding my chopsticks "incorrectly." The notion that this somehow takes away from my ability to identify with Chinese culture is, I rationally understand, flawed. But in my pursuit to try and discover who I am, it's taken an oddly large place.

I'm not sure why I often think that to be a Chinese American means that you relish authentic Chinese food — and by authentic I mostly mean strictly what your grandmother cooks for you — but I do. I've told friends that they don't know what real Chinese food is because all they know is Panda Express. I pride myself on my Cantonese background, which leads me to look favorably on pig's ears and fungus of all shapes and sizes. My innate territorialism regarding my particular definition of what Chinese food is makes the choice to continue eating my dumplings in such a strange fashion slightly fraught. I'm not even sure that anyone besides my family knows that this is how I eat dumplings. In part, I think my reticence derives precisely from a fear that it would make me "less" Chinese.

> I'm not sure why I often think that to be a Chinese American means that you relish authentic Chinese food—and by authentic I mostly mean strictly what your grandmother cooks for you—but I do.

Somehow, I've come to strange terms with these contradictions. 10 Somewhere along the way, dumplings, cut in half with ketchup on the meat and the skin separated as a special entity of its own, have become my comfort food. So whether or not it perverts some thousand-year-old tradition of the "proper" way to eat dumplings, this is what makes me happy. Although I sometimes catch myself overcompensating with extra delight in Chinese delicacies involving jellyfish and sea cucumber that cause most Americans to squirm, eating dumplings in my own style has become the hyphen between Chinese and American in my identity.

Understanding the Text

1. How does Wong define "food"? How does she define "Chinese food"?
2. How does Wong feel that her food preferences define her? Do you agree?
3. What constitutes an "authentic" food experience for Wong?

Reflection and Response

4. Why do you think Wong includes the dictionary definition of "dumpling"? What effect does it have on the rest of the piece?
5. How do you explain the significance of the title? What does it emphasize about Wong's story?

Making Connections

6. Compare Wong's love of dumplings to Jill McCorkle's love of junk food ("Her Chee-to Heart," p. 31) and Camille Kingsolver's love of local food ("Taking Local on the Road," p. 37). What do they suggest about the relationships between food, emotion, and desire?
7. Reflect on the relationship between your food preferences and your identity. Do your food choices express something about your identity or aspects of it? Why or why not?
8. Wong, Michael Pollan ("Eat Food: Food Defined," p. 9), and Bryant Terry ("True Grits," p. 82) define food in relation to what grandmothers would consider authentic. Why do you think this is? Do you connect certain foods to your grandmother or to other family members? Explain.

Doberge Cake after Katrina

Amy Cyrex Sins

When the home of Amy Cyrex Sins was flooded by Hurricane Katrina in August 2005, among her losses was her personal collection of recipes. In her cookbook *Ruby Slippers Cookbook: Life, Culture, Family, and Food after Katrina* (2006), Sins preserves the unique culinary experiences of New Orleans–style cooking. As a longtime New Orleans resident and now an author, Sins is using the proceeds from her cookbook to support the Coalition to Restore Coastal Louisiana. In this essay, published in *Storied Dishes: What Our Family Recipes Tell Us about Who We Are and Where We've Been* (2011), Sins meditates on the loss of her family's recipes.

My first inkling that Katrina was a storm like no other came after I had evacuated to Houston. I watched in horror on national television as the levee on the 17th Street Canal (only ten houses from our own) broke, sending tons of water and debris down our street. This break, which wouldn't have happened if the levees had been properly engineered, caused the major flooding throughout New Orleans. I could see the roofline of our house on the screen, and I could tell that it was flooded but not how deep. Many homes were destroyed beyond re-building.

When disaster struck, it didn't surprise me that the people of New Orleans yearned more than ever for that taste of home, dishes that reminded them of family and normalcy. Centuries of tradition have led to distinctive Creole and Cajun dishes, as well as deep-rooted southern foodways. Many people don't realize how important food is to the people of Louisiana; it is truly a way of life. That's why even though our home was under water, and coated with mold and mud, I mourned the loss of my recipe collection.

Food defines important moments for me. I loved my wedding cake, totally non-traditional — white chocolate filled with raspberry. Our guests still talk about it over five years later. Then there's Doberge Cake, light, fluffy, and moist, a traditional New Orleans treat

> Even though our home was under water, and coated with mold and mud, I mourned the loss of my recipe collection.

piled eight layers high, filled with chocolate custard and slathered with chocolate ganache. My mother-in-law, Janet Sins, always made it for my husband's birthday. For my own, she made a special chicken recipe, known as Birthday Chicken, that she prepared only for my day because it was so much work — layers of chicken, pounded flat and covered with parmesan cheese, green onions, and mushroom-wine sauce. And I wouldn't stop with family; there's so much more — jambalaya at the church fair, fried fish at the grocery during Lent, beignets when your maw maw takes you to Morning Call. Happy, Sad, Momentous, and Every Day, food marks life events.

Hurricane Katrina didn't change that for me; it only made it more poignant. Many days later, my husband and I returned to survey the damage. When we got to our street, we were in shock. Mud, trees, and other unidentifiable objects were piled high; mounds of dirt and debris stacked up as tall as twenty feet. The only way we could access our house was by four-wheel all-terrain vehicle. Incredibly, we found a house from three blocks away sitting in our driveway.

Opening the front door of our house was impossible. Wearing 5 masks, rubber boots, and gloves, we slipped and slid along, climbing mounds to what had been our backyard. Then it hit us — the SMELL. I can only compare it to a port-a-potty on the last day of Mardi Gras. It will stay with me forever.

When we entered through our blown down back doors, we found a six-inch layer of black slimy mud covering the entire first floor. Mold was growing out of control like a fuzzy marine animal climbing our walls.

Nothing was as it had been. Katrina had a capricious sense of humor. A bottle of Sprite had migrated from the kitchen to the living room and was holding up a batch of encyclopedias. My cannister of sugar had been transported to the top shelf of our entertainment center as if for decoration. Only our china cabinet hadn't moved — the one my husband always said contained too much unnecessary stuff. Somewhere in the murky mud that surrounded it were my precious, but unrecognizable, cookbooks.

Everything considered, we were, of course, very lucky. We didn't lose people. My husband had saved our cats, Frank and Dean, named for Frank Sinatra and Dean Martin, and many of our photos. What was left was "stuff" not without emotional attachment, but replicable. Well, mostly replicable.

Lost forever were the family recipes I had collected and cherished. Whenever I had attended a great party or had a fabulous meal at a restaurant or someone brought an excellent dish to a potluck, I would ask for the recipe. There had been food clippings from newspapers (every one from the *Times Picayune* since I had moved to New Orleans), magazine articles, recipes from my mother-in-law, and a few trial-and-error formulas when my friends and I would try to "touch up" recipes from cookbooks.

Most of my favorites came from my mother-in-law who lived only 10 a few miles away. Her home was also flooded and her collection destroyed. She salvaged a few handwritten cards which she stored in ziplock bags. Many were the only remembrances she had in the handwriting of female relatives no longer alive. With her help, and the entire community's, I'm trying to reassemble my recipes; it takes many false attempts and adjustments to recapture the exact flavor and texture.

Take Doberge Cake, for example. On my husband's first birthday after Katrina, the torch passed from my mother-in-law to me to make this all-important confection. Fortunately, I had two cake pans in the galley kitchen of our temporary French Quarter apartment, and I set to work. The cake was the easy part, but re-constructing the family recipe for ganache proved elusive. Janet and I can only remember a few ingredients: corn syrup, chocolate bits, and cream. I've made it several times but my husband George always tells me it's not quite right. "Sorry babe, that's just not the same."

After gaining 15 pounds trying to duplicate Doberge Cake, as well as other pre-Katrina classics, I'm reserving the confection for special occasions! For now, this re-constructed recipe will have to do.

DOBERGE CAKE

Serves 12

The inexperienced baker tends to produce a leaning tower, but with much practice, a perfect upright cake will be possible.

Cake

2 Betty Crocker Butter Yellow Cake mixes

1. Follow package directions to make four layers.
2. Cool layers on wire racks.
3. Using saw-toothed knife, cut each layer horizontally into two. This is easiest if you use toothpicks to mark the halfway point where you intend to cut. You will then have eight layers in all.

Filling

1 c. sugar	1 1/2 t. vanilla extract
1/2 c. flour	3 1/2 oz. Lindt dark chocolate
3 c. milk	bar, chopped
4 eggs	

1. In medium saucepan over medium-high heat, quickly combine sugar and flour. Gradually stir in milk and chopped chocolate. Heat until thick and bubbly and chocolate is completely melted. Reduce heat to very low and cook two minutes more. Remove from heat.
2. Separate eggs into two small bowls. Gradually add cup of filling to yolks to temper them and prevent scrambling. Then add yolk mixture to saucepan. Return to heat and bring to gentle boil. Stir in butter and vanilla.
3. Cover with cling wrap touching mixture to prevent skin from forming and chill in refrigerator one hour.

Ganache

1 lb. (1 box) confectioners' sugar	2 squares (2 oz.) unsweetened chocolate, melted
2 T. light corn syrup	1/2 t. vanilla extract
1/3 c. water	

1. Sift confectioners' sugar into large bowl.
2. In small saucepan, mix corn syrup and water and bring to boil.
3. Remove from heat and pour into confectioners' sugar.
4. Add melted chocolate and vanilla extract and combine all ingredients.

Ganache will be fairly thin, but not runny.

Assembling Cake

1. Smooth filling between layers of cake and stack them. You may hold the confection together with a wooden skewer.
2. Pour ganache over top to cover entire cake. Cool in refrigerator for two hours before serving. Icing will harden. Enjoy!

No matter how dark things may seem at some points of our lives, food helps us regain our bearings and work through our feelings so we can emerge with greater equanimity and renewed harmony.

Understanding the Text

1. What does Sins mean by a "taste of home"?
2. What is Doberge Cake? What does it represent in the essay?

Reflection and Response

3. Sins lost more than directions for cooking when she lost her recipes. What did she lose?
4. How does food define important life events for Sins?
5. Why do you think Sins includes the recipe for Doberge Cake? What does the recipe represent?

Making Connections

6. Sins and Lily Wong ("Eating the Hyphen," p. 40) both imply that food helps define culture and that culture helps define food. Compare how they do this.
7. What does Sins imply that family or regional recipes tell us about ourselves? Describe some family or regional dishes that would help you tell *your* story. What do they say about your relationship with food?

The Eco-Gastronomic Mirror: Narcissism and Death at the Dinner Table

Jordan Shapiro

Jordan Shapiro is known for his work in Jungian and archetypal psychology and interdisciplinary research that involves popular culture, psychology, and technology. He wrote *Freeplay: A Video Game Guide to Maximum Euphoric Bliss* (2012); he coedits the journal *Occupy Psyche: Jungian and Archetypal Perspectives on a Movement*; he teaches at Temple University; and he contributes to *Forbes*. He also owns and operates a coffee shop in Philadelphia, where he currently lives. In the past he has worked as a chef, and he has "cooked almost everything, including black bear shoulder and bison testicles." In this essay, originally published in the journal *Ecopsychology* in 2010, he combines his experiences working in restaurants and his longtime interest in psychology to explore the psychological aspects of our relationship with food.

The dirt beneath my fingernails repulses people. Seeing it, you might feel nauseated. There is no way to romanticize it. They are not the worn hands of a field worker with bark-like wrinkles of toughened skin cultivated by hours of farm labor. No, the greenish black stuff lodged under the tough keratin protein is not soil. I am not a farmer. I am not a gardener. I have not been harvesting root vegetables, sowing seeds, or planting bulbs.

I am a cook. I work with food. I have worked on five-star trendsetting altars of epicurean° opulence,° and I have flipped burgers in greasy spoons. I have mastered the nuances of gently whisking Lyonnais butter into a delicate beurre blanc sauce, and I can smoke a rack of ribs that is best washed down with a pale, bland, American Lager.

As I lift a beer to my lips, you will see those crescents of darkness beneath my fingernails. It is old food lodged under the skin's appendage. Perhaps it is salt, pepper, and sugar that burrowed beneath my nails as I rubbed seasoning onto the flesh of a dead animal awaiting the white-hot charcoal of the barbecue. Perhaps it is the herbed emulsification of fatty fruit triglyceride esters (olive oil) with protein albumen and vitellus (chicken eggs): that ubiquitous dressing called may-

---

epicurean: Dedicated to the pursuit of pleasure, especially of good food.
opulence: Wealth, abundance.

onnaise. Perhaps Miracle Whip coated the undersides of my nails as I distributed it with my hands through tubers (potatoes), bulbs (onions), and petioles (celery stalks) while constructing a simple potato salad.

The potato salad accompanies the St. Louis–style pork ribs. The sharp acidity of the vinegar and tomato-based North Carolina–style barbecue sauce provides a refreshing burst of sweet and sour flavor while cutting through the richness of the mayonnaise and mouth-coating juiciness of the pork fat. Diners inhale these dishes during Fourth of July and other summer holiday picnics. These are foods traditionally enjoyed outdoors. The setting is the pastoral serenity of a public park.

Picnics and barbecues are two of the more common ways that 21st- 5 century Americans interact with the great outdoors. But the exterior setting is hardly necessary; eating is already an interaction with nature. Through food, people both literally and metaphorically consume wilderness and digest the planet. Diet is the environment. We feed on plants and animals, and thus our relationship to flora and fauna is evident in our culinary trends and methods. It is a narcissistic relationship in which humans nail the natural other to the wall like a full-length mirror. The image reflected back — on platters and buffets, in ingredients and recipes — is of our complex link to nature, to death, and to the terra firma that will eventually hold our decomposing bodies.

> Through food, people both literally and metaphorically consume wilderness and digest the planet.

Kitchen Lifestyle, Kitchen Deathstyle

Hollywood movies about the culinary arts such as *Ratatouille* (2007), *Babette's Feast* (1988), and *Big Night* (1996) romanticize the sensory aspect of gourmet construction: the wafting odor of truffles, the precision and color palette of presentation, the musical sounds of clanging porcelain china–like wood chimes, and the clinking rhythms of aluminum, cast iron, and stainless steel pots and pans. In my experience, however, the restaurant cooking line is more like a battlefield than an artist's studio. Feet planted firmly in front of a 12-burner range, I learned to ignore the constant violent burn from tiny droplets of scorching oil. I struggled to hear my coworker's conversation despite the constant racket of the super-powered exhaust fan above my head. Servers screamed. Cooks barked back. I employed garnish to cover up foibles from the sauté pan: A dollop of crème fraiche can mask the charred edge of a wounded chicken breast; a sprig of rosemary can hide the seam where a severed filet of sea bass was mended. When wielding a chef's blade, or flipping the contents of a pan with the flick of my wrist, the realities of life's cycles and death's inevitability were always present and easily ignored.

Behind the scenes, restaurants reek of death. The sweet smell of fruit nectar and fresh herbs is always overpowered by the putrid odor of aging meat and the fetor° of fish water. While diners enjoy the textures of fine linen, the perfume of scented candles, and the sparkle of polished silver and crystal, cooks hide behind the swinging kitchen doors, wading in a cesspool of decomposition. As a professional cook, I often spent 70 or 80 hours a week surrounded by the sensations of food preparation. In my chef's jacket and flame retardant pants, I raced to turn a profit from fruits, vegetables, and animal corpses — speeding to outrun nature's ticking time bomb of decay before net gains turned to net losses.

I took my first cooking job when I was 15. On day one I was sent to the basement walk-in to fetch a pork loin. Instead, I discovered mortality in the form of a young deer's rotting flesh. I was just a gofer. I peeled onions or garlic in between errands. I scrubbed countertops. I spent all night awaiting commands. When Chef ran low on ingredients in his reach-in box, he screamed, "Jap!" The nickname, a popular acronym for "Jewish American Princess," was intentionally demeaning and meant to remind me that I was not yet initiated into the fraternity of male kitchen workers. It was a triple play, scoring insults three ways at once. My Jewish heritage, I could never escape. My upper-middle-class upbringing was invoked as a handicap, not privilege. And I would spend years trying to overcome feelings of inferiority brought on by the misogynist° implications that I was girly. Still a pubescent boy at the time, the banter of the kitchen defined my ideal of adult maleness. Like a microcosm of U.S. patriarchal modernity and its exclusive reliance on rational science, the cooking line taught me that my own masculinity should be marked not only by frying-pan-chemistry's ability to cheat death, but also by the size of the profit one can turn in the process.

"Jap!" He screamed and then took care to remind me that my people were not the chosen ones of the restaurant industry. "Do you even know what pork looks like?" I nodded and rushed down the wobbly wooden stairs to the refrigerator in the basement. My brow was soaked in sweat from the hot kitchen. The chill of cold air blowing over compressed Freon coils made me shiver.

fetor: A bad smell; a stench.
misogynist: Characterized by a hatred of women.

I searched the right side of the walk-in, the image of a pork loin in 10
my mind's eye. The loin cut of pork is the narrow muscle that sits
along the top of a pig's spine. I pictured this tissue considering it as
both muscle and meat, both anatomy and food. I imagined the sawed
off loin ribs that would likely still be attached. I sensed into my
body and felt my own loin running along my back and holding my
body upright. It pressed against my skin and I felt the itchy synthetic fabric from which my chef's whites were sewn. Polyester
pressed into my pores, open from perspiration. I was reminded how
closely related I am to a pig: we are both made of meat.

In my attempt to locate the pork, I surveyed the entire inventory
of refrigerated goods. Hurried, I rushed to search through everything. But I was not prepared for what I found within the thick black
garbage liners on the bottom shelf. At first it just looked like a small
leg of lamb, but as I reached into the bag, I discovered a headless deer.
This was not Venison. Euphemisms meant to obstruct the image are
useless when staring at a skinless corpse. This was deer, dead deer:
the carious corpse of a slaughtered fawn. The membrane and sinew
that covered the muscle was yellow with rot, and I could feel the
heavy and grainy mucus of decomposition on my hands. It was thick
and pasty, at once gooey and dry. It seemed to coat the inside of my
throat as I took a deep breath in through my nose. I smelled the fes-
tering flesh and I felt the odor pass through my nasal cavity and settle on the back of my tongue. I almost gagged.

Today, equipped with the insights of depth psychology, I realize
that this was my misguided 15-year-old initiation into patriarchal
adulthood. It combined lessons of chemistry, business, and my human relationship to the natural other. My education was provided
not only through interaction with male authority figures and the behaviors they modeled, but also through hands-on engagement with
the natural materials of food preparation. I learned that stoicism
must trump squeamishness in the worlds of life, death, and the professional kitchen. I learned to separate matter from meaning. A restaurant education reinforced the Abrahamic° religions' divine directive
to subdue the earth and "have dominion over the fish of the sea, and
over the fowl of the air, and over every living thing that moveth upon
the earth" (Genesis 1:28). In the kitchen, surrounded by oil, steam,
and flame, chemistry united Western religion and Enlightenment
philosophy. Spirit was removed from matter — body from the so-

---

Abrahamic: The monotheistic religions with a spiritual tradition identified with the
patriarch Abraham: Judaism, Christianity, and Islam.

called superior human mind — and a feast was fixed daily in honor of the Cartesian split.°

Fruit and Funerals Like Apples and Oranges

Recently, on a trip to the West Coast, I had a chance to pick oranges off a tree. I tucked them into a plastic shopping bag and then carried them onto a plane. I arrived home to the East Coast and presented the citrus to my 4-year-old son. "Sergey," I asked, "do you want to try the freshest orange you've ever tasted?" He laughed. Not just a giggle or a snicker, but a hysterical belly laugh. He ran to his mother, "Mama, Dad is so silly!" He ran back to me, pointed at the orange and exclaimed, "That orange has a leaf on it. A leaf. Hah. That's crazy! Why does it have a leaf on it? You're a silly magic dad!"

I understood him perfectly. In a world where oranges are found under specialty lighting on custom-built displays, flora and fruit seem counterintuitive together. Flora belongs potted in the garden center at Home Depot. Fruit is erected into pyramids on Wegman's tilt-top produce risers.

I remember feeling the same way Sergey did. As a child, I always 15 enjoyed trips to pick-your-own farms. We would head into Lancaster, Pennsylvania's Amish farmland to pick peaches, apples, or pumpkins. We would trek across the river to New Jersey and fill bushels and baskets with corn, cranberries, and blueberries.

Something about seeing the fruit as an extension of a tree was magical to me. That a plump juicy orange could grow out of a stick was miraculous. I was dumbfounded by the dynamism that seemed frozen in time as well defined and separate categories like wood and fruit morphed together into a single object, blurring the divisions that were emphasized in my school textbooks. It was therefore a numinous° experience to pluck a fruit from the end of a branch. I felt omnipotent and divine. I was able to cut off the life force with my little hands. I was able to render an orange no longer part of nature as I changed it into merely food. Citrus seemed to be carried from living to dead, from plant-life to matter.

Death, when imaged through food, seemed to exist on a continuum. Allowing — no, encouraging — the plant and animal carcasses to become (impossibly) more and more dead transforms foodstuff

---

Cartesian split: The concept that the mind and the body are two distinct things, associated with the French philosopher René Descartes (1596–1650).
numinous: Having a spiritual quality.

into matter. Perhaps I was attracted to cooking in my teens because conveniently, after performing the Cartesian exercise of removing soul from the animal or vegetable body, I could utilize what felt like semi-divine dominance in the form of the culinary arts. The culinary arts, after all, share some of the same symbolic and archetypal° themes as poetic, visual, and performing arts. This is made apparent through a careful analysis of the metaphors at work in the processing of food.

Consider the gastronomic° production cycle of fruit. When I severed a fruit from its tree — from its life source — I imagined that the dying process set in immediately. It started decomposing, rotting. My mother, urging me to eat the brown squishy parts of the banana, called this rotting ripening and explained that with ripening the fruit gets sweeter and better for eating.

Eventually I learned that if it is not embalmed with an antioxidant preservative, if it is not mummified in glass or plastic, fruit will cross the threshold from sweet death to sour death. The process of fermentation sets in and microorganisms feed on the decaying carcass. The natural sugar and carbohydrates are converted into alcohol. Wine or beer is produced. It is a wonderful inebriant,° but according to the metaphorical language of food preparation, it is not yet fully dead. Oenophiles° still speak of its body, its mouth feel. There are impurities: tannins and sediments. It is not fully preserved. It can still turn to vinegar. Symbolically, therefore, more death is imminent.

However, I can immortalize the fruit. I can draw out its essential 20 nature — the essence of the sweet juicy "envelope" of nature's creative potential manifested as seed. Through a process of extraction known as distillation I can transform wine, or beer, into the closest material equivalent to its pure incorporeal fundamental core. Hence the name "spirit." Through engagement with mortality — engagement with the life-and-death cycles of raw cooking ingredients both practically and metaphorically — I can encounter the divine, or pure spirit.

If the metaphoric parallels to religion that I am drawing seem farfetched, consider that spirits' quality supposedly increases with age. A 1926 bottle of Macallan Scotch whiskey sold for $54,000 at Christie's in 2007. While auction houses have clearly proven the financial truism that the age of liquor is proportionate to its market value, critics have long argued about whether or not older actually tastes better.

archetypal: Relating to a universally understood symbol or pattern.
gastronomic: Relating to the art of eating food.
inebriant: Something causing intoxication, especially drunkenness.
oenophile: A lover of wine.

An explanation for this controversy might be found in psychology rather than chemistry. It seems that the general willingness to accept that older equals better (in wine, cheese, meat, and vinegar) is illustrative of a root metaphor involving the human life-and-death cycle. The spirit gains value with age because of the idea that its bodiless immortality has withstood the test of time. The fine spirit has truly attained finality, and it is no longer susceptible to crude somatic vulnerabilities. When no mortal body or matter remains we encounter spirit.

100% Pure and Ready for the Afterlife

The symbolic language of our culinary arts and the ritual techniques of gastronomic processes seem to be narcissistic reflections of humanity's complex relationship with death. In other words, I dealt with the philosophical trauma of my ultimate return to earth through the metaphors of cooking. Nature is reduced to matter, and matter is eventually made pure.

But wasn't it pure to begin with? No, purity is not equivalent to natural. Purity is the freedom from material (and spiritual) pollutants or foreign matter. An apple that I pluck right from the tree, for example, is crisp, sweet, and juicy before any gastronomic procedures. But it is not pure. The poetic chef in me would venture to say that a perfection of esthetic balance exists in the fruit's flavor, texture, and color at the time of harvest. The tender pop of biting through the taut shiny skin releases a burst of liquid slightly thicker than water. The moisture of the juice complements the crunchy starch of the flesh. The sweetness and the acidity of the nectar entwine on your tongue and slide down your throat in a fervid° embrace. You can taste the sun and the rain, the dirt and the tree bark. The seasonal inconsistency of plant and animal flavors and its causal relationship with the weather is evidence that all of nature is married in each bite. The natural ambience — the surroundings of its creation — is present in the fruit itself. It is the landscape in your mouth. But the terrain — the beginnings and endings in dirt — is precisely what gastronomic practice aims to eradicate. It is not pure until we remove every last remnant of its natural origins with culinary techniques.

It seems paradoxical, then, that the American consumer is preoccupied with the geographical and agricultural origins of food. Last

fervid: Intensely passionate.

night, for example, I fried up halloumi cheese imported from Cyprus to a Whole Foods Market in downtown Philadelphia. Halloumi — all cheese, for that matter — is essentially preserved milk, fermented, and brined in salt (a mineral rock). Preservation allows me to enjoy the exotic delicacy despite the fact that the natural life cycle — in which ruminant mammals eat local grasses and other vegetation before producing milk for their young — takes place 5,542 miles away. Tonight my wife and I are going out for sushi. I will most likely order hamachi, because modern transportation technology has made it possible for me to eat fresh-caught (and barely dead) Japanese amberjack native to Northwest Pacific waters (6,794 miles away) without the use of any preservation techniques.

Foods from exotic places have long held cultural appeal. When I began my career as a cook, neither transportation nor industrial preservation was as ubiquitous as it is now. I had never even heard of halloumi, and sushi was a rarity. Each infrequent arrival of an exotic ingredient conjured imagery of foreign lands and distant places. Working with a fresh white truffle, for instance, was tantamount to walking the countryside of the Piedmont city of Alba. After all, the soul of the place was present in the smell, taste, and feel of the tuberous fungi. But the global media has made distant places less alien. Industrialized food distribution has made foreign ingredients more accessible. And geographical exoticism has lost its edge. Now foodies are looking for sophisticated eco-culinary adventure in their own backyards. Trends like the local food movement, emphasizing regional proximity, and the organic farming movement, which promotes unadulterated agriculture, are getting more and more popular.

For example, a recent Walmart press release announced increased partnerships with local growers: "Wal-Mart is working with state departments of agriculture and local farmers to develop or revitalize growing areas for products like corn in Mississippi and cilantro in Southern Florida which had not grown there before or which were once native crops" (Walmart Stores, Inc., 2009). Nativity has become the new exoticism. It is a fashion trend. It is a fad with marketability akin to the hula-hoop, the slinky, and Barack Obama T-shirts.

Walmart barely addresses the political point that local food activists are trying to put forward. That "what we are seeing," as Vandana Shiva writes in *Stolen Harvest* (2000), "is the emergence of food totalitarianism in which a handful of corporations control the entire food chain and destroy alternatives so that people do not have access to diverse, safe foods produced ecologically" (Shiva, 2000, p. 17). But Walmart's marketing department does not miss the metaphorical point.

What captures the consumer's imagination — and therefore his pay-check — is not the political and ecological inequity of corporate indus-trial agriculture, but rather the concept of the sanctity of wilderness.

Therefore, the discussion of food's agricultural origins seems to have become a moralistic one in which words like "holy," "sacred," and "pure" have been translated to "local," "fresh," and "organic." Thus, the media pollinates the cultural gastronomic landscape with sound bites extolling the superiority of free-range beef, chicken, and eggs. Never mind that few take the time to investigate what these words on the label actually mean. The important thing is that the imagery implies that these foods are uncaged, untainted, and therefore holy. After all, William Cronon reminds us that wilderness, post–twentieth century, is "frequently likened to Eden itself" (Cronon, 1989, p. 473). Each nibble, therefore, is like a communion wafer through which you con-sume the holy spirit of a messianic redemption.

Is the soot beneath my fingernails any less repulsive if I tell you I only cook with morally superior local and organic ingredients? I doubt it, because the cultural ambience of food consumption is populated with colliding and contradictory narratives. In one story a bounty of raw ingredients is reduced to depraved matter to preserve the aus-pice° of humanity's dominance over nature. In another story the in-gredients themselves hold the messianic potential to return us to ta-bula rasa° of the Garden of Eden. The former narrative has commodified nature so extremely that the current atmosphere of gastropolitical ac-tivism offers a compensatory swing to the latter. The danger is that the food snob mistakes compensation for consciousness. This is what hap-pens when the sound bite on the end of my fork reflects a fundamen-talist methodology that promotes one moralistic perspective over the other. In both narratives the food acts as a mirror that reflects au-thentic aspects of our human predicament. Both stories are rooted in ideologies that have political, economic, ecological, and social ramifi-cations, but the stories themselves are narcissistic. That is, they mir-ror the Selves we like to see. One may or may not take Genesis 1:27 literally — that humanity was created in God's own image; but un-doubtedly, humanity makes dinner in its own. I wonder what food could look like, taste like, and feel like were we to take it for what it is: neither the villain in a postindustrial corporate economy nor the local sustainable solution to an impending environmental tragedy. Instead, it is a living part of the eco-cycle in which we participate.

auspice: Protection or support.
tabula rasa: Blank slate.

References

Cronon, W. (1989). The trouble with wilderness, or, getting back to the wrong nature. In J. B. Callicott and M. P. Nelson (Eds.), *The great new wilderness debate* (pp. 471–499). Washington: Island Press.

Shiva, V. (2000). *Stolen harvest: The hijacking of the global food supply.* Boston: South End Press.

Walmart Stores, Inc. (2009). Wal-Mart Commits to America's Farmers as Produce Aisles Go Local. (n.d.). Retrieved July 17, 2009, from http://walmartstores.com /FactsNews/NewsRoom/8414.aspx.

Understanding the Text

1. According to Shapiro, eating is necessarily an interaction with the natural world. He explains, "We feed on plants and animals, and thus our relationship to flora and fauna is evident in our culinary trends and methods." What does he mean? What does this tell us about his definition of food?

2. How does Shapiro separate "matter" from "meaning," and how does this affect his definition of food?

3. What is the "cultural gastronomic landscape" (para. 28)? How does it affect how we define food?

Reflection and Response

4. Why is Shapiro's recognition that he and a pig are both "made of meat" important to his argument?

5. Shapiro suggests that we gain something by seeing an orange as the extension of the tree that bears it. What does he imply we gain? Do you agree? What do we gain by seeing an orange as the extension of the tree that bears it?

6. Consider the story Shapiro tells about his son and the orange. Recall a childhood memory that illustrates how you define food. What kind of relationship to food does your story suggest?

Making Connections

7. Shapiro argues that the relationship between food and culture is "populated with colliding and contradictory narratives." What are some of these narratives, and how do they affect how we define food? Locate stories in at least two other readings to support your answer.

8. Shapiro argues that food serves as a mirror that can reflect the human condition. Consider Peter Menzel's photographs ("What the World Eats," p. 90) in relation to Shapiro's argument. What do the photographs tell us about the material lives of the families that are portrayed?

2

What Is the Purpose of Food?

nitially, the purpose of food may seem obvious: we eat food to stay alive, of course. It provides the calories and nutrients we need to maintain our bodies. Sustenance is far from the only reason we eat, however, as the selections in this chapter — by an agriculturalist, nutritionist, photographer, foodie, urban farmer, and farmer-turned-philosopher — show.

Is eating supposed to be pleasurable? social? for our health? The purpose of food can vary greatly depending on your position in society, your goals and values, your culture and country of origin, and your spiritual and political beliefs. Eating with family and friends — sharing meals while sharing company and conversation — is a custom worldwide. Particular foods also hold traditional places in the daily lives of those who prepare and consume them.

Most people would agree that one purpose of food, at least, is nutrition. But how do we know what foods will keep us healthy? In this chapter, Marion Nestle focuses on the effects that food has on our bodies and reminds us that nutrition science can sometimes lead us astray. While Wendell Berry shares with Nestle a belief in healthy eating, he emphasizes that one important purpose of food is pleasure and that truly grasping the pleasure of eating requires an understanding of one's role in its production. Food production is also key for Erica Strauss, while consumption is everything for the young foodies in Michael Idov's account. Masanobu Fukuoka considers a diet that can nourish bodies and souls. Bryant Terry corrects the historical record on soul food. And Peter Menzel and Faith D'Aluisio document varied purposes that food serves in different countries for families of different means and circumstances.

To explore the purpose of food, then, it seems that an understanding of its nutritional components is not enough. Taken together, the readings in this chapter suggest that we need a broader set of considerations to understand the purpose of food in our lives. What roles does food play? Do we eat for nutrition? pleasure? cultural connection? spiritual health? status? What purposes might food be said to serve beyond being something we consume? Is the purpose of food largely cultural, linked to our historical, political, ethnic, and socioeconomic origins? Does the purpose of food complicate what counts as food? How does food nourish us — through certain chemical properties, or through something larger and more difficult to define? What are the different "pleasures" of food? This chapter encourages you to reflect on these questions.

The Pleasures of Eating

Wendell Berry

Wendell Berry has spent his life as a poet and a farmer, drawing on his knowledge of and concern for the land, flora, and fauna in his more than thirty books of essays, poetry, and fiction. A prolific writer and man of letters, he uses his writing as a platform for speaking out about degradation of the land, environmental awareness, and conservation. He is well known for his essays on sustainable agriculture and food, many of which are collected in *Bringing It to the Table: On Farming and Food*, published in 2009. His many awards and lectures demonstrate his ability to connect with his audiences in meaningful ways. In this essay, Berry argues that we should think of eating as an "agricultural act" instead of thinking of food as an "agricultural product." He hopes that this will lead to a greater awareness of the complex relationships we have with our food and our responsibilities in its production.

Many times, after I have finished a lecture on the decline of American farming and rural life, someone in the audience has asked, "What can city people do?"

"Eat responsibly," I have usually answered. Of course, I have tried to explain what I mean by that, but afterwards I have invariably felt there was more to be said than I had been able to say. Now I would like to attempt a better explanation.

I begin with the proposition that eating is an agricultural act. Eating ends the annual drama of the food economy that begins with planting and birth. Most eaters, however, are no longer aware that this is true. They think of food as an agricultural product, perhaps, but they do not think of themselves as participants in agriculture. They think of themselves as "consumers." If they think beyond that, they recognize that they are passive consumers. They buy what they want — or what they have been persuaded to want — within the limits of what they can get. They pay, mostly without protest, what they are charged. And they mostly ignore certain critical questions about the quality and the cost of what they are sold: How fresh is it? How pure or clean is it, how free of dangerous chemicals? How far was it transported, and what did transportation add to the cost? How much did manufacturing or packaging or advertising add to the cost? When the food product has been manufactured or "processed" or "precooked," how has that affected its quality or price or nutritional value?

Most urban shoppers would tell you that food is produced on farms. But most of them do not know what farms, or what kinds of farms, or where the farms are, or what knowledge or skills are involved in farming. They apparently have little doubt that farms will continue to produce, but they do not know how or over what obstacles. For them, then, food is pretty much an abstract idea — something they do not know or imagine — until it appears on the grocery shelf or on the table. *what they think they know.*

The specialization of production induces specialization of consumption. Patrons of the entertainment industry, for example, entertain themselves less and less and have become more and more passively dependent on commercial suppliers. This is certainly true also of patrons of the food industry, who have tended more and more to be mere consumers — passive, uncritical, and dependent. Indeed, this sort of consumption may be said to be one of the chief goals of industrial production. The food industrialists have by now persuaded millions of consumers to prefer food that is already prepared. They will grow, deliver, and cook your food for you and (just like your mother) beg you to eat it. That they do not yet offer to insert it, prechewed, into our mouth is only because they have found no profitable way to do so. We may rest assured that they would be glad to find such a way. The ideal industrial food consumer would be strapped to a table with a tube running from the food factory directly into his or her stomach.

Perhaps I exaggerate, but not by much. The industrial eater is, in fact, one who does not know that eating is an agricultural act, who no longer knows or imagines the connections between eating and the land, and who is therefore necessarily passive and uncritical — in short, a victim. When food, in the minds of eaters, is no longer associated with farming and with the land, then the eaters are suffering a kind of cultural amnesia that is misleading and dangerous. The current version of the "dream home" of the future involves "effortless" shopping from a list of available goods on a television monitor and heating precooked food by remote control. Of course, this implies and depends on a perfect ignorance of the history of the food that is consumed. It requires that the citizenry should give up their hereditary and sensible aversion to buying a pig in a poke. It wishes to make the selling of pigs in pokes an honorable and glamorous activity. The dreams in this dream home will perforce know nothing about the kind or quality of this food, or where it came from, or how it was produced and prepared, or what ingredients, additives, and

when they don't know

where can from

5

residues it contains — unless, that is, the dreamer undertakes a close and constant study of the food industry, in which case he or she might as well wake up and play an active and responsible part in the economy of food.

There is, then, a politics of food that, like any politics, involves our freedom. We still (sometimes) remember that we cannot be free if our minds and voices are controlled by someone else. But we have neglected to understand that we cannot be free if our food and its sources are controlled by someone else. The condition of the passive consumer of food is not a democratic condition. One reason to eat responsibly is to live free.

But if there is a food politics, there are also a food esthetics and a food ethics, neither of which is dissociated from politics. Like industrial sex, industrial eating has become a degraded, poor, and paltry thing. Our kitchens and other eating places more and more resemble filling stations, as our homes more and more resemble motels. "Life is not very interesting," we seem to have decided. "Let its satisfactions be minimal, perfunctory, and fast." We hurry through our meals to go to work and hurry through our work in order to "recreate" ourselves in the evenings and on weekends and vacations. And then we hurry, with the greatest possible speed and noise and violence, through our recreation — for what? To eat the billionth hamburger at some fast-food joint hellbent on increasing the "quality" of our life? And all this is carried out in a remarkable obliviousness to the causes and effects, the possibilities and the purposes, of the life of the body in this world.

One will find this obliviousness represented in virgin purity in the advertisements of the food industry, in which food wears as much makeup as the actors. If one gained one's whole knowledge of food from these advertisements (as some presumably do), one would not know that the various edibles were ever living creatures, or that they all come from the soil, or that they were produced by work. The passive American consumer, sitting down to a meal of pre-prepared or fast food, confronts a platter covered with inert, anonymous substances that have been processed, dyed, breaded, sauced, gravied, ground, pulped, strained, blended, prettified, and sanitized beyond resemblance to any part of any creature that ever lived. The products of nature and agriculture have been made, to all appearances, the products of industry. Both eater and eaten are thus in exile from biological reality. And the result is a kind of solitude, unprecedented in human experience, in which the eater may think of eating as, first, a purely commercial transaction between him and a supplier and then as a purely appetitive transaction between him and his food.

And this peculiar specialization of the act of eating is, again, of 10 obvious benefit to the food industry, which has good reasons to obscure the connection between food and farming. It would not do for the consumer to know that the hamburger she is eating came from a steer who spent much of his life standing deep in his own excrement in a feedlot, helping to pollute the local streams, or that the calf that yielded the veal cutlet on her plate spent its life in a box in which it did not have room to turn around. And, though her sympathy for the slaw might be less tender, she should not be encouraged to meditate on the hygienic and biological implications of mile-square fields of cabbage, for vegetables grown in huge monocultures are dependent on toxic chemicals — just as animals in close confinements are dependent on antibiotics and other drugs.

> Eaters . . . must understand that eating takes place inescapably in the world, that it is inescapably an agricultural act, and how we eat determines, to a considerable extent, how the world is used.

The consumer, that is to say, must be kept from discovering that, in the food industry — as in any other industry — the overriding concerns are not quality and health, but volume and price. For decades now the entire industrial food economy, from the large farms and feedlots to the chains of supermarkets and fast-food restaurants, has been obsessed with volume. It has relentlessly increased scale in order to increase volume in order (probably) to reduce costs. But as scale increases, diversity declines; as diversity declines, so does health; as health declines, the dependence on drugs and chemicals necessarily increases. As capital replaces labor, it does so by substituting machines, drugs, and chemicals for human workers and for the natural health and fertility of the soil. The food is produced by any means or any shortcuts that will increase profits. And the business of the cosmeticians° of advertising is to persuade the consumer that food so produced is good, tasty, healthful, and a guarantee of marital fidelity and long life.

It is possible, then, to be liberated from the husbandry and wifery of the old household food economy. But one can be thus liberated only by entering a trap (unless one sees ignorance and helplessness as the signs of privilege, as many people apparently do). The trap is the ideal of industrialism: a walled city surrounded by valves that let merchandise in but no consciousness out. How does one escape this trap? Only voluntarily, the same way that one went in: by restoring

cosmetician: Someone who sells or applies makeup.

one's consciousness of what is involved in eating; by reclaiming responsibility for one's own part in the food economy. One might begin with the illuminating principle of Sir Albert Howard's, that we should understand "the whole problem of health in soil, plant, animal, and man as one great subject." Eaters, that is, must understand that eating takes place inescapably in the world, that it is inescapably an agricultural act, and how we eat determines, to a considerable extent, how the world is used. This is a simple way of describing a relationship that is inexpressibly complex. To eat responsibly is to understand and enact, so far as we can, this complex relationship. What can one do? Here is a list, probably not definitive:

1. Participate in food production to the extent that you can. If you have a yard or even just a porch box or a pot in a sunny window, grow something to eat in it. Make a little compost of your kitchen scraps and use it for fertilizer. Only by growing some food for yourself can you become acquainted with the beautiful energy cycle that revolves from soil to seed to flower to fruit to food to offal° to decay, and around again. You will be fully responsible for any food that you grow for yourself, and you will know all about it. You will appreciate it fully, having known it all its life.

2. Prepare your own food. This means reviving in your own mind and life the arts of kitchen and household. This should enable you to eat more cheaply, and it will give you a measure of "quality control": you will have some reliable knowledge of what has been added to the food you eat.

3. Learn the origins of the food you buy, and buy the food that is produced closest to your home. The idea that every locality should be, as much as possible, the source of its own food makes several kinds of sense. The locally produced food supply is the most secure, freshest, and the easiest for local consumers to know about and to influence.

4. Whenever possible, deal directly with a local farmer, gardener, or orchardist. All the reasons listed for the previous suggestion apply here. In addition, by such dealing you eliminate the whole pack of merchants, transporters, processors, packagers, and advertisers who thrive at the expense of both producers and consumers.

offal: Scrap waste.

5. Learn, in self-defense, as much as you can of the economy and technology of industrial food production. What is added to the food that is not food, and what do you pay for those additions?

6. Learn what is involved in the best farming and gardening.

7. Learn as much as you can, by direct observation and experience if possible, of the life histories of the food species.

The last suggestion seems particularly important to me. Many people are now as much estranged from the lives of domestic plants and animals (except for flowers and dogs and cats) as they are from the lives of the wild ones. This is regrettable, for these domestic creatures are in diverse ways attractive; there is such pleasure in knowing them, too.

It follows that there is great displeasure in knowing about a food economy that degrades and abuses those arts and those plants and animals and the soil from which they come. For anyone who does know something of the modern history of food, eating away from home can be a chore. My own inclination is to eat seafood instead of red meat or poultry when I am traveling. Though I am by no means a vegetarian, I dislike the thought that some animal has been made miserable in order to feed me. If I am going to eat meat, I want it to be from an animal that has lived a pleasant, uncrowded life outdoors, on bountiful pasture, with good water nearby and trees for shade. And I am getting almost as fussy about food plants. I like to eat vegetables and fruits that I know have lived happily and healthily in good soil, not the products of the huge, bechemicaled factory-fields that I have seen, for example, in the Central Valley of California. The industrial farm is said to have been patterned on the factory production line. In practice, it looks more like a concentration camp.

The pleasure of eating should be an extensive pleasure, not that of   15
the mere gourmet. People who know the garden in which their vegetables have grown and know that the garden is healthy and remember the beauty of the growing plants, perhaps in the dewy first light of morning when gardens are at their best. Such a memory involves itself with the food and is one of the pleasures of eating. The knowledge of the good health of the garden relieves and frees and comforts the eater. The same goes for eating meat. The thought of the good pasture and of the calf contentedly grazing flavors the steak. Some, I know, will think of it as bloodthirsty or worse to eat a fellow creature you have known all its life. On the contrary, I think it means that you eat with understanding and with gratitude. A significant part of the pleasure of eating is in one's accurate consciousness of the lives and

the world from which food comes. The pleasure of eating, then, may be the best available standard of our health. And this pleasure, I think, is pretty fully available to the urban consumer who will make the necessary effort.

I mentioned earlier the politics, esthetics, and ethics of food. But to speak of the pleasure of eating is to go beyond those categories. Eating with the fullest pleasure — pleasure, that is, that does not depend on ignorance — is perhaps the profoundest enactment of our connection with the world. In this pleasure we experience and celebrate our dependence and our gratitude, for we are living from mystery, from creatures we did not make and powers we cannot comprehend. When I think of the meaning of food, I always remember these lines by the poet William Carlos Williams, which seem to me merely honest:

> There is nothing to eat,
> seek it where you will,
> but the body of the Lord.
> The blessed plants
> and the sea, yield it
> to the imagination intact.

Understanding the Text

1. What is an "industrial eater"?
2. Why does Berry think it is important to understand the connection between eating and the land?
3. According to Berry, how does the separation of food from farming and agriculture benefit the food industry?

Reflection and Response

4. Berry wrote this essay in 1989. Do you notice substantial changes from what he describes? Do you think he would be pleased with how farming and agricultural practices have changed since then? Why or why not?
5. Berry suggests that freedom depends on eating responsibly and understanding our place in the agricultural economy. Why does he think eating responsibly is a necessary condition of democracy? Explain your answer. Do you agree? Why or why not?
6. Why do you think Berry includes the poem by William Carlos Williams at the end of his essay? What does it add? How does it connect to the larger purpose of Berry's essay?

Making Connections

7. What is the "pleasure of eating," according to Berry? Compare the way Berry describes the purpose of food to the ways Jill McCorkle ("Her Chee-to Heart, p. 31) and Jordan Shapiro ("The Eco-Gastronomic Mirror," p. 50) describe it.

8. Berry argues that eating is necessarily an "agricultural act" and makes seven suggestions for responsible eating. Compare them to Michael Pollan's rules for choosing foods to eat ("Eat Food: Food Defined," p. 9). What values do they share? Are they rules or suggestions you have tried or would consider trying? Which ones? What might you gain (or lose)? What might you learn about your food (and yourself)?

9. Berry argues that there is a "food politics" that is impossible to separate from a "food esthetics" and a "food ethics." What is a "food politics"? Think about the community in which you live. What kinds of local food movements, organizations, programs, or activities exist that could be identified as political in nature (overtly or subtly)? Research at least one of them, and use the views of Berry, Eliot Coleman ("Real Food, Real Farming," p. 236), and Bill McKibben ("The Only Way to Have a Cow," p. 200) to analyze its potential for contributing to awareness of the public's relationships with and responsibilities to food production.

Eating Made Simple

Marion Nestle

Marion Nestle is a professor in both the Department of Nutrition, Food Studies, and Public Health and the Department of Sociology at New York University. She has also spent much of her career in public service, consulting on government policies around food and health. She is the author of several books, including *What to Eat* (2007), *Food Politics: How the Food Industry Influences Nutrition and Health* (2007), *Safe Food: The Politics of Food Safety* (2010), and the most recently published *Why Calories Count: From Science to Politics* (2012). Nestle's research focuses on food and nutrition policy and analysis and the social, political, and environmental influences on food choice. She regularly writes about her work in the *San Francisco Chronicle*, *The Atlantic*, and her blog *Food Politics*. In this essay, which originally appeared in *Scientific American*, Nestle provides advice on how to sort out the often confusing and sometimes contradictory messages about nutrition and dietary advice.

As a nutrition professor, I am constantly asked why nutrition advice seems to change so much and why experts so often disagree. Whose information, people ask, can we trust? I'm tempted to say, "Mine, of course," but I understand the problem. Yes, nutrition advice seems endlessly mired in scientific argument, the self-interest of food companies, and compromises by government regulators. Nevertheless, basic dietary principles are not in dispute: eat less; move more; eat fruits, vegetables, and whole grains; and avoid too much junk food.

"Eat less" means consume fewer calories, which translates into eating smaller portions and steering clear of frequent between-meal snacks. "Move more" refers to the need to balance calorie intake with physical activity. Eating fruits, vegetables, and whole grains provides nutrients unavailable from other foods. Avoiding junk food means to shun "foods of minimal nutritional value" — highly processed sweets and snacks laden with salt, sugars, and artificial additives. Soft drinks are the prototypical° junk food; they contain sweeteners but few or no nutrients.

If you follow these precepts, other aspects of the diet matter much less. Ironically, this advice has not changed in years. The noted cardiologist Ancel Keys (who died in 2004 at the age of 100) and his wife, Margaret, suggested similar principles for preventing coronary heart disease nearly 50 years ago.

prototypical: Serving as an example of a type.

But I can see why dietary advice seems like a moving target. Nutrition research is so difficult to conduct that it seldom produces unambiguous results. Ambiguity requires interpretation. And interpretation is influenced by the individual's point of view, which can become thoroughly entangled with the science.

Nutrition Science Challenges

This scientific uncertainty is not overly surprising given that humans 5 eat so many different foods. For any individual, the health effects of diets are modulated° by genetics but also by education and income levels, job satisfaction, physical fitness, and the use of cigarettes or alcohol. To simplify this situation, researchers typically examine the effects of single dietary components one by one.

Studies focusing on one nutrient in isolation have worked splendidly to explain symptoms caused by deficiencies of vitamins or minerals. But this approach is less useful for chronic conditions such as coronary heart disease and diabetes that are caused by the interaction of dietary, genetic, behavioral, and social factors. If nutrition science seems puzzling, it is because researchers typically examine single nutrients detached from food itself, foods separate from diets, and risk factors apart from other behaviors. This kind of research is "reductive" in that it attributes health effects to the consumption of one nutrient or food when it is the overall dietary pattern that really counts most.

> If nutrition science seems puzzling, it is because researchers typically examine single nutrients detached from food itself, foods separate from diets, and risk factors apart from other behaviors.

For chronic diseases, single nutrients usually alter risk by amounts too small to measure except through large, costly population studies. As seen recently in the Women's Health Initiative, a clinical trial that examined the effects of low-fat diets on heart disease and cancer, participants were unable to stick with the restrictive dietary protocols. Because humans cannot be caged and fed measured formulas, the diets of experimental and control study groups tend to converge, making differences indistinguishable over the long run — even with fancy statistics.

modulate: Modify or control.

It's the Calories

Food companies prefer studies of single nutrients because they can use the results to sell products. Add vitamins to candies, and you can market them as health foods. Health claims on the labels of junk foods distract consumers from their caloric content. This practice matters because when it comes to obesity — which dominates nutrition problems even in some of the poorest countries of the world — it is the calories that count. Obesity arises when people consume significantly more calories than they expend in physical activity.

America's obesity rates began to rise sharply in the early 1980s. Sociologists often attribute the "calories in" side of this trend to the demands of an overworked population for convenience foods — prepared, packaged products and restaurant meals that usually contain more calories than home-cooked meals.

But other social forces also promoted the calorie imbalance. The 10 arrival of the Reagan administration in 1980 increased the pace of industry deregulation, removing controls on agricultural production and encouraging farmers to grow more food. Calories available per capita in the national food supply (that produced by American farmers, plus imports, less exports) rose from 3,200 a day in 1980 to 3,900 a day two decades later.

The early 1980s also marked the advent of the "shareholder value movement" on Wall Street. Stockholder demands for higher short-term returns on investments forced food companies to expand sales in a marketplace that already contained excessive calories. Food companies responded by seeking new sales and marketing opportunities. They encouraged formerly shunned practices that eventually changed social norms, such as frequent between-meal snacking, eating in book and clothing stores, and serving larger portions. The industry continued to sponsor organizations and journals that focus on nutrition-related subjects and intensified its efforts to lobby government for favorable dietary advice. Then and now food lobbies have promoted positive interpretations of scientific studies, sponsored research that can be used as a basis for health claims, and attacked critics, myself among them, as proponents of "junk science." If anything, such activities only add to public confusion.

Supermarkets as "Ground Zero"

No matter whom I speak to, I hear pleas for help in dealing with supermarkets, considered by shoppers as "ground zero" for distinguishing health claims from scientific advice. So I spent a year visiting supermarkets to help people think more clearly about food choices. The result was my book *What to Eat.*

Supermarkets provide a vital public service but are not social services agencies. Their job is to sell as much food as possible. Every aspect of store design — from shelf position to background music — is based on marketing research. Because this research shows that the more products customers see, the more they buy, a store's objective is to expose shoppers to the maximum number of products they will tolerate viewing.

If consumers are confused about which foods to buy, it is surely because the choices require knowledge of issues that are not easily resolved by science and are strongly swayed by social and economic considerations. Such decisions play out every day in every store aisle.

Are Organics Healthier?

Organic foods are the fastest-growing segment of the industry, in part because people are willing to pay more for foods that they believe are healthier and more nutritious. The U.S. Department of Agriculture forbids producers of "Certified Organic" fruits and vegetables from using synthetic pesticides, herbicides, fertilizers, genetically modified seeds, irradiation, or fertilizer derived from sewage sludge. It licenses inspectors to ensure that producers follow those rules. Although the USDA is responsible for organics, its principal mandate is to promote conventional agriculture, which explains why the department asserts that it "makes no claims that organically produced food is safer or more nutritious than conventionally produced food. Organic food differs from conventionally grown food in the way it is grown, handled and processed."

This statement implies that such differences are unimportant. Critics of organic foods would agree; they question the reliability of organic certification and the productivity, safety, and health benefits of organic production methods. Meanwhile the organic food industry longs for research to address such criticisms, but studies are expensive and difficult to conduct. Nevertheless, existing research in this area has established that organic farms are nearly as productive as conventional farms, use less energy, and leave soils in better condition. People who eat foods grown without synthetic pesticides ought to have fewer such chemicals in their bodies, and they do. Because the organic rules require pretreatment of manure and other steps to reduce the amount of pathogens in soil treatments, organic foods should be just as safe — or safer — than conventional foods.

Similarly, organic foods ought to be at least as nutritious as conventional foods. And proving organics to be more nutritious could help justify their higher prices. For minerals, this task is not difficult. The mineral content of plants depends on the amounts present in the soil in which they are grown. Organic foods are cultivated in richer soils, so their mineral content is higher.

But differences are harder to demonstrate for vitamins or antioxidants (plant substances that reduce tissue damage induced by free radicals); higher levels of these nutrients relate more to a food plant's genetic strain or protection from unfavorable conditions after harvesting than to production methods. Still, preliminary studies show benefits: organic peaches and pears contain greater quantities of vitamins C and E, and organic berries and corn contain more antioxidants.

Further research will likely confirm that organic foods contain higher nutrient levels, but it is unclear whether these nutrients would make a measurable improvement in health. All fruits and vegetables contain useful nutrients, albeit in different combinations and concentrations. Eating a variety of food plants is surely more important to health than small differences in the nutrient content of any one food. Organics may be somewhat healthier to eat, but they are far less likely to damage the environment, and that is reason enough to choose them at the supermarket.

Dairy and Calcium

Scientists cannot easily resolve questions about the health effects of dairy foods. Milk has many components, and the health of people who consume milk or dairy foods is influenced by everything else they eat and do. But this area of research is especially controversial because it affects an industry that vigorously promotes dairy products as beneficial and opposes suggestions to the contrary.

Dairy foods contribute about 70 percent of the calcium in American diets. This necessary mineral is a principal constituent of bones, which constantly lose and regain calcium during normal metabolism. Diets must contain enough calcium to replace losses, or else bones become prone to fracture. Experts advise consumption of at least one gram of calcium a day to replace everyday losses. Only dairy foods provide this much calcium without supplementation.

But bones are not just made of calcium; they require the full complement of essential nutrients to maintain strength. Bones are stronger in people who are physically active and who do not smoke cigarettes or drink much alcohol. Studies examining the effects of single nutrients in dairy foods show that some nutritional factors — magnesium, potassium, vitamin D, and lactose, for example — promote calcium retention in bones. Others, such as protein, phosphorus, and sodium, foster calcium excretion. So bone strength depends more on overall patterns of diet and behavior than simply on calcium intake.

Populations that do not typically consume dairy products appear to exhibit lower rates of bone fracture despite consuming far less calcium than recommended. Why this is so is unclear. Perhaps their diets contain less protein from meat and dairy foods, less sodium from processed foods, and less phosphorus from soft drinks, so they retain calcium more effectively. The fact that calcium balance depends on multiple factors could explain why rates of osteoporosis (bone density loss) are highest in countries where people eat the most dairy foods. Further research may clarify such counterintuitive observations.

In the meantime, dairy foods are fine to eat if you like them, but they are not a nutritional requirement. Think of cows: they do not drink milk after weaning, but their bones support bodies weighing 800 pounds or more. Cows feed on grass, and grass contains calcium in small amounts — but those amounts add up. If you eat plenty of fruits, vegetables and whole grains, you can have healthy bones without having to consume dairy foods.

A Meaty Debate

Critics point to meat as the culprit responsible for elevating blood cholesterol, along with raising risks for heart disease, cancer, and other conditions. Supporters cite the lack of compelling science to justify such allegations; they emphasize the nutritional benefits of meat protein, vitamins, and minerals. Indeed, studies in developing countries demonstrate health improvements when growing children are fed even small amounts of meat. [25]

But because bacteria in a cow's rumen attach hydrogen atoms to unsaturated fatty acids, beef fat is highly saturated — the kind of fat that increases the risk of coronary heart disease. All fats and oils contain some saturated fatty acids, but animal fats, especially those from beef, have more saturated fatty acids than vegetable fats. Nutritionists recommend eating no more than a heaping tablespoon (20 grams) of saturated fatty acids a day. Beef eaters easily meet or exceed this limit. The smallest McDonald's cheeseburger contains 6 grams of saturated fatty acids, but a Hardee's Monster Thickburger has 45 grams.

Why meat might boost cancer risks, however, is a matter of speculation. Scientists began to link meat to cancer in the 1970s, but even after decades of subsequent research they remain unsure if the relevant factor might be fat, saturated fat, protein, carcinogens,° or something else related to meat. By the late 1990s experts could conclude only that eating beef probably increases the risk of colon and rectal cancers and possibly enhances the odds of acquiring breast, prostate and perhaps other cancers. Faced with this uncertainty, the American Cancer Society suggests selecting leaner cuts, smaller portions, and alternatives such as chicken, fish, or beans — steps consistent with today's basic advice about what to eat.

Fish and Heart Disease

Fatty fish are the most important sources of long-chain omega-3 fatty acids. In the early 1970s Danish investigators observed surprisingly low frequencies of heart disease among indigenous populations in Greenland that typically ate fatty fish, seals, and whales. The researchers attributed the protective effect to the foods' content of omega-3 fatty acids. Some subsequent studies — but by no means all — confirm this idea.

Because large, fatty fish are likely to have accumulated methylmercury and other toxins through predation, however, eating them raises questions about the balance between benefits and risks. Understandably, the fish industry is eager to prove that the health benefits of omega-3s outweigh any risks from eating fish.

Even independent studies on omega-3 fats can be interpreted 30 differently. In 2004 the National Oceanic and Atmospheric Administration — for fish, the agency equivalent to the USDA — asked the Institute of Medicine (IOM) to review studies of the benefits and risks of consuming seafood. The ensuing review of the research on heart disease risk illustrates the challenge such work poses for interpretation.

The IOM's October 2006 report concluded that eating seafood reduces the risk of heart disease but judged the studies too inconsistent to decide if omega-3 fats were responsible. In contrast, investigators from the Harvard School of Public Health published a much more positive report in the *Journal of the American Medical Associa-*

carcinogen: Any substance that directly causes cancer.

tion that same month. Even modest consumption of fish omega-3s, they stated, would cut coronary deaths by 36 percent and total mortality by 17 percent, meaning that not eating fish would constitute a health risk.

Differences in interpretation explain how distinguished scientists could arrive at such different conclusions after considering the same studies. The two groups, for example, had conflicting views of earlier work published in March 2006 in the *British Medical Journal.* That study found no overall effect of omega-3s on heart disease risk or mortality, although a subset of the original studies displayed a 14 percent reduction in total mortality that did not reach statistical significance. The IOM team interpreted the "nonsignificant" result as evidence for the need for caution, whereas the Harvard group saw the data as consistent with studies reporting the benefits of omega-3s. When studies present inconsistent results, both interpretations are plausible. I favor caution in such situations, but not everyone agrees.

Because findings are inconsistent, so is dietary advice about eating fish. The American Heart Association recommends that adults eat fatty fish at least twice a week, but U.S. dietary guidelines say: "Limited evidence suggests an association between consumption of fatty acids in fish and reduced risks of mortality from cardiovascular disease for the general population . . . however, more research is needed." Whether or not fish uniquely protects against heart disease, seafood is a delicious source of many nutrients, and two small servings per week of the less predatory classes of fish are unlikely to cause harm.

Sodas and Obesity

Sugars and corn sweeteners account for a large fraction of the calories in many supermarket foods, and virtually all the calories in drinks — soft, sports, and juice — come from added sugars.

In a trend that correlates closely with rising rates of obesity, daily 35 per capita consumption of sweetened beverages has grown by about 200 calories since the early 1980s. Although common sense suggests that this increase might have something to do with weight gain, beverage makers argue that studies cannot prove that sugary drinks alone — independent of calories or other foods in the diet — boost the risk of obesity. The evidence, they say correctly, is circumstantial. But pediatricians often see obese children in their practices who consume more than 1,000 calories a day from sweetened drinks alone, and several studies indicate that children who habitually consume sugary beverages take in more calories and weigh more than those who do not.

Nevertheless, the effects of sweetened drinks on obesity continue to be subject to interpretation. In 2006, for example, a systematic review funded by independent sources found sweetened drinks to promote obesity in both children and adults. But a review that same year sponsored in part by a beverage trade association concluded that soft drinks have no special role in obesity. The industry-funded researchers criticized existing studies as being short-term and inconclusive, and pointed to studies finding that people lose weight when they substitute sweetened drinks for their usual meals.

These differences imply the need to scrutinize food industry sponsorship of research itself. Although many researchers are offended by suggestions that funding support might affect the way they design or interpret studies, systematic analyses say otherwise. In 2007 investigators classified studies of the effects of sweetened and other beverages on health according to who had sponsored them. Industry-supported studies were more likely to yield results favorable to the sponsor than those funded by independent sources. Even though scientists may not be able to prove that sweetened drinks cause obesity, it makes sense for anyone interested in losing weight to consume less of them.

The examples I have discussed illustrate why nutrition science seems so controversial. Without improved methods to ensure compliance with dietary regimens, research debates are likely to rage unabated. Opposing points of view and the focus of studies and food advertising on single nutrients rather than on dietary patterns continue to fuel these disputes. While we wait for investigators to find better ways to study nutrition and health, my approach — eat less, move more, eat a largely plant-based diet, and avoid eating too much junk food — makes sense and leaves you plenty of opportunity to enjoy your dinner.

Understanding the Text

1. What is nutrition science? Why is nutrition science "reductive"?
2. What nutritional principles do experts agree on, according to Nestle?
3. If the basic principles are not in dispute, why is there so much conflicting nutritional advice? How does Nestle suggest reconciling it?

Reflection and Response

4. Nestle explains that nutrition science is controversial. Why is it so difficult to conduct nutrition research, and what makes the results so controversial? Select three of her examples to illustrate your position.

5. Think about what you eat. What have you learned about your own overall nutrition from reading Nestle's essay? Are there changes you think you should make? Why or why not?

Making Connections

6. What possible connections exist between the flavor industry described by Eric Schlosser ("Why the Fries Taste Good," p. 20) and the nutrition research described by Nestle? How might Masanobu Fukuoka ("Living by Bread Alone," p. 87) analyze these connections?

7. Nestle served as a policy maker for the federal government nutrition guidelines. How do you think Nestle would interpret and evaluate the USDA's Food Pyramid in relation to the Food Plate guidelines (p. 112)? Which one do you think she would prefer and why?

8. Think about the story of nutrition in America that Nestle tells in relation to the optimism Michelle Obama expresses in "The Business Case for Healthier Food Options" (p. 115). What does each emphasize? What values do they share? How does evidence presented by Nestle support, contradict, or complicate Obama's evidence? Do you think Nestle would share Obama's optimism if she considered the evidence Obama presents? Why or why not?

9. Messages regarding nutrition and dietary advice surround us, from stories in the media about cutting-edge studies to advertising and packaging labels. Find several pieces of nutrition advice that employ nutrition science as evidence for why consumers should adopt the advice or buy the product. How do they use nutrition science? What would Nestle, Dhruv Khullar ("Why Shame Won't Stop Obesity," p. 127), and Wendell Berry ("The Pleasures of Eating," p. 64) say about the advice? What do you think of the advice? Would you follow it?

Reclaiming True Grits

Bryant Terry

Bryant Terry is a chef, author, and food justice activist. He has written three books, including *Vegan Soul Kitchen* (2009) and the most recent, *The Inspired Vegan* (2012). He also hosts a Web series, *Urban Organic*. Terry traces his interest in cooking, farming, food justice, and public health to his upbringing in Memphis, Tennessee, where, he says, his grandparents taught him the value of growing your own fruits and vegetables and preparing your own food. After completing chef's training at the Natural Gourmet Institute for Health and Culinary Arts and a master's degree in American history at New York University, he settled in Oakland, California. His research interests focus on history, politics, and food, but his passion centers on empowering people to make healthy choices even if their local communities make that difficult to do. In this blog post published on *The Root*, Terry provides a historical overview of soul food, rejecting the notion that it is necessarily bad for you and using the discussion to comment on the way African American cuisine is portrayed in the media.

Mention "soul food" and you will hear scores of health and medical professionals claim that it is the downfall of the health and well-being of African Americans. It is true that African Americans have some of the highest rates of obesity, diabetes, heart disease, and some cancers of any group in this country. But frankly, I'm getting sick of soul food being held partially responsible for this. The majority of people imagine the traditional soul food diet as unsophisticated and unhealthy fare comprised of high-calorie, low-nutrient dishes replete with salt, sugar, and bad fats. Rather than vilifying traditional soul food, let's focus on the real culprit, what I like to call instant soul food.

In reality, soul food is good for you. In order to understand why, you have to understand grits. As seen with instant grits, mass production and distribution has diminished the product's superb quality and has obscured the distinctive characteristics that make down-home hominy so darn desirable in the first place. The taste of instant grits boxed up in a factory can never compare to the complex nutty flavor of grits stone-ground in a Mississippi mill. So it's understandable that those who have only had that watered-down stuff (read: many of my friends in the Northeast) scoff at the mention of grits.

Similar to instant grits, instant soul food is a dishonest representation of African American cuisine. And to be clear, when I refer to instant soul food, I'm not just describing the processing, packaging, and mass marketing of African American cuisine in the late 1980s. I'm also alluding to the oversimplified version of the cuisine that was constructed in the popular imagination in the late 1960s.

The term "soul food" first emerged during the black liberation movement as African Americans named and reclaimed their diverse traditional foods. Clearly, the term was meant to celebrate and distinguish African American cooking from general Southern cooking, and not ghettoize it. But in the late 1960s, soul food was "discovered" by the popular media and constructed as the newest exotic cuisine for white consumers to devour. Rather than portray the complexity of this cuisine and its changes throughout the late 19th and 20th centuries, many writers played up its more exotic aspects (e.g., animal entrails) and simply framed the cuisine as a remnant of poverty-driven antebellum° survival food.

To paraphrase food historian Jessica B. Harris, "soul food" was simply what Southern black folks ate for dinner. 5

Sadly, over the past four decades most of us have forgotten that what many African Americans in the South ate for dinner just two generations ago was diverse, creative, and comprised of a lot of fresh, local, and homegrown nutrient-dense food.

Most self-proclaimed soul food restaurants, a considerable amount of soul food cookbooks, and the canned and frozen soul food industry reinforce this banal portrayal of African American cuisine. Moreover, film and television routinely bombard viewers with crass images of African American eating habits and culinary practices that further distort and demonize soul food.

> Sadly, over the past four decades most of us have forgotten that what many African Americans in the South ate for dinner just two generations ago was diverse, creative, and comprised of a lot of fresh, local, and homegrown nutrient-dense food.

Don't get me wrong, I'm all for fried chicken, mac-and-cheese, collard greens, and peach cobbler being reinterpreted. But romanticizing comfort foods that should be eaten occasionally and presenting these foods as standard fare not only rewrites history, but it also normalizes unhealthy eating habits for African Americans who are unaware of their historical cuisine.

---

antebellum: Existing before a war, especially (and in this case) referring to the American Civil War (1861–1865).

When I think about the soul food that my grandparents and their parents ate, I do have some fond memories of deep-fried meats, over-cooked leafy greens, and sugary desserts occasionally making a cameo on our menu. But I also recall lightly sautéed okra, corn, and tomatoes recently harvested from their "natural" backyard garden in South Memphis. Divine recollections abound of butchered-that-morning herb-roasted chicken from Paw-Paw's coop; "grit cakes" fashioned from breakfast leftovers and then grilled alongside pulled pork; Ma'Dear's chutney made from peaches that came from Miss Cole's mini-orchard next door; and fresh watermelon purchased from a flatbed truck on the side of the road and served with salt sprinkled on each slice.

There are African Americans like the late chef and cookbook author 10 Edna Lewis; food historian Jessica B. Harris; and the chef-owner of Farmer Brown Restaurant in San Francisco, Jay Foster, who acknowl-edge a more complex culinary heritage and understand the African American legacy of being "green." It's time, however, that we all reclaim real Soul Food by learning from elders; rediscovering heirloom vari-etals°; planting home and community gardens; shopping at the farm-er's market; eating what's in season; pickling, canning, and preserving for leaner months; getting back into the kitchen and cooking; and shar-ing meals with family and friends. While these actions may not solve all the health issues in our communities, they will get the ball rolling.

☆ Obviously, there are complex social, economic, demographic, and environmental factors that explain why diseases such as diabetes and high blood pressure are so rife within African American communities. *Yes, we can* experience real change consisting of personal, family, community, and structural shifts by making our voices heard and pressuring our elected officials to create national, state, and local poli-cies that ensure that *all* Americans have access to healthy, affordable food. The task won't be easy, but employing the same grit that carried our ancestors through the worst of times can pull us through anything.

PAN-FRIED GRIT CAKES WITH CARAMELIZED SPRING ONIONS, GARLIC, AND THYME

Yield: Serves 4–6
Soundtrack: Green Onions by Booker T. & the MG's
      Mark my word, after making and eating this dish while listening to Green Onions, they both will be on heavy rotation for a few months, if not longer. I enjoy these tasty cakes as a

---

varietals: A variety of heirloom vegetables that represent biological diversity.

savory dinner side or as a light meal with a green salad. You can omit the spring onions, cayenne, garlic, and thyme and eat these with pure maple syrup as a breakfast treat.

For a lower-fat version, they can be baked on a lightly greased baking sheet at 325°F until crisp, about 15 minutes each side. They can also be lightly brushed with olive oil and grilled for 10 minutes on each side.

Extra-virgin olive oil
1 large bunch of spring onions, trimmed and sliced thinly
1/8 teaspoon cayenne pepper
3 garlic cloves, minced

2 cups whole milk
1 cup water
1 cup stone-ground corn grits
Coarse sea salt
1/2 teaspoon fresh thyme

- In a medium sauté pan combine 1/2 tablespoon of the olive oil, the spring onions, and the cayenne pepper. Warm the heat to medium-low and sauté gently until well caramelized, 10–15 minutes. Add the garlic and sauté until golden, 2–3 minutes. Remove from heat and set aside.
- In a medium saucepan combine the milk with the water, cover, and bring to a boil, about 3 minutes. Uncover and whisk the grits into the liquid until no lumps remain.
- Reduce the heat to low and simmer for 15 minutes, stirring every 2–3 minutes with a wooden spoon to prevent the grits from sticking to the bottom of the pan.
- Add the spring onion–olive oil mixture, 1/2 teaspoon salt, and thyme and stir well. Cook for an additional 5 minutes, stirring from time to time.
- Pour the grits into a 2-quart rectangular baking dish or a comparable mold and spread them out with a rubber spatula (the grits should be about 1/2 inch thick). Refrigerate and allow it to rest until firm, about 3 hours or overnight.
- Preheat the oven to 250°F.
- Slice the grits into 2-inch by 2-inch squares.
- Line a couple of large plates with paper towels. In a wide heavy skillet over medium-high heat warm 1 tablespoon of olive oil. When the oil is hot, panfry the cakes for 2 to 3 minutes per side, until they are golden brown and crispy on the outside (do this in several batches to avoid overcrowding the pan). Transfer the cooked cakes from the skillet to the plates to drain, and then hold them in the oven until all the cakes are cooked.
- Serve immediately.

Understanding the Text

1. What is "soul food"? What is African American cuisine? Is there a difference?

2. What is the difference between Terry's description of soul food and what he calls "distorted portrayals" of soul food? Give some examples of "authentic" and "distorted" portrayals.

Reflection and Response

3. Why do you think Terry emphasizes the popular media's role in the characterization of soul food?

4. Have you ever eaten soul food? What do you think of when you think of soul food? Why do you think it is called soul food?

Making Connections

5. Compare Terry's description of "true grits" to Lily Wong's description of Chinese dumplings ("Eating the Hyphen," p. 40) and Amy Cyrex Sins's description of Doberge Cake ("Doberge Cake after Katrina," p. 45). What do they say about the purpose and meaning of food? What do they say about the relationships between food, culture, race, and ethnicity?

6. How might Camille Kingsolver ("Taking Local on the Road," p. 37) reflect on Terry's meditation on soul food? What would she notice?

7. Go online and explore the blog posts of Bryant Terry and Natasha Bowens ("Brightening Up the Dark Farming History of the Sunshine State," p. 252). What similarities do you notice in their explorations of the intersections between race and food? What differences emerge? Why do you think they each have chosen blogging as a way to promote their ideas?

[handwritten annotations: "Taste is important", "we eat to nourish the body", " Nestle comments", "name points"]*

Living by Bread Alone

Masanobu Fukuoka

Masanobu Fukuoka was a Japanese philosopher and farmer dedicated to natural farming practices. As a young man, he had a profound spiritual experience while recovering from a serious illness, which led him to leave his work as a research scientist and return to his family's farm on an island in southern Japan. Here he began experimenting with organic farming practices, even after World War II, when he lost most of his farmland to the forced redistribution policies of the American occupying forces. He began writing books and traveling the world to give lectures to share his agricultural philosophy of natural farming. He received many awards and much recognition worldwide for his important contributions to the international organic farming movement. He died in 2008 at the age of 95. His 1975 book *The One-Straw Revolution* has sold more than one million copies and has been translated into more than 20 languages. In this excerpt from it, he argues that our spiritual health is connected to what we eat and that to truly nourish ourselves and live healthy lives, we need to eat what he calls a natural diet.

[handwritten annotations: "science tells us this is good for our body"]

There is nothing better than eating delicious food, but for most people eating is just a way to nourish the body, to have energy to work and to live to an old age. Mothers often tell their children to eat their food — even if they do not like the taste — because it is "good" for them.

But nutrition cannot be separated from the sense of taste. Nutritious foods, good for the human body, whet the appetite and are delicious on their own account. Proper nourishment is inseparable from good flavor.

> Nutrition cannot be separated from the sense of taste.

Not too long ago the daily meal of the farmers in this area consisted of rice and barley with *miso*° and pickled vegetables. This diet gave long life, a strong constitution, and good health. Stewed vegetables and steamed rice with red beans was a once-a-month feast. The farmer's healthy, robust body was able to nourish itself well on this simple rice diet.

The traditional brown-rice-and-vegetable diet of the East is very different from that of most Western societies. Western nutritional science believes that unless certain amounts of starch, fat, protein, minerals, and vitamins are eaten each day, a well-balanced diet and good

---

miso: A traditional Japanese seasoning made from fermented soybeans.

health cannot be preserved. This belief produced the mother who stuffs "nutritious" food into her youngster's mouth.

One might suppose that Western dietetics, with its elaborate theo- 5 ries and calculations, could leave no doubts about proper diet. The fact is, it creates far more problems than it resolves.

One problem is that in Western nutritional science there is no effort to adjust the diet to the natural cycle. The diet that results serves to isolate human beings from nature. A fear of nature and a general sense of insecurity are often the unfortunate results.

Another problem is that spiritual and emotional values are entirely forgotten, even though foods are directly connected with human spirit and emotions. If the human being is viewed merely as a physiological° object, it is impossible to produce a coherent understanding of diet. When bits and pieces of information are collected and brought together in confusion, the result is an imperfect diet which draws away from nature.

"Within one thing lie all things, but if all things are brought together not one thing can arise." Western science is unable to grasp this precept of Eastern philosophy. A person can analyze and investigate a butterfly as far as he likes, but he cannot make a butterfly.

If the Western scientific diet were put into practice on a wide scale, what sort of practical problems do you suppose would occur? High-quality beef, eggs, milk, vegetables, bread, and other foods would have to be readily available all year around. Large-scale production and long-term storage would become necessary. Already in Japan, adoption of this diet has caused farmers to produce summer vegetables such as lettuce, cucumbers, eggplants, and tomatoes in the winter. It will not be long before farmers are asked to harvest persimmons in spring and peaches in the autumn.

It is unreasonable to expect that a wholesome, balanced diet can be 10 achieved simply by supplying a great variety of foods regardless of the season. Compared with plants which ripen naturally, vegetables and fruits grown out-of-season under necessarily unnatural conditions contain few vitamins and minerals. It is not surprising that summer vegetables grown in the autumn or winter have none of the flavor and fragrance of those grown beneath the sun by organic and natural methods.

Chemical analysis, nutritional ratios, and other such considerations are the main causes of error. The food prescribed by modern science is far from the traditional Oriental diet, and it is undermining the health of the Japanese people.

physiological: Relating to the functions of the body.

Understanding the Text

1. What does Fukuoka argue is the purpose of food?
2. What is the relationship between food and spiritual well-being?
3. What does Fukuoka argue is the best way to nourish the body?

Reflection and Response

4. What do the foods we eat say about our spiritual values? In what ways might eating be called a spiritual act?
5. Why does Fukuoka critique modern science's food prescriptions? What beliefs about food does Western nutrition science privilege? What does it ignore?

Making Connections

6. Compare Fukuoka's concerns about nutrition science to Marion Nestle's ("Eating Made Simple," p. 72). What values do they share? How are they different? Which approach do you think is more effective? Why?
7. How might Bryant Terry ("Reclaiming True Grits," p. 82) respond to Fukuoka's essay? Why do you conclude this? Provide textual examples from both essays to support your conclusions.
8. Fukuoka argues that Western nutrition science "with its elaborate theories and calculations" actually "creates far more problems than it resolves" (para. 5). Using library resources, identify and research two or three of the problems it creates. Analyze the problems using the argument made by Fukuoka and at least one other author from this book. Do you agree that they are "problems"? Why or why not?

What the World Eats: Guatemala, India, Mali, and the United States

Peter Menzel and Faith D'Aluisio

The award-winning photographer Peter Menzel is known for his international coverage of science and environmental issues. His photographs have been published in *Life*, *National Geographic*, and the *New York Times Magazine*, and his images have won prestigious awards, including a number of World Press Photo and Picture of the Year awards. Faith D'Aluisio worked as a television news producer before she became the editor and lead writer for the *Material World* book series, which she cocreated with Menzel. Menzel and D'Aluisio have coauthored many books, including *Man Eating Bugs* (1998) and the award-winning *Hungry Planet: What the World Eats* (2005), from which these images are taken.

Eating meals with family and friends has long been a tradition in most cultures. But increasing globalization and the expansion of the global food industry have led to rapid changes in food customs. Menzel and D'Aluisio set out to explore how these global shifts are affecting families around the world. They joined people on shopping outings, participated in neighborhood feasts, and sat down to dinner with 25 families in 21 countries. They met one family who hunted seals for food and another who consumed six gallons of Coca-Cola in one week. Part of how they documented their findings was with images of families photographed with all of the food that they consumed in a week. In the photographs included here, we meet four of these families — from Guatemala, India, Mali, and the United States. D'Aluisio and Menzel, while emphasizing that the families represent themselves (and that they are not statistical representations of their countries), also ask us to consider the ways these photographs help us better understand our world and the impacts of globalization on food.

Guatemala—The Mendozas The Mendozas and a servant, shown in their courtyard in Todos Santos Cuchumatán, Guatemala. They use a gas stovetop, a wood stove, and a refrigerator.

India—The Patkars The Patkars, shown in the living room of their home in Ujjain, Madhya Pradesh, India. They use a gas stove and a refrigerator-freezer.

Mali—The Natomos The Natomos, shown on the roof of their mud-brick home in Kouakourou, Mali. They use a wood fire and natural drying.

United States—The Cavens The Cavens, shown in the kitchen of their home in American Canyon, California. They use an electric stove, a microwave oven, an outdoor barbecue, a refrigerator-freezer, and a freezer.

Understanding the Text

1. What do we learn about the families pictured by seeing the food they consumed in one week? What might we conclude about their health, socioeconomic status, values, culture, and lifestyle?

2. What *don't* we learn about these families that we might wonder or want to know? What questions about their relationships with food go unanswered?

Reflection and Response

3. If you were to be photographed with your food, what would be portrayed? What would we learn about you from the photograph? What would be impossible to capture that might be important to know about your relationship with food?

4. What argument is implied by the photo essay? What do you think the authors hope we will learn?

5. Menzel and D'Aluisio have said that one of the reasons they set out to document what the world eats is because our food choices and traditions are rapidly changing in the face of globalizing food markets. Do you see evidence of globalization in these photographs? Explain your answer by making specific references to details in the photographs.

Making Connections

6. Michael Idov ("When Did Young People Start Spending 25% of Their Paychecks on Pickled Lamb's Tongues?" p. 101) writes about Diana Chang and her friends' practice of photographing what they eat. Compare the purpose Menzel's photographs serve to the purpose of those "foodies" take to document their dining experiences.

7. Locate several images of food and people in your community. What do the images tell us about the purpose food serves in the lives of the people portrayed in the image? How would Michael Pollan ("Eat Food: Food Defined," p. 9), Wendell Berry ("The Pleasures of Eating," p. 64), and Marion Nestle ("Eating Made Simple," p. 72) analyze these photographs?

Zombies vs. The Joy of Canning: Motivation in the Productive Home

Erica Strauss

After attending culinary school and working in restaurants in the Seattle area for ten years, Erica Strauss took her interest in food and gardening to a new level. Her garden includes an impressive array of amazing fruits and vegetables, much of which she cooks fresh, using elaborate recipes that she shares on her Web site and some of which she dries, pickles, and freezes for later use. She keeps an exhaustive blog, *Northwest Edible Life: Life on Garden Time,* that documents her gardening triumphs (and defeats); her impressive growing, food storage, and cooking knowledge; and her tips on motherhood, daily living, and the cultivation of a slower life in a fast-paced world. With an impressive and exhaustive array of food knowledge and advice, a political edge that keeps it interesting, and an authorial voice that aims to delight on a regular basis, her blog captures in writing what she lives, thinks, and values in her life as a self-described "urban farmer" and "radical home-maker." In this blog post, Strauss talks about why she grows and stores her own food.

H ey, we were planning on getting together later today, right?" I asked my friend.

"Yeah, but after dinner."

"Can we push that back to later in the week?" I was exhausted from *Can-o-Rama* and the idea of a social commitment after dinner was more than I could handle.

"Sure. What's up?"

"I'm pretty tired. I stayed up until 2 in the morning yesterday wrap- 5 ping up a weekend of canning."

Long pause.

"Um. . . . *why*?!?" my friend laughed.

I muttered something about trying to have my year's supply of canned tomatoes be home-canned.

"Wow, ok. You're really crazy!"

Why? Why do I do this? 10

I ask myself this question with some frequency, actually. When I have a list of a million things that all need doing and very short windows of time in which to do them, I ask myself what the point of playing urban farmer really is.

Chickens, crops, children, canning, cooking — not necessarily in that order.

Chickens, crops, cooking and canning are entirely optional (children are optional too, I suppose, but only *before* you have them). Most people don't do these things. I have realized this lately. Most people don't even cook. Maybe they heat stuff up, but balls-to-the-wall, from-scratch cooking? That's more unusual than the popularity of cookbooks and *Food TV* shows and cooking blogs would lead you to believe.

Most people consider real, honest-to-God, from-scratch food to be entertainment, not a thrice-daily reality.

So, *why?* Why can my own tomatoes? Why grow my own lettuce? 15 Why make my own deodorant? Why use cloth diapers on my son? Why cook from scratch? Why check the thrift store first?

In a nutshell: why voluntarily take on the complications and efforts of the productive home when the economic system I live in means I simply don't have to? Why make life harder?

There's a lot of answers to that question floating around the world of the self-proclaimed Radical Homemakers, Urban Householders, and Punk Domestic badasses.

A lot of the answers are political-economic. You'll hear that we owe it to local farmers to source directly from them and provide them with a market for their goods. You'll hear that rejecting industrial food undermines soul-less corporate interests and is, therefore, a radical political statement. At the micro-economic level you'll hear about the money that can be saved if you can your own tomatoes (a dubious claim unless your garden is putting out *a lot* of excellent-quality canning tomatoes).

There's rallying cries about supporting different markets — local markets, sustainable markets, alternative markets. Anything but the international, corporate-dominated, local-to-nowhere market we currently enjoy.

"Occupy your food supply! Make your own jam!"

"Be prepared for zombies! Grow a garden!"

"Take out insurance against midwestern crop failures — support your local farmers!"

These claims are how the lifestyle of the productive home is sold. 20 They say: be a part of something bigger. Be a part of a movement. Help to change the world. Join our gang, we jump you in with homemade scones and really delicious bing cherry jam. You'll love our global fight for justice! We wage our battle at the fair-trade, shade-grown coffee shop!

All these motivations are very good reasons to attempt to make your home a place of greater productivity and less consumption. And I'm not saying the world couldn't use a little changing.

But all that political spitfire, as much as I enjoy it occasionally, isn't *really* why I do any of this. I don't bake my own bread to fuck over Wonder Bread (owned by Hostess) or can my own tomatoes to stick it to Muir Glen (owned by General Mills).

While I do have some grave concerns about the just-in-time food distribution system that connects most people with their calories, I don't expect hoards of zombies to suck my brains out or neighbors to take my butternut squash at gunpoint any time soon.

The drought in the Midwest is bad. It's going to be very, very bad for farmers and ranchers and very bad for companies and consumers that rely on cheap cereal grains and products made from them. It's going to cost taxpayers a bundle, even though most will have no idea that they are paying for it, and the knock-on to the supply/demand curve will send grocery prices higher more or less across the board.

But that has almost *nothing* to do with why I visit the farmer's mar-   25
ket, or buy boxes of fruit in season from the family farmer just over the mountains in Central Washington.

Really, I can my tomatoes, make jam, keep chickens, bake bread and — perhaps most consumingly — grow a rather large garden — because I *enjoy* doing these things. Even if once a year in late August that means a few late-nights in front of the canning pot, I still *enjoy* this life.

I think, against the backdrop of big reasons why productive home-keeping is *A Very Important Movement* and all that, the simple pleasures that come from nurturing and creating in the home are sometimes lost.

When we feel like we are obligated to do something, because doing that thing is how we make our political statement in a world gone mad, or keep our families safe against unseen, unknown, and as-yet-unrealized threats, or protect our assets against the vagaries of a complicated global economic system, we are acting from fear or from anger.

We are stretching out our hand to try to take some measure of control back from that which seems so out-of-control.

We are saying with clenched fist, "You and your peak oil and BPA   30
and your global banking crisis and your housing collapse and your high-fructose-corn-syrup, pink-slime, diabetes-nation food system, you can push me into the dirt. But I will rise back up and when I do,

I'll be holding these homegrown, organic cantaloupes, motherfucker! Yeah!"

There's nothing wrong with this, to a point. Anger that changes behaviors and fear that motivates people to examine their deep values can be a catalyst for great and positive change. But at the end of a long, long, long day of canning, or weeding, or sowing, something greater than fear and anger has to carry you along.

After 16 hours of processing tomatoes, if you have the energy to be fist-raising, passionately upset about anything, you should look really into anger management classes.

Nah, when push comes to shove, you have to do this stuff because you like it. You have to *like* patiently reducing strawberry syrup to get just the right texture in your jam. You have to *like* bullshitting with farmers and ranchers and going out on field trips to where the food is grown. You have to get a small thrill when you harvest an egg that is still warm, or find yourself covered with sticky gold from the bee-hives you've helped along.

You have to be in love with the miracle that is a squash seed — no bigger than a fingernail but able to produce hundreds of pounds of food in a single summer with only a little help from you, the gardener. You have to find a certain calm prayerfulness in the act of working your earth, even as your To Do list presses in on you ceaselessly.

You have to love food enough to work for it, and not in an abstract 35 trade-space kind of way. Not in the, "An hour writing this code for the latest version of Microsoft Excel pays me enough to buy a month's worth of hamburgers on the road!" kind of way.

You have to be okay getting your hands dirty, and your brow sweaty, and your forearms scratched from the cuts of a thousand blackberry brambles. You have to not just survive that kind of labor, but revel in it.

> You have to love food enough to work for it.

Right now, we do have a choice — those #10 cans of tomatoes are cheap and easy to buy. Those pears from Argentina are available in June. That feedlot ground beef is on special for $2.49 a pound. McDonald's is on the way and Hot Pockets and Lean Cuisines are in the freezer section.

So why go to all that trouble? Why not run out and grab a can of crushed tomatoes and a jar of jam right alongside the Lean Cuisines and Hot Pockets?

Why?

Because I have a pantry that reflects a summer spent in relaxing 40 work and joyful creation.

Because cooking dinner makes me proud.
Because the food is delicious.
Because this kind of work makes me happy.
That's why. And that's enough.

Understanding the Text

1. Why does Strauss can her own tomatoes? shop at the farmer's market? keep chickens? What purposes do these practices serve in her life and the life of her family?
2. What is an urban farmer? Why does Strauss identify as one?
3. What is a "productive home"?

Reflection and Response

4. Strauss writes a blog about her life, her gardening practices, her food production, and her values. If you were to write a blog documenting your "food life," what would we learn about you and your food?
5. The way Strauss describes it, canning tomatoes sounds like a lot of hard work. Why does it make her happy? What intrinsic pleasures does it bring? Why might we conclude that she "love[s] food enough to work for it" (p. 99)?

Making Connections

6. What aspects of the food production chain are visible in Strauss's home? How would Michael Pollan ("Eat Food: Food Defined," p. 9) and Wendell Berry ("The Pleasures of Eating," p. 64) comment on her goals and values? What do you think of her goals and values?
7. If food is a mirror through which we can better understand ourselves, as Jordan Shapiro argues ("The Eco-Gastronomic Mirror," p. 50), what kind of reflection would Strauss see? Explain your answer, and compare her reflection to the one you imagine for at least one other author in this collection.
8. Strauss is not the only blogger writing about food, cooking, and gardening. Search the Internet for blogs about food, cooking, eating, and gardening. Find blogs that support a movement or advocate a practice. Select two or three and analyze what they tell us (implicitly or explicitly) about the food values and food politics they are promoting. Compare them to Strauss's blog and to one another. Use specific textual examples to support your analysis.

When Did Young People Start Spending 25% of Their Paychecks on Pickled Lamb's Tongues?

Michael Idov

Michael Idov was born in 1976 in Riga, a city long fought over by Germany and Russia, at the time under communist control. In 1990, shortly before the collapse of the Soviet Union, Idov, then only thirteen, began writing for *Soviet Youth*, in which he interviewed a writer who criticized the Communist Party, a dangerous act at the time. Soon after, his family immigrated to the United States.

Idov is a staff writer for *New York Magazine*, where this essay was first published. His articles also have appeared in *Slate* and *The New Republic*. After suffering through a failed attempt to run a New York coffee shop, he authored the novel *Ground Up*, which is loosely based on the experience. In this essay, Idov examines foodie trends in youth culture and provides a portrait of the life of a young foodie in New York City.

On the Tuesday before we meet, Diane Chang sends me a list of places where she wants to eat in the coming week. Here it is, in alphabetical order: ABC Kitchen, Abistro, Bhojan, Bianca, Cafe Katja, Char No. 4, Coppelia, Cotan, Diner, Eisenberg's, Han Joo Chik BBQ, Henan Feng Wei, Marlow & Sons, Schnitzi, St. Anselm, Sun in Bloom, Tanoreen, Upstate Craft Beer & Oyster Bar, Vinegar Hill House, and Wondee Siam. For our dinner, she eventually settles on Wondee Siam II, on Ninth and 54th (but emphatically not the original Wondee Siam, on Ninth and 53rd).

Chang arrives at the tiny Thai place with her friends Jasmine, a stylist, and Marcos, a graphic designer. They, too, have their food bona fides: Marcos snaps quick photos of each dish as it is placed on the table; Jasmine's phone holds carefully curated favorite-restaurant lists for New York and L.A. Both are a little older — 30-plus to Chang's 27 — but Chang is clearly the group's leader. She has picked the place, orders for everyone (shrimp salad, deep-fried catfish, and crispy pork off the restaurant's "secret menu"), and generally steers the conversation toward the plates in front of us.

Petite and stylish, with a self-consciously goofy smile, Chang works in online and social-media marketing. She is, in culinary parlance, a civilian — her job has nothing to do with New York's sprawling food industry or with the chattering class that's gathered around it. Her leisure time and modest discretionary income, however, are devoted almost entirely to food and restaurants.

"I'm not a foodie, I just like what I like," She says. "Yes, I know, it's just like hipsters saying, 'I'm not a hipster.'" (The cliché cracks her up.) "But it's like when my boss says, 'Oh, you're such a foodie.' I'm like, *Oh God.* When I hear the word *foodie,* I think of Yelp. I don't want to be lumped in with Yelp." Just then, her iPhone goes off, and I glimpse her screen saver. It's a close-up photo of a pile of gnarly, gristly pig's feet, skin singed and torn, half-rendered fat and pearlescent cartilage beaming back the flash. The dish is from a tiny food stall in Taipei, she tells me. "It's braised in a soy-based sauce, and they serve it on rice with pickled mustard greens."

There have, of course, always been people in this town for whom 5 food is a serious cultural pursuit. Traditionally, they have been older, white, and affluent. Knowing the newest and finest restaurants to frequent and where to find the very best things to eat have long been essential New York status markers. One of the main hallmarks of twenty-something life, on the other hand, has typically been to not give a shit what and where you eat. As recently as the late nineties, a steady diet of burritos and takeout Chinese, with an ironic-but-not-really TV dinner thrown in now and then, was part of the Generation X ethic. An abiding interest in food was something for old people or snobs, like golf or opera. The notion of idolizing chefs, filling notebooks with restaurant "life lists," or talking about candied foie gras on a date was out-and-out bizarre.

> Food is now viewed as a legitimate option for a hobby, a topic of endless discussion, a playground for one-upmanship, and a measuring stick of cool.

Lately, however, food has become a defining obsession among a wide swath of the young and urbane. It is not golf or opera. It's more like indie rock. Just like the music of, say, Drag City bands on a nineties campus, food is now viewed as a legitimate option for a hobby, a topic of endless discussion, a playground for one-upmanship, and a measuring stick of cool. "It's a badge of honor," says Chang. "Bragging rights." She says she disliked M. Wells, last year's consensus "It" restaurant, partly because of "the fact that everybody loves it, and I just don't want to believe the hype." The quest for ever greater obscurity, a central principle of the movement, reaches a kind of event horizon in Chang's friend James Casey, the publisher of an idiosyncratic annual food magazine called *Swallow.* Lately, Casey has been championing the theory that mediocre food is better than good, the equivalent of a jaded indie kid extolling the virtues of Barry Manilow.

Food's transformation from a fusty° hobby to a youth-culture phenomenon has happened remarkably fast. The simultaneous rise of social networks and camera phones deserves part of the credit (eating, like sex, is among the most easily chronicled of pursuits), but none of this would have happened without the grassroots revolution in fine dining. "You can now eat just as quality food with a great environment without the fuss and the feeling of sitting at the grown-up table," says Chang's friend Amy, who is, incidentally, a cook at the very grown-up Jean Georges.

The timeline looks roughly like this: In 1998, Mario Batali gutted the space that was once home to the stodgy Coach House and replaced it with the loud and brilliant Babbo. The *Times* later cited Babbo's "Led Zeppelin soundtrack" as "one of the dividing lines between a restaurant with three stars, which it unequivocally deserves, and one with the highest rating of four." That missed the point. The whole *idea* was to fuse fine dining and rock and roll. Anthony Bourdain's 2000 *Kitchen Confidential* destroyed the archetype of the foofy French chef in a toque and replaced it with an image of cooks as young tattooed badasses. Then, in 2004, a young neurotic chef named David Chang (no relation to Diane) opened Momofuku Noodle Bar, serving what Bourdain has called the kind of food that chefs themselves like to eat after-hours — that is, simple, ingredient-driven food, often global, that is unfailingly delicious but not necessarily expensive or stuffy. Somewhere along the line, young people even began to view cooking as a form of artistic expression. The idea of eating well wasn't just democratized. It was now, improbably enough, edgy.

Diane Chang is a prime specimen of the new breed of restaurant-goer. The species is obsessive and omnivorous. Although they lean toward cheap ethnic food and revile pretension, they do not ultimately discriminate by price point or cuisine. They might hit a vegan joint like Sun in Bloom one day, its neighbor Bark Hot Dogs the next, then subsist on ramen for a week before blowing a paycheck on a sixteen-course lunch at Ko. They are not especially concerned with locavorism or sustainability or foraging. Sometimes nirvana simply takes the form of an authentic, ice-cold Mexican Coke. They abhor restaurant clichés (Carnegie Deli, Peter Luger) and studiously avoid chains (Olive Garden, McDonald's) but are not above the occasional ironic trip

fusty: Old-fashioned.

to either. They consume food media — blogs, books, *Top Chef,* and other "quality" TV shows but definitely not Food Network — like so many veal sweetbreads. *Lucky Peach,* Chang's quarterly journal, is required reading. They talk about food and restaurants incessantly, and their social lives are organized around them. Some are serious home cooks who seek to duplicate the feats of their chef-heroes in their own kitchens; others barely use a stove. Above all, they are avowed culinary agnostics whose central motivation is simply to hunt down and enjoy the next most delicious meal, all the better if no one else has yet heard of it. Dish snapshots and social-network check-ins are a given.

As Chang and her friends plow through the menu at Wondee Siam, 10 I feel no need to raise the subject of food. Discounting Marcos's recent singlehood, which quickly turns into a discussion of his "Single Man diet," the topic is virtually the only one on the table. A conversational pattern recurs: a restaurant name-drop, a quick Zagat-style assessment, next topic. The amazing Chinese New Year dinner at a Vietnamese place on Orchard ("You have to know the chef"). Lone Star barbecue ("So. Delicious"). A server at Roberta's ("stuck-up"). Red Rooster ("My girlfriend is really good friends with the chef," but "it's just a scene"). This leads to a sidebar on "scene" restaurants — Miss Lily's, La Esquina, the Smile — with the conclusion that the food is always disappointing.

At one point, Chang turns to me. "So what's your favorite restaurant in New York?" she asks. Without thinking, I give my standby answer, which hasn't changed in the past four years or so: Eleven Madison Park. I feel the air whoosh out of the room. "Ah." There falls a pause while I savor, perhaps for the first time, at age 35, the full extent of feeling old and out of touch. It's not that the group doesn't respect chef Daniel Humm. It's that my answer is so pathetically predictable. I should have said Torrisi, I think. No, Parm. They are probably way over Torrisi already. On the food-as-indie-rock matrix, I have just accidentally confessed to loving the Dave Matthews Band. Chang gives me a forgiving look and reaches for more crispy pork.

Diane Chang was born in a predominantly Chinese community in San Gabriel Valley, near Los Angeles. Her early life was steeped in the tastes and aromas of Sichuan cuisine. Chang's China-born grandmother, "an amazing, amazing cook," taught her traditional dishes. As for the local options, "We had Sizzler," she deadpans. She hadn't tried American food until grade school, when the one-two punch of sugar and salt predictably floored her. "Like, Lunchables? So much better than the fish my grandmother just spent two hours on," she says, laughing. "Then you get older and you wise up." But not before gaining fifteen pounds on UCLA cafeteria food. At the dorm, Chang had an all-day unlimited cafeteria pass, "like a MetroCard for food," so she ended up popping in for a snack every couple of hours. Trying to right her ways, she developed an eating disorder, and gave up carbs. "Bread is her greatest frenemy," says her friend Katherine, a former food-magazine staffer. "Who is she kidding? She loves food too much to deny herself anything."

In 2006, after moving out of the dorm, Chang grew more serious about food as a hobby. She cycled through several identities, from going vegetarian to joining a group called the Burger Club, which was exactly what it sounds like — friends and strangers comparison-eating their way through the L.A. hamburger scene. She began to hit progressively more obscure places, spurred on by blogs and trying to one-up friends. Chang's college years coincided with the first explosion of websites like Chowhound — "The ones that were super bare-bones," she says, "just people talking about food. The food blogs are still big, but they really had their moment in the early aughts. And I think that's why food became such a thing." She ate at obscure L.A. haunts, and began frequenting a nameless pop-up Burmese restaurant that operated on weekends out of someone's garage. After one visit, she got food poisoning. She later reasoned that by Sunday evening, when she had eaten it, the chicken was no longer fresh. So she stopped going — on Sundays.

This was also the time when her trips to New York began, for job interviews and, of course, food. On one such sojourn, Chang managed to get into Momofuku Ko in the first months of its existence, despite the furious loading and reloading of the restaurant's website at precisely 10 a.m. that landing a reservation requires. She impulsively booked a party of four — the maximum number Ko's arcane rules allow — and then realized she had no idea whom to invite along. "I was just out of college at the time, so nobody had money," she remembers. "I was super-poor. It's like, which one of my friends will shell out 160 bucks for a lunch?" The impasse lasted until Chang's then-boyfriend found a way to expense half of the outing as client entertainment. The lunch took up three hours, involved sixteen courses, and left Chang, the would-be un-foodie, unimpressed. "Remember when he just made burritos?" she asks, sighing, the culinary equivalent of claiming R.E.M. sold out after *Chronic Town.*

Besotted with New York, she landed a job and moved here in January 2010. "I was about to be paid close to nothing, but I decided that the pay cut was worth it to live in one of the most exhilarating cities 15 in the world." She bunked with an old friend in an apartment on the corner of Allen and Broome. It was a perfect young food lover's destination: one foot in Chinatown, one on the LES.° The first thing she did on her first day as a New Yorker was get coffee from 88 Orchard, then banana bread from Babycakes, dumplings from Vanessa's, and finally a litchi martini at Congee Village. Her first real New York restaurant experience, however, was Blue Hill, with the same ex-boyfriend who footed the bill for Ko. "Since food was a major part of our relationship, we knew we had to pick somewhere delicious for dinner," Chang remembers. "I was a big fan of Dan Barber." She had acorn-squash pasta that she didn't like: too stringy. "Honestly, I don't remember too much about the meal," she says, a statement directly contradicted by the previous one, "but the whole experience resonates to this day because I felt kind of out of place among a lot of older, more affluent people. But, oddly enough, wondering how the cost of the meal will affect my budget made me feel more of a New Yorker."

Chang earns about $70,000 a year; her rent in Park Slope, where she lives now ("the worst food destination ever"), runs $1,100 a month. As for the rest, "I spend it all on food," she says flatly. During the one week I asked Chang to keep tabs on her restaurant-going and market purchases, she ate at fourteen restaurants, pizza joints, and cafes, and spent $350. The largest single bill she racked up was $58, although Han Joo, a Korean barbecue spot in Flushing famous for its slanted grills that pour rendered pork fat onto kimchee, required a $38 cab ride. Chang also made a few dishes at home, including potatoes with crème fraîche and smoked paprika (a re-creation of a brunch favorite from Vinegar Hill House), pozole, chile verde, a red-lentil soup with pistou, and a fennel salad, the last two from *New York Times* recipes. When it comes to grocery shopping, Chang hits the nearby Grand Army Plaza farmers' market every Saturday and buys the rest of her provisions in precision-targeted outings: meat at the Park Slope outpost of the cult upstate butcher Fleisher's, spices at Sahadi's. During the week she recorded her purchases, there was only one backslide into the mainstream. After the $20 organic chicken she saw at the farmers' market proved a little too expensive, she grabbed a couple of shrink-wrapped chicken breasts at Key Food.

About two months after we first meet, I am having dinner with Chang at Williamsburg's St. Anselm, one of the few places she has yet to cross off her original list. We order butcher's steak, grilled artichoke hearts

LES: Lower East Side.

("Don't you always feel so humbled eating an artichoke?"), a patty melt, and a couple of other dishes I strain to remember two days later; Chang will probably be able to recall them, in succession, two years from now. She photographs each, and shares them on Instagram. Chang keeps a blog, of course. It's called Beets N' Jamz (she pairs meals she's eaten recently, i.e., a breakfast taco from Brooklyn Taco, with songs, i.e., Fleetwood Mac's "Hypnotized," and refers to herself as D.J. Panko). It replaces her two previous bread-focused blogs called Lotta Loaf and Baguettaboutit. But these days Chang is much more interested in throwing real-life parties. "Diane is very good about bringing people together," says her friend Katherine, "and it will always involve food." Her first year in New York, Chang organized an Oktoberfest picnic for a dozen people in Brooklyn Bridge Park. She made pretzels, pigs in a blanket, and curried ketchup, all from scratch. Chang's birthdays are equally elaborate culinary group outings: In 2010, she went to Spicy & Tasty, a cult Sichuan eatery in Flushing. Last year, she considered Tanoreen, a Middle Eastern restaurant in Bay Ridge, but decided instead on Tulcingo del Valle, an unassuming Mexican place in Hell's Kitchen. She also tried to start a Barbecue Club on the model of her Burger Club in L.A., but found the scene too limited. "You've got Fatty 'Cue, Fette Sau, Rub, you have Hill Country, Dinosaur . . . but then it's like, where are you going to go, Dallas BBQ? Burgers are so much easier in New York. I'm kind of sick of burgers a little bit, though." Which doesn't prevent her from sampling my patty melt.

Aside from Robert Sietsema and Jonathan Cold, with their tight focus on rustic and ethnic food, Chang doesn't trust food critics. She used to simply go on friends' recommendations, but the blogs changed the game. Now the choice of a place for dinner turns into an oft-tortuous multistep process. When someone recommends a place, Chang goes online. Despite her distrust of Yelp and sites like it, she still reads them compulsively, at least to look at the photos. "It doesn't matter if it's good or bad," she says. "I just want to know." Last night, she had three options, she tells me. "And I was just stressing out and stressing out about it. The reason I ended up choosing Neptune was, like, 'Okay, I mean, that's the one from way out of left field, no one ever talks about it, maybe I'll stumble across a gem.' But it's like, I also realize, there's not a single restaurant no one has ever talked about any more."

Sometimes, of course, this approach misfires. Neptune, an obscure Polish restaurant on First Avenue, proved the biggest disappointment of the fourteen places where Chang ate that week. The idea belonged to Chang's then-boyfriend, another card-carrying food fanatic. (For the couple's first date, they had gone to a festival called "Egg Rolls and

Egg Creams.") Telling me about the Neptune debacle, Chang sounds depressed, apologetic even. "We happened to be in Union Square, which always throws us off in our food choices," she says. She had suggested ABC Kitchen for her favorite cumin-carrot salad and a glass of wine. Maybe Cotan for Japanese? Or Zabb Elee for Thai? But no, the boyfriend insisted on Neptune. He felt really bad, she says. "It was the first time he's ever struck out picking a restaurant." They broke up not long afterward.

Understanding the Text

1. What is "foodie culture"? What does it say about the purpose of food?
2. What role does social networking play in foodie culture?
3. What does it mean for food to be a "serious cultural pursuit"? How does Diane Chang pursue food? What does her pursuit say about her values?

Reflection and Response

4. Are you mesmerized or baffled by the obsessions of Diane Chang and her cohort? What about this "foodie" lifestyle stands out to you? Explain your answers with textual examples.
5. Why do foodies photograph their food? What role do photographs play in Diane Chang's pursuit of food?

Making Connections

6. Compare Jordan Shapiro's description of food production in restaurants ("The Eco-Gastronomic Mirror," p. 50) to Idov's description of food consumption in restaurants. What purposes do restaurants serve? What does restaurant culture tell us about the purpose of food?
7. Idov describes the ways "food has become a defining obsession among a wide swath of the young and urbane." Research "foodie" culture — either locally or in another region of interest. What purpose does foodie culture serve for this particular constituency? What role does food play in the participants' lives? How are they defined by their food? In what ways do the participants treat food as a "serious cultural pursuit"? What do you learn about their values and cultural identities? Compare what you learn in your research to the story Idov tells.

3 What Determines What We Eat?

We wake up in the morning and decide what to eat for breakfast. We go to the cafeteria or the fridge or a restaurant, and we make choices about what to select from the display or order from the menu. We might select an apple or some raspberries, or we might opt for a doughnut or a granola bar. In one sense, then, *we* determine what we eat. But our food choices aren't made in a vacuum; many larger political, social, economic, environmental, and cultural factors help direct what choices are available (and where) and if they are affordable (and for whom).

A variety of factors, then, determine what we eat—whether we realize it or not. Various laws, policies, patents, and trade agreements play a role in determining what food choices are available to us. Federal guidelines make recommendations about health. Restaurant options and portion sizes help dictate what we choose. Government agencies regulate buying and selling options. International trade agreements affect what is available and where. Corporate interests and farming practices—and disputes between corporations and farmers—play a part in determining what is planted and harvested, and how it is processed and made available for public consumption.

We are thus surrounded by institutions, agencies, corporations, and businesses that affect our food choices, as the readings in this chapter demonstrate. While Michelle Obama argues for making healthier food options visible and available to children, she also acknowledges the difficulties involved. Brian Wansink and Collin Payne address one of these difficulties when they look at how classic recipes have changed over time. Dhruv Khullar addresses another in his discussion of the prevalence of readily available junk food and how this reality helps determine what we eat. James Surowiecki examines a controversial proposal to ban large sodas as a way of discussing how the government plays a role in determining what we consume. Gary Paul Nabhan and Vandana Shiva each discuss how globalization affects food availability and food choices in their accounts of cross-border food trade and the effects of global food markets on local food cultures, respectively. Donald Barlett and James Steele investigate the role of corporations and the courts in food production and food availability.

The complex mix of laws, social realities, health guidelines, seed patents, and trade agreements discussed in these selections are not usually on our minds when we ask "What's for dinner?" But international trade, federal health recommendations, corporate interests, farming practices, and even seed patents impact the answer in important ways. The readings in this chapter ask us to attend to this broad range of factors that determine what we eat.

The Food Plate and Food Pyramid Nutritional Guidelines

United States Department of Agriculture

The U.S. Department of Agriculture established the Center for Nutrition Policy and Promotion in 1994 to promote the nutrition and well-being of Americans. One of the core ways the center supports this objective is through the advancement of dietary guidelines and the promotion of guidance systems like MyPyramid and MyPlate. The Food Pyramid was introduced in 1992, updated in 2005, and replaced in 2010 by MyPlate. These visual diagrams are widely used as educational tools for translating nutritional guidelines into simple images of how much to eat of what kinds of food on a daily basis.

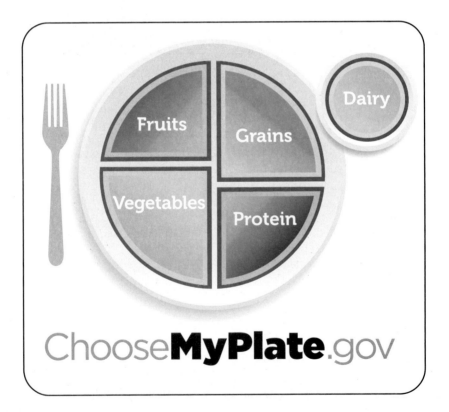

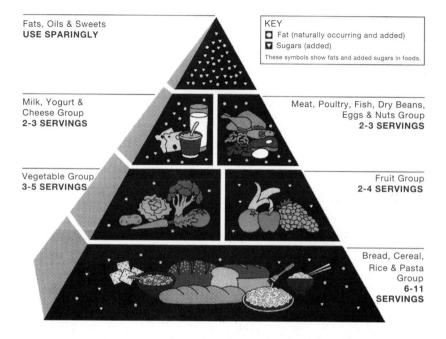

Fats, Oils & Sweets
USE SPARINGLY

KEY
▢ Fat (naturally occurring and added)
◩ Sugars (added)
These symbols show fats and added sugars in foods.

Milk, Yogurt &
Cheese Group
2-3 SERVINGS

Meat, Poultry, Fish, Dry Beans,
Eggs & Nuts Group
2-3 SERVINGS

Vegetable Group
3-5 SERVINGS

Fruit Group
2-4 SERVINGS

Bread, Cereal,
Rice & Pasta
Group
**6-11
SERVINGS**

Understanding the Text

1. What did the Food Pyramid prioritize? What kinds of recommendations did it give?

2. How is the new MyPlate different in scope and purpose? What goals do they share?

Reflection and Response

3. Why do you think the USDA continues to rely on visual images to promote nutrition? Which visual do you think will lead to better health education? To healthier eating? Why?

4. What social, cultural, and economic tendencies are the federal nutritional guidelines working against?

5. Were you aware of these guidelines before reading them here? Where did you encounter them? Have you studied them in school? Have you tried to live by them?

Making Connections

6. Review Michael Pollan's "rules" ("Eat Food: Food Defined," p. 9). How do they compare to the USDA's advice? What would he applaud in this advice? What might he question? Would he see this as a good way to decide what to eat? Why or why not?

7. Do you think the federal government should play a role in nutrition education? Why or why not? Select two or three selections in this collection and two or three sources you find through library research to help you construct your argument. Select at least one source that presents a challenge to your position. Refute that challenge as part of your support for your position.

The Business Case for Healthier Food Options

Michelle Obama

Michelle Obama is the wife of the forty-fourth president of the United States, Barack Obama, and the first African American First Lady. She grew up on the South Side of Chicago, studied sociology and African American studies at Princeton University, and then studied law at Harvard University. As First Lady, she has focused on promoting healthy food choices. Her program Let's Move! aims to raise a healthier generation of kids through programs that increase healthy food options and physical education in schools and the availability of fresh, healthy food in all neighborhoods and communities (not just affluent ones). As part of this effort, she initiated a kitchen garden at the White House, which is the subject of her book *American Grown: The Story of the White House Kitchen Garden and Gardens across America* (2012). In the following opinion piece from the *Wall Street Journal*, Obama challenges conventional wisdom and lays out the case for why healthier food options make good business sense.

For years, America's childhood obesity crisis was viewed as an insurmountable problem, one that was too complicated and too entrenched to ever really solve. According to the conventional wisdom, healthy food simply didn't sell—the demand wasn't there and higher profits were found elsewhere—so it just wasn't worth the investment.

But thanks to businesses across the country, today we are proving the conventional wisdom wrong. Every day, great American companies are achieving greater and greater success by creating and selling healthy products. In doing so, they are showing that what's good for kids and good for family budgets can also be good for business.

Take the example of Walmart. In just the past two years, the company reports that it has cut the costs to its consumers of fruits and vegetables by $2.3 billion and reduced the amount of sugar in its products by 10%. Walmart has also opened 86 new stores in underserved communities and launched a labeling program that helps customers spot healthy items on the shelf. And today, the company is not only seeing increased sales of fresh produce, but

> American companies are achieving greater and greater success by creating and selling healthy products. In doing so, they are showing that what's good for kids and good for family budgets can also be good for business.

also building better relationships with its customers and stronger connections to the communities it serves.

Walmart isn't alone in discovering that healthier products sell. Disney is eliminating ads for junk foods from its children's programming and improving the food served in Disney theme parks. Walgreens is adding fresh fruits and vegetables to its stores in underserved communities. And restaurants around the country are cutting calories, fat, and sodium from menus and offering healthier kids' meals.

These companies and so many others are responding to clear 5 trends in consumer demand. Today, 82% of consumers feel that it's important for companies to offer healthy products that fit family budgets, according to the Edelman public relations firm. Meanwhile, a study conducted by Nielsen revealed that even when many families are operating on tight budgets, sales of fresh produce actually increased by 6% in 2012. And in 2011, the Hudson Institute reported that in recent years, healthier foods have generated more than 70% of the growth in sales for consumer packaged-goods companies — and when these companies sell a high percentage of healthier foods, they deliver significantly higher returns to their shareholders.

These trends don't just matter for businesses that produce and sell food. They matter for every business in America. We spend $190 billion a year treating obesity-related health conditions like diabetes and heart disease, and a significant portion of those costs are borne by America's businesses. That's on top of other health-related costs like higher absenteeism and lower worker productivity, costs that will continue to rise and threaten the vitality of American businesses until this problem is solved once and for all.

That's why American businesses are stepping up to invest in building a healthier future for our kids. In doing so, they are joining leaders from every sector across the country. Over the past few years, through Let's Move!—our nationwide campaign to help kids grow up healthy—we've seen teachers bringing physical education back into schools. We've seen mayors building safe spaces where children can play, faith leaders educating their congregations about healthy eating, and parents preparing healthier meals and snacks for their kids. And we've seen Republicans and Democrats working together in Congress to pass groundbreaking legislation to improve school lunches.

And we're starting to see real results. In Mississippi, obesity rates have dropped by 13% for elementary school–aged kids. States like California, and cities like New York and Philadelphia, have also seen measurable declines in childhood obesity.

So it's clear that we are moving in the right direction. But we also know that the problem is nowhere near being solved. We need more leaders from all across the country to step up, and I stand ready to work with business leaders who are serious about taking meaningful steps to forge a healthier future. We need every business in America to dig deeper, get more creative, and find new ways to generate revenue by giving American families better information and healthier choices. We know this can be done in a way that's good for our kids and good for businesses.

That's why, even though we still have a long way to go, I have never 10 been more optimistic about our prospects for solving this problem. And I am confident that, with leadership from America's business community, we can give all our children the bright, healthy futures they so richly deserve.

Understanding the Text

1. According to Michelle Obama, what is the conventional wisdom about healthy food?

2. How are businesses proving the conventional wisdom wrong?

3. What role does Walmart play in the solution to the obesity crisis?

Reflection and Response

4. Obama argues that American companies are responding to consumer demands for healthier food options. How does she support this argument? Does she make an effective case? What, if any, evidence does she leave out that might be important to consider?

5. What is the rhetorical impact of Michelle Obama's optimism? Is it warranted? Why or why not? How might her optimism be tied to her role as First Lady?

6. Describe Michelle Obama's idea of a healthy lifestyle. Is such a lifestyle easy to achieve? Why or why not? What factors help determine whether an individual can achieve such a lifestyle?

Making Connections

7. As first lady, Michelle Obama helped launch MyPlate and her accompanying program Let's Move! to promote nutrition education and to provide real support for families to make healthier choices for their children. Go online and analyze the goals of her programs and initiatives. Were you aware of these initiatives? What kind of impact do you think Michelle Obama has? What role might she play in determining what Americans have for dinner? Is this an appropriate role for the First Lady? Why or why not?

8. Michelle Obama was instrumental in the creation of the White House kitchen garden. Go online or to your library and find out more about the development of this garden. What role does it play in the solution to the problem of childhood obesity that she describes in this article? Compare her efforts to promote healthy eating nationwide to Erica Strauss's efforts to promote healthy homegrown food on her blog ("Zombies vs. The Joy of Canning," p. 96). What are some important similarities and differences? Taken together, what do they teach us about what determines what people eat?

The Joy of Cooking Too Much: 70 Years of Calorie Increases in Classic Recipes

Brian Wansink and Collin R. Payne

Brian Wansink is the John Dyson Professor of Consumer Behavior at Cornell University and the award-winning author of more than 150 academic articles and books, including *Mindless Eating: Why We Eat More Than We Think*, published in 2006. His areas of expertise include eating behavior, nutrition science, and food psychology. His research has contributed to marketing changes and policies, some of which are aimed at reducing portion sizes and preventing overeating. Collin R. Payne was a postdoctoral research associate at Cornell University before becoming a professor of marketing in the College of Business at New Mexico State University. He specializes in consumer behavior and social marketing. In this academic article, originally published in *Annals of Internal Medicine* in 2009, Wansink and Payne examine the classic recipes in various editions of *The Joy of Cooking*, concluding that serving sizes and calories have increased since 1936.

B*ackground:* Obesity has been associated with the expanding portion sizes of away-from-home foods (1). Although portion size norms and calorie density have increased outside the home, they could also have a parallel or referred impact on serving sizes in the home (2, 3). Cookbook recipes might provide a longitudinal° gauge of how serving sizes and calorie density have changed inside homes. One cookbook, *The Joy of Cooking*, has been updated approximately every 10 years since 1936 (4) and could provide a glimpse into the changing norms of U.S. food preparation and serving sizes over the past 70 years (5).

Objective: To assess changes in calorie density and serving sizes of household meals since 1936, as reflected in recipes in *The Joy of Cooking*.

Methods: We content-analyzed the seven editions of *The Joy of Cooking* (1936, 1946, 1951, 1963, 1975, 1997, and 2006) to determine how serving sizes and calorie density have changed over the past 70 years [see the table on p. 120]. Since the first edition in 1936, only 18 recipes have been continuously published in each subsequent edition. By using standard nutritional analysis techniques, we determined serving size calorie levels for each recipe in each edition.

---

longitudinal: Involving information gathered over a long period of time.

We performed all analyses of variance by using SPSS statistical software, version 12.0 (SPSS, Chicago, Illinois). We considered a P value less than 0.05 to be statistically significant.

Results: Over the past 70 years, the total caloric content increased 5 for 14 of the 18 recipes. Because of changes in ingredients, the mean average calories in a recipe increased by 928.1 (from 2123.8 calories [95% CI, 1638.7 to 2608.9 calories] to 3051.9 calories [CI, 2360.7 to 3743.1 calories]), representing a 43.7% increase ($P < 0.001$). As the table indicates, mean average calories per serving increased for 17 of 18 recipes and was influenced by both changes in ingredients and changes in serving size. The resulting increase of 168.8 calories (from 268.1 calories [CI, 210.4 to 325.8 calories] to 436.9 calories [CI, 359.1 to 514.7 calories]) represents a 63.0% increase ($P < 0.001$) in calories per serving. Given that the average 2006 recipe had 1.1 fewer servings than in 1936, the average calorie density per serving size has increased by 37.4% ($P < 0.001$).

Over the 70-year history of *The Joy of Cooking*, the recommended serving sizes were altered at 3 points. Between 1946 and 1951, 3 of 18 recipes increased their serving size by an average of 32.5%. Between 1951 and 1963, 4 recipes increased their serving size by an average of 20.0%. Between 1997 and 2006, 5 recipes increased their serving size by an average of 21.1%. Only 3 recipes decreased their serving size at

Average Caloric Content and Number of Servings in *The Joy of Cooking*, by Publication Year

Characteristic	Publication Year			
	1936	1946	1951	1963
Mean total calories	2123.8	2122.3	2089.9	2250.0
per recipe (SD)	(1050.0)	(1002.3)	(1009.6)	(1078.6)
Mean average calories	268.1	271.1	280.9	294.7
per serving (SD)	(124.8)	(124.2)	(116.2)	(117.7)
Mean number of servings	12.9	12.9	13.0	12.7
per recipe (SD)	(13.3)	(13.3)	(14.5)	(14.6)

	1975	1997	2006
Mean total calories	2234.2	2249.6	3051.9
per recipe (SD)	(1089.2)	(1094.8)	(1496.2)
Mean average calories	285.6	288.6	384.4
per serving (SD)	(118.3)	(122.0)	(168.3)
Mean number of servings	12.4	12.4	12.7
per recipe (SD)	(14.3)	(14.3)	(13.0)

any point in the past 70 years, but all three were compensated by subsequent increases in later years.

Discussion: The mean average calorie density in 18 classic recipes has increased 35.2% per serving over the past 70 years. This is due mostly to the use of higher-calorie ingredients and partly to serving sizes that showed small increases in the late 1940s and early 1960s and a 33.2% increase since 1996.

The calories and portion sizes of classic recipes may reflect prevailing tastes and norms. Yet, they may also establish or reinforce exaggerated norms in other settings, such as new families. Although this study is largely descriptive, it implies a prescriptive recommendation for families. The serving size and calorie composition of classic recipes need to be downsized to counteract growing waistlines.

> The serving size and calorie composition of classic recipes need to be downsized to counteract growing waistlines.

Conclusion: Calorie density and serving sizes in recipes from *The Joy of Cooking* have increased since 1936.

References

1. Nielsen SJ, Popkin BM. Patterns and trends in food portion sizes, 1977–1998. JAMA. 2003;289:450–3. [PMID: 12533124]

2. Wansink B, van Ittersum K. Portion size me: downsizing our consumption norms. J Am Diet Assoc. 2007;107:1103–6. [PMID: 17604738]

3. Smiciklas-Wright H, Mitchell DC, Mickle SJ, Goldman JD, Cook A. Foods commonly eaten in the United States, 1989–1991 and 1994–1996: are portion sizes changing? J Am Diet Assoc. 2003;103:41–7. [PMID: 12525792]

4. Rombauer IS, Becker MR, Becker E, eds. The Joy of Cooking. New York: Bobbs-Merrill; 1936, 1946, 1951, 1963, 1975; New York: Scribner; 1997, 2006.

5. Wansink B. Environmental factors that increase the food intake and consumption volume of unknowing consumers. Annu Rev Nutr. 2004;24:455–79. [PMID: 15189128]

Understanding the Text

1. What did Wansink and Payne set out to learn in their study of *The Joy of Cooking* recipes? What method did they use?

2. What conclusion did they reach? On what is this conclusion based?

3. What does the table show?

Reflection and Response

4. This article was published in an academic journal. What do you learn about academic research from reading this article? What is the value of this kind of research about food? What are some practical uses of such research?

5. Why did they choose to analyze recipes from *The Joy of Cooking*? Are you familiar with this cookbook? Do you know anyone who uses it?

Making Connections

6. What would Marion Nestle ("Eating Made Simple," p. 72) and Michelle Obama ("The Business Case for Healthier Food Options," p. 115) think of this study? Use textual evidence to support your response.

7. What role do recipes play in our food choices? What would Wansink and Payne think of the recipes included by Amy Cyrex Sins ("Doberge Cake after Katrina," p. 45) and Bryant Terry ("Reclaiming True Grits," p. 82)?

Downsizing Supersize

James Surowiecki

James Surowiecki is an American journalist who has written about finance for a range of prominent publications, including *Fortune*, *Talk*, *New York*, the *Wall Street Journal*, the *New York Times Magazine*, the *Washington Post*, *Lingua Franca*, *Wired*, and *Slate*. He earned a doctoral degree in American history from Yale University before becoming a journalist. Since 2000 he has been a staff writer for the *New Yorker*, where he writes the regular financial column "The Financial Page." His book *The Wisdom of Crowds: Why the Many Are Smarter Than the Few and How Collective Wisdom Shapes Business, Economics, Societies, and Nations* was published in 2004. In this article, originally published in the *New Yorker* in August 2012, Surowiecki uses the occasion of the proposal by New York mayor Michael Bloomberg to ban the sale of large sodas to explore the role of government in regulating what we eat (and drink).

In an era of political polarization, Michael Bloomberg has the rare ability to come up with policies that enrage everyone. His latest pet project—banning large sodas, as a way of fighting obesity in New York—has been ridiculed by both Jon Stewart and John Boehner. And a recent Board of Health hearing on the plan saw Democratic and Republican politicians alike lining up to attack the idea, which would prohibit restaurants, delis, sports arenas, movie theatres, and food carts from selling any soft drinks larger than 16 ounces. Critics dismiss the ban as yet another expression of Bloomberg's nanny-state mentality and as a "feel-good placebo" that's doomed to fail. They're right that the ban is blatantly paternalist. But that doesn't mean it won't work.

It's true that the ban will be easy to circumvent: if you want to drink 32 ounces, you can just buy two 16-ounce servings. But Bloomberg's proposal makes clever use of what economists call "default bias." If you offer a choice in which one option is seen as a default, most people go for that default option. People who are automatically enrolled in a retirement plan, for instance, are more likely to stay with their original plan than those who choose plans for themselves. In countries where people have to choose to be an organ donor, most people aren't donors; in countries where people have to actively say they don't want to be an organ donor, most are donors. The soda ban makes 16 ounces or less the default option for soda drinkers; if they want more, they'll have to make an extra effort.

An executive at the American Beverage Association has dismissed the plan, saying that "150 years of research finds that people consume what they want." Actually, the research shows that what people "want" has a lot to do with how choices are framed. In one well-known study, researchers put a bowl of M&M's on the concierge desk of an apartment building, with a scoop attached and a sign below that said "Eat Your Fill." On alternating days, the experimenters changed the size of the scoop—from a tablespoon to a quarter-cup scoop, which was four times as big. If people really ate just "what they want," the amounts they ate should have remained roughly the same. But scoop size turned out to matter a lot: people consumed much more when the scoop was big. This suggests that most of us don't have a fixed idea of how much we want; instead, we look to outside cues—like the size of a package or cup—to instruct us. And since the 1970s the portion sizes offered by food companies and restaurants have grown significantly larger. In 1974, the biggest drink McDonald's offered was 21 ounces. Today, that's roughly the size of a "small" drink at Burger King. In effect, the scoops have gotten bigger, and consumption has risen accordingly.

If all this sounds as if New York's soda consumers were about to become the subjects of an elaborate social-science experiment designed to reshape their behavior and desires, well, that's kind of true.

Of course, if you don't want the large soda, you needn't order it. Yet the mere existence of the supersize can change your idea of how much you want to drink. In a classic experiment by Itamar Simonson and Amos Tversky, people asked to choose between a cheap camera and a pricier one with more features were divided more or less equally between the two options. But when a third option—a fancy, very expensive camera—was added to the mix most people went for the mid-range camera. The very expensive camera made the middle one seem less extravagant. In the same way, the fact that a large soda is now 40 ounces makes a 20-ounce soda feel sensible. Bloomberg's ban is designed to flip this effect on its head: if the largest soda you can order is 16 ounces, a can of Coke may start to seem like more than enough. Some food researchers doubt that this will work, since so many of us are used to the idea of large servings. But even our experience of feeling satiated is highly malleable. In one experiment, people ate meals of dramatically different sizes in the dark, and those who were given much less food did not feel hungrier than the others or rate their meals as much smaller. So once people have a few 16-ounce drinks they may find that 16 ounces is plenty.

Many economists would say that, if we want to discourage soda 5
consumption, taxing it—the way we do alcohol and tobacco—would
be more efficient than a ban. Some European countries do have such
taxes, but the idea has been a political non-starter in New York. In
any case, perhaps the most cunning aspect of Bloomberg's proposed
ban is that it would function as a kind of stealth tax on consumption,
while leaving average-sized sodas untouched. Currently, on a per-
ounce basis, large drinks are much cheaper than smaller ones—which
encourages people to supersize. The soda ban should shift this. Two
16-ounce servings are bound to be more expensive than one 32-ounce
serving, which creates another disincentive to drink more.

If all this sounds as if New York's soda consumers were about to become the subjects of an elaborate social-science experiment designed to
reshape their behavior and desires, well, that's kind of true. But then
we've been the subject of just such an experiment, run by beverage and
fast-food companies, for the past 40 years. If Bloomberg has his way, we
may start feeling like we're white rats in a maze, but at least there's a
good chance we'll be thinner rats.

Understanding the Text

1. What is "default bias"?
2. Why do some economists argue that taxing soda consumption would
   discourage it?
3. What does it mean to "supersize"?

Reflection and Response

4. Describe two different kinds of economic or social science research
   Surowiecki employs. What do we learn about human behavior from such
   research? How does he use this research in his essay?
5. According to Surowiecki, Michael Bloomberg's critics are right that the soda
   ban is "blatantly paternalist" (para. 1). Does this kind of legislation represent a
   valid role for the government? In what ways might the public perceive this kind
   of government intervention? Is this intervention similar to or different from the
   USDA's nutritional guidelines? Explain your answer.

Making Connections

6. Research Michael Bloomberg's proposal and find out what happened to the
   over-16-ounce soda ban. Was his proposed ban enacted? In what ways did
   the public view the proposal and the eventual outcome?

7. Do you think Surowiecki thinks the ban might work? Do you think he supports it? Locate textual evidence to support your response. Do you think it would work? Would you support it? Why or why not?

8. Compare Michael Bloomberg's approach to health, as described by Surowiecki, to Michelle Obama's approach ("The Business Case for Healthier Food Options" p. 115). What values do they share? In what ways do their methods differ?

Why Shame Won't Stop Obesity

Dhruv Khullar

Dhruv Khullar wrote this piece in 2012 for the *Bioethics Forum*, the blog published by the *Hastings Center Report*, while studying medicine at Yale University and public policy at the Harvard Kennedy School as a Zuckerman Fellow. Khullar's interest in public health and social justice has led him to do research that bridges the gap between medicine and public policy. He considers obesity a public health as well as a social justice issue, one that disproportionately affects the poor and minority groups. He is particularly interested in publishing his research for the general public in the hope that sound research can play a larger role in public discussion of health policies. In this essay, Khullar offers specific suggestions for reversing the trend of junk food and fast food being more readily available and cheaper than healthy food choices.

I am still in medical school, but today I sigh the frustrated, disapproving sigh of a fully trained doctor. "You know," I scold the middle-aged man in front of me, "you really should start eating better."

Like many patients I saw in clinic that morning, this man is obese. His diabetes is poorly controlled. His blood pressure is through the roof. And he hasn't lost a single pound in months.

Oh well, it's lunchtime and I'm hungry. I slip off to the hospital cafeteria and begin to ponder why these patients can't seem to lead a healthier lifestyle. As I wait in line, I consider a more pressing problem: should I get the fried chicken or the four-cheese pizza? I settle on popcorn shrimp and some curly fries. Only then do I ask myself what exactly I would have recommended my patients eat—besides maybe a side of cheesy broccoli and some bruised bananas—had they joined me for lunch.

This, sadly, is the case in the cafeteria of a major hospital, an institution devoted to preserving and promoting health. It is a stark and telling microcosm of a much broader issue—one in large part responsible for the skyrocketing rates of obesity and associated disease in this country.

Americans today are exposed to an unprecedented amount of readily available high-fat, high-calorie, and low-nutrient foods. We are saturated with junk food advertising. We are eating more and more meals outside the home, and portion sizes are bigger than ever. Healthy options are more frequently the exception than the rule. 5

It is hardly surprising, then, that we find ourselves in the midst of an obesity epidemic. Nearly three-quarters of Americans are overweight or obese, and a report by United Healthcare predicts that half of all American adults will develop diabetes or prediabetes by the end of the decade. The report further estimates that diabetes—which increases one's risk of stroke, cardiovascular disease, kidney failure, blindness, and amputations—will cost our society $500 billion a year by 2020.

In an effort to combat this disturbing trend, Georgia—the state with the nation's second highest obesity rates—recently launched a provocative and controversial ad campaign. It emphasizes the role of parents in failing to recognize and address childhood obesity. In the commercials, obese children sullenly ask questions like, "Mom, why am I fat?" and drive home poignant messages like, "It's hard to be a little girl, when you're not," or "Being fat takes the fun out of being a kid."

One might argue that Georgia's campaign is a bold and necessary step in the right direction, and to the extent that it raises awareness and sparks constructive conversation, it may be. However, these commercials miss the point. Shaming children and parents into losing weight is unlikely to be an effective strategy. It increases stigma on those already struggling with the psychosocial° consequences of being overweight, and shifts the focus of obesity control efforts to personal responsibility at a time when, for many individuals, options for improving eating habits may be limited.

While taking responsibility for one's health is certainly part of the solution, we must also recognize that we have created a food environment so ripe for obesity that to expect anything else would be irrational. Even for the most knowledgeable and resourceful among us, consistently eating well is a challenge. It is difficult to distinguish healthy options from unhealthy ones, and purchasing the right foods once they are identified is no cakewalk. Furthermore, people living in low-income areas have limited access to healthy food options for a variety of reasons, a barrier that contributes to their particularly high risk for being obese.

---

psychosocial: Relating to the interconnection of individual thoughts and behavior and external social factors.

There is much we can and should do to reverse the current trend.   10
An important step would be to provide monetary incentives to promote the production of and access to fresh, healthy food. By subsidizing fresh fruits and vegetables and supporting restaurants and vendors
that offer healthy alternatives, we might create an economic environment more conducive to healthy eating. Making healthy options
more accessible and affordable, especially for those living in low-
income areas of the country, is a vital component of reducing the
burden of obesity. When you can buy 2,000 calories for under $10 at
your neighborhood McDonald's, but have trouble getting your hands
on an apple, it's difficult to justify trying to shame anyone into skin-
niness.

Another important measure would be to minimize junk food advertising, especially to children. Each year, the food industry spends
nearly $2 billion marketing its products to children, and evidence
suggests that children exposed to junk food advertising express
greater preference for these types of foods. Asking the industry to
refrain from advertising foods that contain unhealthful amounts of
sugar, salts, and fats to youth could also encourage the production
of healthier options. I think that initially the guidelines should be
voluntary, but significant public and political pressure should
be placed on the food industry to adopt them. If it becomes clear
over time that they are unwilling to do so, then federal regulations
may be needed.

A third initiative might center on education and empowering youth
to make informed decisions. Instituting nutrition and health curric-
ulums into public schools would help children learn how to read
nutrition labels and identify healthy foods, as well as understand
the negative long-term consequences of obesity. Today's youth may
be the first generation of Americans to live shorter, more disease-
riddled lives than their parents—a staggering prediction based
largely on the rapid rise in childhood obesity. Let this not be our
legacy.

Understanding the Text

1. What realization does Khullar have when he makes his trip to the cafeteria?
2. What dilemma does Khullar describe? What solutions does he propose?

Reflection and Response

3. Why does Khullar claim that shame will not help reduce the obesity epidemic? Does he make a good case? Why or why not? Do you agree with him? Why or why not?

4. Khullar indicates that personal responsibility for food choices is not the only factor that affects what people eat. On what does he base this conclusion? What evidence does he give?

Making Connections

5. According to Khullar, what determines what we eat? In what ways do Brian Wansink and Collin Payne ("The Joy of Cooking Too Much," p. 119) and Michael Bloomberg (as described in James Surowiecki's "Downsizing Supersize," p. 123) agree with him? Are there authors in this collection who would disagree? How and why?

6. Do your eating habits and food choices reflect your values regarding food, or are they determined by other factors? Explain your answer using Khullar's argument, at least one other source from this book, and at least two other sources located in your campus library.

Monsanto's Harvest of Fear

Donald L. Barlett and James B. Steele

Donald L. Barlett and James B. Steele have reported and written together for more than four decades. As a widely acclaimed and award-winning investigative reporting team, these two American journalists have wowed audiences with their in-depth reporting and careful research and analysis of the complex issues and institutions of their times. They began working together in the 1970s at the *Philadelphia Inquirer*, then moved to *Time*, and now are contributing editors at *Vanity Fair*. They have won many prominent journalism awards, including the Pulitzer Prize (twice) and the National Magazine Award (twice). They have also coauthored eight books, including *The Betrayal of the American Dream* (2012). In this selection from a longer article that first appeared in *Vanity Fair* in May 2008, Barlett and Steele investigate the role of the Monsanto corporation and the legal system in American food production.

Gary Rinehart clearly remembers the summer day in 2002 when the stranger walked in and issued his threat. Rinehart was behind the counter of the Square Deal, his "old-time country store," as he calls it, on the fading town square of Eagleville, Missouri, a tiny farm community 100 miles north of Kansas City.

The Square Deal is a fixture in Eagleville, a place where farmers and townspeople can go for lightbulbs, greeting cards, hunting gear, ice cream, aspirin, and dozens of other small items without having to drive to a big-box store in Bethany, the county seat, 15 miles down Interstate 35.

Everyone knows Rinehart, who was born and raised in the area and runs one of Eagleville's few surviving businesses. The stranger came up to the counter and asked for him by name.

"Well, that's me," said Rinehart.

As Rinehart would recall, the man began verbally attacking him, 5 saying he had proof that Rinehart had planted Monsanto's genetically modified (G.M.) soybeans in violation of the company's patent. Better come clean and settle with Monsanto, Rinehart says the man told him—or face the consequences.

Rinehart was incredulous, listening to the words as puzzled customers and employees looked on. Like many others in rural America, Rinehart knew of Monsanto's fierce reputation for enforcing its patents and suing anyone who allegedly violated them. But Rinehart wasn't a farmer. He wasn't a seed dealer. He hadn't planted any seeds or sold any seeds. He owned a small—a *really* small—country store in a town of 350 people. He was angry that somebody could just barge into the store and embarrass him in front of everyone. "It made me and my business look bad," he says. Rinehart says he told the intruder, "You got the wrong guy."

When the stranger persisted, Rinehart showed him the door. On the way out the man kept making threats. Rinehart says he can't remember the exact words, but they were to the effect of: "Monsanto is big. You can't win. We will get you. You will pay."

Scenes like this are playing out in many parts of rural America these days as Monsanto goes after farmers, farmers' co-ops, seed dealers—anyone it suspects may have infringed its patents of genetically modified seeds. As interviews and reams of court documents reveal, Monsanto relies on a shadowy army of private investigators and agents in the American heartland to strike fear into farm country. They fan out into fields and farm towns, where they secretly videotape and photograph farmers, store owners, and co-ops; infiltrate community meetings; and gather information from informants about farming activities. Farmers say that some Monsanto agents pretend to be surveyors. Others confront farmers on their land and try to pressure them to sign papers giving Monsanto access to their private records. Farmers call them the "seed police" and use words such as "Gestapo" and "Mafia" to describe their tactics.

When asked about these practices, Monsanto declined to comment specifically, other than to say that the company is simply protecting its patents. "Monsanto spends more than $2 million a day in research to identify, test, develop, and bring to market innovative new seeds and technologies that benefit farmers," Monsanto spokesman Darren Wallis wrote in an e-mailed letter to *Vanity Fair*. "One tool in protecting this investment is patenting our discoveries and, if necessary, legally defending those patents against those who might choose to infringe upon them." Wallis said that, while the vast majority of farmers and seed dealers follow the licensing agreements, "a tiny fraction" do not, and that Monsanto is obligated to those who do abide by its rules to enforce its patent rights on those who "reap the benefits of the technology without paying for its use." He said only a small number of cases ever go to trial.

Some compare Monsanto's hard-line approach to Microsoft's zealous efforts to protect its software from pirates. At least with Microsoft the buyer of a program can use it over and over again. But farmers who buy Monsanto's seeds can't even do that. 10

The Control of Nature

For centuries—millennia—farmers have saved seeds from season to season: they planted in the spring, harvested in the fall, then reclaimed and cleaned the seeds over the winter for re-planting the next spring. Monsanto has turned this ancient practice on its head.

Monsanto developed G.M. seeds that would resist its own herbicide, Roundup, offering farmers a convenient way to spray fields with weed killer without affecting crops. Monsanto then patented the seeds. For nearly all of its history the United States Patent and Trademark Office had refused to grant patents on seeds, viewing them as life-forms with too many variables to be patented. "It's not like describing a widget," says Joseph Mendelson III, the legal director of the Center for Food Safety, which has tracked Monsanto's activities in rural America for years.

Indeed not. But in 1980 the U.S. Supreme Court, in a five-to-four decision, turned seeds into widgets, laying the groundwork for a handful of corporations to begin taking control of the world's food supply. In its decision, the court extended patent law to cover "a live human-made microorganism." In this case, the organism wasn't even a seed. Rather, it was a *Pseudomonas* bacterium developed by a General Electric scientist to clean up oil spills. But the precedent was set, and Monsanto took advantage of it. Since the 1980s, Monsanto has become the world leader in genetic modification of seeds and has won 674 biotechnology patents, more than any other company, according to U.S. Department of Agriculture data.

Farmers who buy Monsanto's patented Roundup Ready seeds are required to sign an agreement promising not to save the seed produced after each harvest for re-planting, or to sell the seed to other farmers. This means that farmers must buy new seed every year. Those increased sales, coupled with ballooning sales of its Roundup weed killer, have been a bonanza for Monsanto.

This radical departure from age-old practice has created turmoil 15 in farm country. Some farmers don't fully understand that they aren't supposed to save Monsanto's seeds for next year's planting. Others do, but ignore the stipulation rather than throw away a perfectly usable product. Still others say that they don't use Monsanto's genetically modified seeds, but seeds have been blown into their fields by wind or deposited by birds. It's certainly easy for G.M. seeds to get mixed in with traditional varieties when seeds are cleaned by commercial dealers for re-planting. The seeds look identical; only a laboratory analysis can show the difference. Even if a farmer doesn't buy

G.M. seeds and doesn't want them on his land, it's a safe bet he'll get a visit from Monsanto's seed police if crops grown from G.M. seeds are discovered in his fields.

Most Americans know Monsanto because of what it sells to put on our lawns—the ubiquitous weed killer Roundup. What they may not know is that the company now profoundly influences—and one day may virtually control—what we put on our tables. For most of its history Monsanto was a chemical giant, producing some of the most toxic substances ever created, residues from which have left us with some of the most polluted sites on earth. Yet in a little more than a decade, the company has sought to shed its polluted past and morph into something much different and more far-reaching—an "agricultural company" dedicated to making the world "a better place for future generations." Still, more than one Web log claims to see similarities between Monsanto and the fictional company "U-North" in the movie *Michael Clayton*, an agribusiness giant accused in a multibillion-dollar lawsuit of selling an herbicide that causes cancer.

> Most Americans know Monsanto because of what it sells to put on our lawns—the ubiquitous weed killer Roundup. What they may not know is that the company now profoundly influences—and one day may virtually control—what we put on our tables.

Monsanto's genetically modified seeds have transformed the company and are radically altering global agriculture. So far, the company has produced G.M. seeds for soybeans, corn, canola, and cotton. Many more products have been developed or are in the pipeline, including seeds for sugar beets and alfalfa. The company is also seeking to extend its reach into milk production by marketing an artificial growth hormone for cows that increases their output, and it is taking aggressive steps to put those who don't want to use growth hormone at a commercial disadvantage.

Even as the company is pushing its G.M. agenda, Monsanto is buying up conventional-seed companies. In 2005, Monsanto paid $1.4 billion for Seminis, which controlled 40 percent of the U.S. market for lettuce, tomatoes, and other vegetable and fruit seeds. Two weeks later it announced the acquisition of the country's third-largest cottonseed company, Emergent Genetics, for $300 million. It's estimated that Monsanto seeds now account for 90 percent of the U.S. production of soybeans, which are used in food products beyond counting. Monsanto's acquisitions have fueled explosive growth, transforming the St. Louis–based corporation into the largest seed company in the world.

In Iraq, the groundwork has been laid to protect the patents of Monsanto and other G.M.-seed companies. One of L. Paul Bremer's last acts as head of the Coalition Provisional Authority was an order stipulating that "farmers shall be prohibited from re-using seeds of protected varieties." Monsanto has said that it has no interest in doing business in Iraq, but should the company change its mind, the American-style law is in place.

To be sure, more and more agricultural corporations and individual farmers are using Monsanto's G.M. seeds. As recently as 1980, no genetically modified crops were grown in the U.S. In 2007, the total was 142 million acres planted. Worldwide, the figure was 282 million acres. Many farmers believe that G.M. seeds increase crop yields and save money. Another reason for their attraction is convenience. By using Roundup Ready soybean seeds, a farmer can spend less time tending to his fields. With Monsanto seeds, a farmer plants his crop, then treats it later with Roundup to kill weeds. That takes the place of labor-intensive weed control and plowing. 20

Monsanto portrays its move into G.M. seeds as a giant leap for mankind. But out in the American countryside, Monsanto's no-holds-barred tactics have made it feared and loathed. Like it or not, farmers say, they have fewer and fewer choices in buying seeds.

And controlling the seeds is not some abstraction. Whoever provides the world's seeds controls the world's food supply.

Under Surveillance

After Monsanto's investigator confronted Gary Rinehart, Monsanto filed a federal lawsuit alleging that Rinehart "knowingly, intentionally, and willfully" planted seeds "in violation of Monsanto's patent rights." The company's complaint made it sound as if Monsanto had Rinehart dead to rights:

> During the 2002 growing season, Investigator Jeffery Moore, through surveillance of Mr. Rinehart's farm facility and farming operations, observed Defendant planting brown bag soybean seed. Mr. Moore observed the Defendant take the brown bag soybeans to a field, which was subsequently loaded into a grain drill and planted. Mr. Moore located two empty bags in the ditch in the public road right-of-way beside one of the fields planted by Rinehart, which contained some soybeans. Mr. Moore collected a small amount of soybeans left

in the bags which Defendant had tossed into the public right-of-way. These samples tested positive for Monsanto's Roundup Ready technology.

Faced with a federal lawsuit, Rinehart had to hire a lawyer. Monsanto eventually realized that "Investigator Jeffery Moore" had targeted the wrong man, and dropped the suit. Rinehart later learned that the company had been secretly investigating farmers in his area. Rinehart never heard from Monsanto again: no letter of apology, no public concession that the company had made a terrible mistake, no offer to pay his attorney's fees. "I don't know how they get away with it," he says. "If I tried to do something like that it would be bad news. I felt like I was in another country."

Gary Rinehart is actually one of Monsanto's luckier targets. Ever 25
since commercial introduction of its G.M. seeds, in 1996, Monsanto has launched thousands of investigations and filed lawsuits against hundreds of farmers and seed dealers. In a 2007 report, the Center for Food Safety, in Washington, D.C., documented 112 such lawsuits, in 27 states.

Even more significant, in the Center's opinion, are the numbers of farmers who settle because they don't have the money or the time to fight Monsanto. "The number of cases filed is only the tip of the iceberg," says Bill Freese, the Center's science-policy analyst. Freese says he has been told of many cases in which Monsanto investigators showed up at a farmer's house or confronted him in his fields, claiming he had violated the technology agreement and demanding to see his records. According to Freese, investigators will say, "Monsanto knows that you are saving Roundup Ready seeds, and if you don't sign these information-release forms, Monsanto is going to come after you and take your farm or take you for all you're worth." Investigators will sometimes show a farmer a photo of himself coming out of a store, to let him know he is being followed.

Lawyers who have represented farmers sued by Monsanto say that intimidating actions like these are commonplace. Most give in and pay Monsanto some amount in damages; those who resist face the full force of Monsanto's legal wrath. . . .

The Milk Wars

Jeff Kleinpeter takes very good care of his dairy cows. In the winter he turns on heaters to warm their barns. In the summer, fans blow gentle breezes to cool them, and on especially hot days, a fine mist floats down to take the edge off Louisiana's heat. The dairy has gone "to the ultimate end of the earth for cow comfort," says Kleinpeter, a fourth-generation dairy farmer in Baton Rouge. He says visitors marvel at what he does: "I've had many of them say, 'When I die, I want to come back as a Kleinpeter cow.'"

Monsanto would like to change the way Jeff Kleinpeter and his family do business. Specifically, Monsanto doesn't like the label on Kleinpeter Dairy's milk cartons: "From Cows *Not* Treated with rBGH." To consumers, that means the milk comes from cows that were not given artificial bovine growth hormone, a supplement developed by Monsanto that can be injected into dairy cows to increase their milk output.

No one knows what effect, if any, the hormone has on milk or the 30 people who drink it. Studies have not detected any difference in the quality of milk produced by cows that receive rBGH, or rBST, a term by which it is also known. But Jeff Kleinpeter—like millions of consumers—wants no part of rBGH. Whatever its effect on humans, if any, Kleinpeter feels certain it's harmful to cows because it speeds up their metabolism and increases the chances that they'll contract a painful illness that can shorten their lives. "It's like putting a Volkswagen car in with the Indianapolis 500 racers," he says. "You gotta keep the pedal to the metal the whole way through, and pretty soon that poor little Volkswagen engine's going to burn up."

Kleinpeter Dairy has never used Monsanto's artificial hormone, and the dairy requires other dairy farmers from whom it buys milk to attest that they don't use it, either. At the suggestion of a marketing consultant, the dairy began advertising its milk as coming from rBGH-free cows in 2005, and the label began appearing on Kleinpeter milk cartons and in company literature, including a new Web site of Kleinpeter products that proclaims, "We treat our cows with love . . . not rBGH."

The dairy's sales soared. For Kleinpeter, it was simply a matter of giving consumers more information about their product.

But giving consumers that information has stirred the ire of Monsanto. The company contends that advertising by Kleinpeter and other dairies touting their "no rBGH" milk reflects adversely on Monsanto's product. In a letter to the Federal Trade Commission in February 2007, Monsanto said that, notwithstanding the overwhelming evidence that there is no difference in the milk from cows treated with its product, "milk processors persist in claiming on their labels and in advertisements that the use of rBST is somehow harmful, either to cows or to the people who consume milk from rBST-supplemented cows."

Monsanto called on the commission to investigate what it called the "deceptive advertising and labeling practices" of milk processors such as Kleinpeter, accusing them of misleading consumers "by falsely claiming that there are health and safety risks associated with milk from rBST-supplemented cows." As noted, Kleinpeter does not make any such claims—he simply states that his milk comes from cows not injected with rBGH.

Monsanto's attempt to get the F.T.C. to force dairies to change their advertising was just one more step in the corporation's efforts to extend its reach into agriculture. After years of scientific debate and public controversy, the F.D.A. in 1993 approved commercial use of rBST, basing its decision in part on studies submitted by Monsanto. That decision allowed the company to market the artificial hormone. The effect of the hormone is to increase milk production, not exactly something the nation needed then—or needs now. The U.S. was actually awash in milk, with the government buying up the surplus to prevent a collapse in prices.

Monsanto began selling the supplement in 1994 under the name Posilac. Monsanto acknowledges that the possible side effects of rBST for cows include lameness, disorders of the uterus, increased body temperature, digestive problems, and birthing difficulties. Veterinary drug reports note that "cows injected with Posilac are at an increased risk for mastitis," an udder infection in which bacteria and pus may be pumped out with the milk. What's the effect on humans? The F.D.A. has consistently said that the milk produced by cows that receive rBGH is the same as milk from cows that aren't injected: "The public can be confident that milk and meat from BST-treated cows is safe to consume." Nevertheless, some scientists are concerned by the lack of long-term studies to test the additive's impact, especially on children. A Wisconsin geneticist, William von Meyer, observed that when rBGH was approved the longest study on which the F.D.A.'s approval was based covered only a 90-day laboratory test with small animals. "But people drink milk for a lifetime," he noted. Canada and the European Union have never approved the commercial sale of the artificial hormone. Today, nearly 15 years after the F.D.A. approved rBGH, there have still been no long-term studies "to determine the safety of milk from cows that receive artificial growth hormone," says Michael Hansen, senior staff scientist for Consumers Union. Not only have there been no studies, he adds, but the data that does exist all comes from Monsanto. "There is no scientific consensus about the safety," he says.

However F.D.A. approval came about, Monsanto has long been wired into Washington. Michael R. Taylor was a staff attorney and executive assistant to the F.D.A. commissioner before joining a law firm in Washington in 1981, where he worked to secure F.D.A. approval of Monsanto's artificial growth hormone before returning to the F.D.A. as deputy commissioner in 1991. Dr. Michael A. Friedman, formerly the F.D.A.'s deputy commissioner for operations, joined Monsanto in 1999 as a senior vice president. Linda J. Fisher was an assistant administrator at the E.P.A. when she left the agency in 1993. She became a vice president of Monsanto, from 1995 to 2000, only to return to the E.P.A. as deputy administrator the next year. William D. Ruckelshaus, former E.P.A. administrator, and Mickey Kantor, former U.S. trade representative, each served on Monsanto's board after leaving government. Supreme Court justice Clarence Thomas was an attorney in Monsanto's corporate-law department in the 1970s. He wrote the Supreme Court opinion in a crucial G.M.-seed patent-rights case in 2001 that benefited Monsanto and all G.M.-seed companies. Donald Rumsfeld never served on the board or held any office at Monsanto, but Monsanto must occupy a soft spot in the heart of the former defense secretary. Rumsfeld was chairman and C.E.O. of the pharmaceutical maker G. D. Searle & Co. when Monsanto acquired Searle in 1985, after Searle had experienced difficulty in finding a buyer. Rumsfeld's stock and options in Searle were valued at $12 million at the time of the sale.

From the beginning some consumers have consistently been hesitant to drink milk from cows treated with artificial hormones. This is one reason Monsanto has waged so many battles with dairies and regulators over the wording of labels on milk cartons. It has sued at least two dairies and one co-op over labeling.

Critics of the artificial hormone have pushed for mandatory labeling on all milk products, but the F.D.A. has resisted and even taken action against some dairies that labeled their milk "BST-free." Since BST is a natural hormone found in all cows, including those not injected with Monsanto's artificial version, the F.D.A. argued that no dairy could claim that its milk is BST-free. The F.D.A. later issued guidelines allowing dairies to use labels saying their milk comes from "non-supplemented cows," as long as the carton has a disclaimer saying that the artificial supplement does not in any way change the milk. So the milk cartons from Kleinpeter Dairy, for example, carry a label on the front stating that the milk is from cows not treated with rBGH, and the rear panel says, "Government studies have shown no significant difference between milk derived from rBGH-treated and non-rBGH-treated cows." That's not good enough for Monsanto.

The Next Battleground

As more and more dairies have chosen to advertise their milk as "No rBGH," Monsanto has gone on the offensive. Its attempt to force the F.T.C. to look into what Monsanto called "deceptive practices" by dairies trying to distance themselves from the company's artificial hormone was the most recent national salvo. But after reviewing Monsanto's claims, the F.T.C.'s Division of Advertising Practices decided in August 2007 that a "formal investigation and enforcement action is not warranted at this time." The agency found some instances where dairies had made "unfounded health and safety claims," but these were mostly on Web sites, not on milk cartons. And the F.T.C. determined that the dairies Monsanto had singled out all carried disclaimers that the F.D.A. had found no significant differences in milk from cows treated with the artificial hormone.

Blocked at the federal level, Monsanto is pushing for action by the   40
states. In the fall of 2007, Pennsylvania's agriculture secretary, Dennis Wolff, issued an edict prohibiting dairies from stamping milk containers with labels stating their products were made without the use of the artificial hormone. Wolff said such a label implies that competitors' milk is not safe, and noted that non-supplemented milk comes at an unjustified higher price, arguments that Monsanto has frequently made. The ban was to take effect February 1, 2008.

Wolff's action created a firestorm in Pennsylvania (and beyond) from angry consumers. So intense was the outpouring of e-mails, letters, and calls that Pennsylvania governor Edward Rendell stepped in and reversed his agriculture secretary, saying, "The public has a right to complete information about how the milk they buy is produced."

On this issue, the tide may be shifting against Monsanto. Organic dairy products, which don't involve rBGH, are soaring in popularity. Supermarket chains such as Kroger, Publix, and Safeway are embracing them. Some other companies have turned away from rBGH products, including Starbucks, which has banned all milk products from cows treated with rBGH. Although Monsanto once claimed that an estimated 30 percent of the nation's dairy cows were injected with rBST, it's widely believed that today the number is much lower.

But don't count Monsanto out. Efforts similar to the one in Pennsylvania have been launched in other states, including New Jersey, Ohio,

Indiana, Kansas, Utah, and Missouri. A Monsanto-backed group called AFACT—American Farmers for the Advancement and Conservation of Technology—has been spearheading efforts in many of these states. AFACT describes itself as a "producer organization" that decries "questionable labeling tactics and activism" by marketers who have convinced some consumers to "shy away from foods using new technology." AFACT reportedly uses the same St. Louis public-relations firm, Osborn & Barr, employed by Monsanto. An Osborn & Barr spokesman told the *Kansas City Star* that the company was doing work for AFACT on a pro bono basis.

Even if Monsanto's efforts to secure across-the-board labeling changes should fall short, there's nothing to stop state agriculture departments from restricting labeling on a dairy-by-dairy basis. Beyond that, Monsanto also has allies whose foot soldiers will almost certainly keep up the pressure on dairies that don't use Monsanto's artificial hormone. Jeff Kleinpeter knows about them, too.

He got a call one day from the man who prints the labels for his 45 milk cartons, asking if he had seen the attack on Kleinpeter Dairy that had been posted on the Internet. Kleinpeter went online to a site called StopLabelingLies, which claims to "help consumers by publicizing examples of false and misleading food and other product labels." There, sure enough, Kleinpeter and other dairies that didn't use Monsanto's product were being accused of making misleading claims to sell their milk.

There was no address or phone number on the Web site, only a list of groups that apparently contribute to the site and whose issues range from disparaging organic farming to downplaying the impact of global warming. "They were criticizing people like me for doing what we had a right to do, had gone through a government agency to do," says Kleinpeter. "We never could get to the bottom of that Web site to get that corrected."

As it turns out, the Web site counts among its contributors Steven Milloy, the "junk science" commentator for FoxNews.com and operator of junkscience.com, which claims to debunk "faulty scientific data and analysis." It may come as no surprise that earlier in his career, Milloy, who calls himself the "junkman," was a registered lobbyist for Monsanto.

Understanding the Text

1. What are genetically modified seeds? What are Roundup Ready seeds?
2. Why is Monsanto trying to protect its patent?
3. How has Monsanto changed farming practices? What ancient practices are being eliminated?

Reflection and Response

4. What's at stake in the legal battles between Monsanto and the farmers accused of misusing patented seeds? Why is Monsanto trying to protect its interests so vigorously? Why and how are some farmers fighting back?
5. Barlett and Steele's investigative reporting is aimed at exposing Monsanto's ruthless tactics, legal and otherwise. How do they do this? What rhetorical strategies do they employ? How and why are their strategies effective?
6. Why does Monsanto care about how dairy farmers advertise their products? Should Monsanto have a say? Who should decide?

Making Connections

7. Describe Monsanto's tactics for protecting its own interests. Are they justified? Why or why not? Which authors in this collection would critique Monsanto's tactics? Would any defend them? Use textual evidence to support your answers.
8. Barlett and Steele claim that Monsanto "profoundly influences—and one day may virtually control—what we put on our tables" (para. 16). How do they support this argument? What evidence is presented in Vandana Shiva's essay ("Soy Imperialism and the Destruction of Local Food Cultures," p. 143) that could be used to support this claim? What evidence could be used to complicate or argue against it? Using your campus library resources, locate at least two other sources that discuss the impact of Monsanto on food production to develop your response to these questions. Use textual evidence to support your responses.

Soy Imperialism and the Destruction of Local Food Cultures

Vandana Shiva

Vandana Shiva was a leading physicist in India before she became an internationally known environmental and antiglobalization activist. She is particularly dedicated to the protection of local food cultures and the preservation of heirloom seeds in India. She is the recipient of many international awards and the author of more than 20 books, including *Staying Alive: Women, Ecology, and Development* (1988); *Stolen Harvest: The Hijacking of the Global Food Supply* (2000); and *Earth Democracy: Justice, Sustainability, and Peace* (2005). She is a leader in the International Forum on Globalization and director of the Research Foundation on Science, Technology, and Ecology. In this selection from *Stolen Harvest*, Shiva issues a stinging critique of the way global food markets are destroying local food cultures. She argues that particular economic and political trends of globalization are threatening India's local food culture.

The diversity of soils, climates, and plants has contributed to a diversity of food cultures across the world. The maize-based food systems of Central America, the rice-based Asian systems, the teff-based Ethiopian diet, and the millet-based foods of Africa are not just a part of agriculture; they are central to cultural diversity. Food security is not just having access to adequate food. It is also having access to culturally appropriate food. Vegetarians can starve if asked to live on meat diets. I have watched Asians feel totally deprived on bread, potato, and meat diets in Europe.

India is a country rich in biological diversity and cultural diversity of food systems. In the high Himalayan mountains, people eat pseudocereals such as amaranth, buckwheat, and chenopods. The people of the arid areas of Western India and semiarid tracts of the Deccan live on millets. Eastern India is home to rice and fish cultures, as are the states of Goa and Kerala. Each region also has its culturally specific edible oil used as a cooking medium. In the North and East it is mustard, in the West it is [peanut], in the Deccan it is sesame, and in Kerala it is coconut.

The diversity of oilseeds has also contributed to diversity of cropping systems. In the fields, oilseeds have always been mixed with cereals. Wheat is intercropped with mustard and sesame is intercropped with millets. A typical home garden could have up to 100 different species growing in cooperation.

The story of how the soybean displaced mustard in India within a few months of open imports is a story being repeated with different foods, crops, and cultures across the world, as subsidized exports from industrialized countries are dumped on agricultural societies, destroying livelihoods, biodiversity, and cultural diversity of food. The flooding of domestic markets with artificially cheap imports is stealing local markets and livelihoods from local farmers and local food processors. The expansion of global markets is taking place by extinguishing local economies and cultures.

"Mustard Is Our Life"

For Bengalis, Hilsa fish fried in mustard oil is the ultimate delight, and North Indians like their *pakoras* fried in it because of the unique taste and aroma. In the South, mustard seeds are the preferred seasoning for many dishes. Mustard oil is used as the cooking medium in the entire North Indian belt—the standard oil of Bihar, Bengal, Orissa, and East Uttar Pradesh, used for flavoring and cooking.

Mustard, which was developed as a crop in India, is not just useful as an edible oil. It is an important medicine in the indigenous system of health care. It is used for therapeutic massages and for muscular and joint problems. Mustard oil with garlic and turmeric is used for rheumatism and joint pains. Mustard oil is also used as a mosquito repellent, a significant contribution in a region where the resurgence of malaria is responsible for the death of thousands.

There are many other personal and health care uses for mustard seeds and oil, and diverse varieties and species of mustard are grown and used for different purposes.[1] During the Deepavali celebration, mustard oil is used to light *diya* lamps. This is not just a celebratory tradition, but an ecological method of pest control at a time when the change in seasons causes an outbreak of disease and pests. The smoke from the mustard oil used to light the *deepavali* lamp acts as an environmental purifier and pest-control agent, reducing the spread of diseases that destroy stored grains and cleaning the atmosphere of homes and villages. As these mustard-oil lamps have been replaced by candles made of paraffin wax, an environmentally cleansing festival is transformed into an environmentally polluting one.

Indigenous° oilseeds, being high in oil content, are easy to process at small-scale, decentralized levels with eco-friendly and health-friendly technologies. These oils are thus available to the poor at low

indigenous: Occurring naturally in a particular place.

cost. Hundreds and thousands of artisans are self-employed in rural India by extracting oil from locally produced crops for oil edible by humans and oil cake edible by cattle. The bulk of oilseed processing is done by over 1 million *ghanis* (expellers) and 20,000 small and tiny crushers that account for 68 percent of edible oils processed.[2] The oil extracted through these cold-pressing indigenous technologies is fresh, nutritious, unadulterated, and contains natural flavor.[3]

Women in the *bastis*, or slums, usually buy small quantities of mustard oil extracted on their local *ghani* in front of their eyes. This direct, community supervision over processing is the best guarantee for food safety. Yet these community-based systems of food and health safety were quickly dismantled in the name of food safety in 1998, when local processing of mustard oil was banned and free imports of soybean oil were installed in response to a mysterious contamination of Delhi's edible-oil supply.

The sudden lack of availability of mustard oil posed serious prob- 10 lems for poor women. Their children would not eat food cooked in imported palm oil or soybean oil, and were going to bed hungry. Being poor, they could not afford to buy the packaged oil that was the only form in which oil was available after the ban on local processors. For although the Chinese and Japanese eat soybean products as fermented foods, in most cultures outside East Asia, soybean products are not eaten. In spite of decades of promotion through free distribution in schools, soybean has not been adopted in India as a preferred choice for either oil or protein.

The Dropsy Epidemic

During August 1998, a tragedy unfolded in Delhi due to a massive adulteration° of mustard oil with seeds of the weed *Argemone mexicana*, as well as other adulterants such as diesel, waste oil, and industrial oil.

Consumption of the adulterated oil had led to an epidemic of what was called "dropsy" and referred to a range of signs and symptoms affecting multiple organs and systems. These included nausea, vomiting, diarrhea, abdominal swelling, liver toxicity, kidney damage, cardiotoxicity, breathlessness due to retention of fluids in the lungs, and death due to heart failure. The link between dropsy and adulterated edible oil was first established by an Indian doctor in Bengal in 1926. By early September 1998, the official death toll was 41, and 2,300 people had been affected.

---

adulteration: The process of adding extraneous or inferior ingredients.

Mustard-oil sales were banned in Delhi, Assam, Bihar, Haryana, Madhya Pradesh, Orissa, Uttar Pradesh, West Bengal, Arunachal Pradesh, Sikkum, Tripura, and Karnataka. In July, India announced that it would import 1 million tons of soybeans for use as oilseeds, over the protests of citizen groups and the Agriculture Ministry, which challenged the necessity and safety of the imports. Later, free imports of soybeans were instituted. Not only was there no guarantee that these soybeans would not be contaminated with genetically engineered soybeans, the moves profoundly jeopardized the local oil-processing industry and with it the food culture and economy that depended on it.

On September 4, the government banned the sale of all unpackaged edible oils, thus ensuring that all household and community-level processing of edible oils stopped, and edible oil became fully industrialized. The food economy of the poor, who depend on unpackaged oil since it is cheaper and they can buy it in small quantities, was completely destroyed.

The highest-level political and economic conflicts between freedom and slavery, democracy and dictatorship, diversity and monoculture have thus entered into the simple acts of buying edible oils and cooking our food.

The adulteration that triggered these dire effects remains mysterious in origin. First, in the past local traders had adulterated particular brands of oils in remote and marginalized regions to cheat consumers in a way that would go unnoticed; however, the mustard-oil adulteration affected nearly all brands, and India's capital, Delhi, was the worst-affected region. Such an adulteration triggered an immediate response and could not have been initiated by an individual local trader.

Second, while corrupt traders had adulterated mustard oil with argemone° in the past, before the 1998 tragedy, the adulterating agent was never found to be more than 1 percent of the oil. This time, contaminated oil contained up to 30 percent argemone and other agents. The high level of adulteration with argemone and other toxic substances such as diesel and waste oil clearly indicated that the tragedy was not the result of the normal business of adulteration.

According to the health minister of Delhi, the adulteration was not possible without an organized conspiracy. It was done in such a way that it could kill people quickly and conspicuously, and an immedi-

---

argemone: A flowering plant commonly known as prickly poppy; its oil is sometimes mixed with edible oils even though it is considered toxic.

ate ban on mustard oil and free import of soybeans and other oil-seeds for oil became inevitable. The Rajasthan Oil Industries Association claimed that a "conspiracy" was being hatched to undermine the mustard-oil trade, and felt that "invisible hands of the multinationals" were involved.

Multinational Companies Gain from the Mustard-Oil Tragedy

During the oil crisis, the Indian soybean lobby organized a major conference, "Globoil India 98," to promote the globalization and monoculturization of India's edible-oil economy. The U.S. Soybean Association was present at this conference to push for soybean imports.[4] According to *Business Line*, "U.S. farmers need big new export markets. . . . India is a perfect match."[5]

Multinational companies (MNCs) did gain from the mustard-oil tragedy. The ban on local processing has destroyed the domestic, small-scale edible-oil economy. It has criminalized the small-scale oil processor. It has criminalized the small trader. And it has destroyed the local market for farmers. Mustard prices have crashed from Rs.° 2,200 to Rs. 600–800 per 100 kilograms.

The dangers of this destruction are tremendous. If traders cannot 20 sell mustard oil, they will not buy mustard from farmers, and farmers will stop growing mustard. This will lead to the extinction of a crop that is the very symbol of spring. Once mustard oil has gone out of cultivation, even after the ban is lifted on mustard oil, we will be forced to continue an enforced dependence on soybeans for edible oil.

Calgene, now owned by Monsanto, has patented the Indian mustard plant, the *India brassica.* If India wanted to reintroduce mustard later, it would have to depend on genetically engineered, patented mustard varieties. Farmers and consumers would be dependent on Monsanto for patented seeds of both soybean and mustard.

Such a reliance on imported oilseeds can easily trigger violence and instability. The food riots in Indonesia in the late 1990s were largely based on the fact that Indonesia had been made cripplingly dependent on imported soybeans for oil. When the Indonesian currency collapsed, the price of cooking oils shot up, and violence was the result.

Nor does the destruction of the domestic oil industry ensure greater food safety, as is argued by the government. It is an established

Rs.: Rupees (the currency of India).

fact that U.S. exports are heavily adulterated through what has been called purposeful contamination, or "blending." The toxic weed parthenium, which has spread across India, has been traced to wheat shipments from the United States.

More significantly, the adulteration of genetic engineering takes place at the genetic level and is hence invisible. Instead of toxic seeds like those of argemone being added *externally*, genetic engineering in effect allows food adulteration to be done *internally* by introducing genes for toxins from bacteria, viruses, and animals into crops. Genetic engineering is adulterating foods with toxins from rats and scorpions.

It is estimated that over 18 million acres were planted with genetically engineered Roundup Ready soybeans in 1998. The soybeans are engineered by Monsanto to contain a bacterial gene that confers tolerance to the herbicide Roundup, also manufactured by Monsanto. This soybean has been genetically engineered not in order to improve its yield or healthfulness. The sole purpose of Roundup Ready soybeans is to sell more chemicals for seeds tailored to these chemicals.

The United States has been unable to sell its genetically engineered soybeans to Europe because of European consumers' demands that such foods be labeled, something that is ardently opposed by agribusiness interests and their allies. According to former U.S. president Jimmy Carter, such labeling would make U.S. exports rot at ports around the world. (A wide-ranging coalition of U.S. scientists, health professionals, consumers, farmers, and religious leaders have filed a lawsuit demanding mandatory labeling.)

U.S. companies are therefore desperate to dump their genetically engineered soybeans on countries such as India. The mustard-oil tragedy is a perfect "market opening." For while the Indian government lost no time imposing packaging and labeling restrictions on the indigenous edible-oil industry, it has taken no steps to require segregation and labeling of genetically engineered soybeans.

A new soybean-futures exchange has been opened in India. According to Harsh Maheshwari of the Soya Association, the most conservative estimate of its activity is a turnover of $2.3 billion. Some say it will be five times more. The Council for Scientific Research and the Technology Mission on oilseeds have announced steps to promote the use of soybeans for food. Every agency of government in the United States and India is being used by the soybean lobby to destroy agricultural and food diversity in order to spread the soybean monoculture.

While the profits for agribusiness grow, the prices U.S. farmers receive for soybeans have been crashing. Both U.S. farmers and Indian farmers are losers in a globalized free-trade system that benefits global corporations.

Global Merchants of Soybeans

In 1921, 36 firms accounted for 85 percent of U.S. grain exports. By 30 the end of the 1970s, six giant "Merchants of Grain" controlled more than 90 percent of exports from the United States, Canada, Europe, Argentina, and Australia. Today, Cargill and Continental each control 25 percent of the grain trade.

Referring to this concentration of power, former Representative James Weaver (D-OR) said,

> These companies are giants. They control not only the buying and the selling of grain but the shipment of it, the storage of it, and everything else. It's obscene. I have rallied against them again and again. I think food is the most—hell, whoever controls the food supply has really got the people by the scrotum. And yet we allow six corporations to do this in secret. It's mind-boggling![6]

The United States is the world's biggest producer of soybeans, an East Asian crop that is also the United States' biggest export commodity. Twenty-six percent of U.S. acreage is under soybean cultivation. This production doubled between 1972 and 1997, from 34.6 million to 74.2 million metric tons. More than half of this crop is exported as soybeans or as soybean oil.

The U.S. acreage planted with genetically engineered soybeans has shot up from 0.5 million hectares in 1996 to 18 million hectares° in 1998, accounting for 40 percent of the country's genetically engineered crops.[7] It is thus becoming inevitable that conventional soybeans will be mixed with genetically engineered soybeans in export shipments.

In the United States, soybeans are used for cattle feed, fish feed, adhesives, pesticides, plastics, solvents, soaps, paints, and inks.[8] Eighty percent of industrially processed foods now have soybeans in them, as European consumers discovered when they tried to boycott foods with Monsanto Roundup Ready soybeans.

Brazil follows the United States in soybean production, producing 35 30.7 million metric tons in 1997. Argentina is the third-biggest producer. Acreage in Argentina under soybean cultivation has increased from none in the 1960s to nearly 7 million hectares in 1998, with

---

hectare: A metric unit of measure equal to 10,000 square meters.

more than half planted with transgenic varieties. India's acreage under soybean cultivation has also increased from zero in the 1960s to nearly 6 million hectares in 1998.

The soybean trade, like trade in other agricultural commodities, is controlled by six Merchants of Grain: Cargill, Continental (now owned by Cargill), Louis Dreyfus, Bunge, Mitsui Cook, and Andre & Company.[9] These companies also control the storage and transport facilities, and hence the prices of commodities.

Soybean Patents and Seed Monopoly

Not only is the soybean trade controlled by multinational corporations; soybean cultivation is becoming increasingly monopolized through control over the seed itself.

Monsanto has bought up the seed business of corporations such as Cargill, Agracetus, Calgene, Asgrow Seed, Delta and Pine Land, Holden, Unilever, and Sementes Agrocetes. It owns the broad species patents on soybean. A subsidiary of W. R. Grace, Agracetus owns patent on all transgenic° soybean varieties and seeds, regardless of the genes used, and all methods of transformation.

Agracetus's extraordinarily broad soybean patent has been challenged by Rural Advancement Foundation International, a public-interest group. Dr. Geoffrey Hawtin, director-general of the International Plant Genetic Resources Institute in Rome, Italy, expressed his concern at such patenting:

> The granting of patents covering all genetically engineered varieties of a species, irrespective of the genes concerned or how they were transferred, puts in the hands of a single inventor the possibility to control what we grow on our farms and in our gardens. At a stroke of a pen the research of countless farmers and scientists has potentially been negated in a single, legal act of economic hijack.[10]

While Monsanto had originally challenged the patent, it has withdrawn the challenge after buying Agracetus.

Monsanto also owns a patent on herbicide-resistant plants. This patent covers herbicide-resistant corn, wheat, rice, soybean, cotton, sugar beet, oilseed, rape, canola, flax, sunflower, potato, tobacco, alfalfa, poplar, pine, apple, and grape. It also covers methods for weed

transgenic: Containing genetic material into which DNA from another organism has been introduced.

control, planting of seeds, and application of glyphosate (a herbicide). Thus Monsanto controls the entire production process of these plants, from breeding to cultivation to sale.

The Roundup Ready soybean has been genetically engineered to be resistant to Monsanto's broad-spectrum herbicide Roundup. The three new genes genetically engineered into the soybean—from a bacterium, a cauliflower virus, and a petunia—don't do a thing for the taste or nutritional value of the bean. Instead, the unusual genetic combination—which would never be created by nature—makes the soybean resistant to a weed-killer. Normally soybeans are too delicate to spray once they start sprouting from the ground. But now, since two of its products—the bean and the weed-killer—are so closely linked, Monsanto gets to sell more of both.[11] Monsanto claims this will mean more soybean yields from each crop, but they cannot guarantee it.

Industrial Processing

From seed to distribution to processing, soybeans are associated with concentration of power. While the oil content of coconut is 75 percent, [peanut] 55 percent, sesame 50 percent, castor 56 percent, and niger 40 percent, the oil content of soybeans is only 18 percent. However, textbooks state that "soybean yields abundant supply of oil" and "soybeans have oil content higher than other pulses."[12]

Being low in oil content, soybean oil is extracted at large solvent-extraction plants. (Solvent extraction was first applied in the United States to extract grease from garbage, bones, and cracking and packing house waste.) Chlorinated solvents such as chloroethylene are used to extract the oil.

Food safety is necessarily sacrificed in large-scale industrial processing since: 45

- the processing allows mixing of non-edible oils with edible oils,
- the processing is based on the use of chemicals,
- processing creates saturated fats,
- the long-distance transport lends itself to risks of adulteration, adds "food miles" in the form of CO_2 pollution, and contributes to climate change, and
- consumers are denied the right to know what ingredients have been used and what processing has been used to produce industrial oils.

Are Soy Products Healthy?

Soybeans and soybean products are being pushed as global substitutes for diverse sources of foods in diverse cultures. They are being promoted as substitutes for the diverse oilseeds and pulses of India and for cereals and dairy products worldwide. The American Soybean Association is promoting "analogue" dals—soybean extrusions shaped into pellets that look like black gram, green gram, pigeon pea, lentil, and kidney bean. The diet they envision would be a monoculture of soybean; only its appearance would be diverse.

However, even though the promotion of soybean-based foods is justified on grounds of health and nutrition, studies show that this sudden shift to soybean-based diets can be harmful to health. Soybean foods, in both raw and processed form, contain a number of toxic substances at concentration levels that pose significant health risks to humans and animals.

Soybeans have trypsin inhibitors that inhibit pancreatic processes, cause an increase in pancreatic size and weight, and can even lead to cancer.[13] In the United States, pancreatic cancer is the fifth most common fatal cancer, and its incidence is rising. The highest concentrations of trypsin inhibitors are found in soybean flour, which is a soy-based product that is not consumed in traditional soybean-eating cultures, which specialize in the consumption of fermented soybean products.[14]

Soybeans also have lectins that interfere with the immune system and the microbial ecology of the gut. When injected into rats, lectins isolated from soybeans were found to be lethal. When administered orally, these lectins inhibited rat growth.[15] Soybeans also contain phytic acid, which interferes in the absorption of essential minerals such as calcium, magnesium, zinc, copper, and iron. Given that deficiencies in calcium and iron are major symptoms of malnutrition in women and children in countries such as India, compromising the body's absorption of these essential minerals can have serious consequences.[16]

The most significant health hazard posed by diets rich in soybeans 50 is due to their high estrogen content, especially in genetically engineered soybeans. The devastating impact of estrogenic compounds was highlighted when women born to mothers who took synthetic estrogens were found to have three times more miscarriages than other women and a greater incidence of a rare form of malignant vaginal cancer. Men born to mothers who took these synthetic estrogens had higher infertility levels than other men.[17]

Since soybeans are being used widely in all food products, including baby food, high doses of estrogen are being consumed by children, women, and men. Infants fed with soy-based formula are daily ingesting a dose of estrogens equivalent to that of 8 to 12 contraceptive pills.[18] According to New Zealand ecologist Richard James, soybean products are "unsafe at any speed and in any form."[19] The globalization of soybean-based foods is a major experiment being carried out on present and future generations. It is an unnecessary experiment, since nature has given us a tremendous diversity of safe foods, and diverse cultures have selected and evolved nutritious foods from nature's diversity.

During the mustard-oil crisis in 1998, women from the slums of Delhi, organized by a women's group called "Sabla Sangh," invited me to discuss with them the roots of the crisis. They said that "mustard is our life. . . . We want our cheap and safe mustard oil back." Ultimately, a women's alliance for food rights was formed. We held protests and distributed pure organic mustard oil as part of the Sarson Satyagraha, a program of non-cooperation against laws and policies that were denying people safe, cheap, and culturally appropriate foods.

The National Alliance for Women's Food Rights has challenged the ban on small-scale processing and local sales of open oil in the Supreme Court of India. We are building direct producer-consumer alliances to defend the livelihood of farmers and the diverse cultural choices of consumers. We protest soybean imports and call for a ban on the import of genetically engineered soybean products. As the women from the slums of Delhi sing, "Sarson Bachao, Soya Bhagao," or "Save the Mustard, Dump the Soya."

The highest-level political and economic conflicts between freedom and slavery, democracy and dictatorship, diversity and monoculture have thus entered into the simple acts of buying edible oils and cooking our food. Will the future of India's edible-oil culture be based on mustard and other edible oilseeds, or will it become part of the globalized monoculture of soybean, with its associated but hidden food hazards?

Notes

1. Some of these diverse varieties include Indian mustard, *Brassica juncea*; black mustard, *Brassica nigra*; turnip rape; brown and yellow *Brassica campestris*; Indian rape; and rocket cross.
2. "Conspiracy in Mustard Oil Adulteration," *The Hindu*, September 17, 1998.
3. Status Paper on "Ghani Oil Industry," Mumbai: KVIC.
4. "Oilseeds Sector Needs to Be Liberalized: U.S. Soya Body," *Economic Times*, September 22, 1998.
5. *Business Line,* October 12, 1998.
6. A. V. Krebs, "The Corporate Reapers: The Book of Agribusiness," Washington, DC: Essential Books, 1992.

7. Clive James, "Global Status of Transgenic Crops in 1997," ISAAA Briefs, Cambridge, MA: MIT Press, 1996. Also, Greg D. Horstmeier, "Lessons from Year One: Experience Changes How Farmers Will Grow Roundup Ready Beans in 98," *Farm Journal*, January 1998, p. 16.

8. American Soybean Association, "Soy Stats, 1998."

9. A. V. Krebs.

10. Brian Belcher and Geoffrey Hawtin, "A Patent on Life Ownership of Plant and Animal Research," Ottawa, Canada: International Development Research Centre, 1991.

11. Vandana Shiva, *Mustard or Soya? The Future of India's Edible Oil Culture*, New Delhi: Navdanya, 1998.

12. Dr. Irfan Khan, *Genetic Improvement of Oilseed Crops,* New Delhi: Ukaaz Publications, 1996, p. 334.

13. M. G. Fitzpatrick, "Report on Soybeans and Related Products: An Investigation into Their Toxic Effects," New Zealand: Allan Aspell and Associates, Analytical Chemists and Scientific Consultants, March 31, 1994, p. 5.

14. B. A. Charpentier and D. E. Lemmel, "A Rapid Automated Procedure for the Determination of Trypsin Inhibitor Activity in Soy Products and Common Food Stuffs," *Journal of Agricultural and Food Chemistry,* Vol. 32, 1984, p. 908.

15. I. E. Liener and M. J. Pallansch, "Purification of a Toxic Substance from Defatted Soy Bean Flour," *Journal of Biological Chemistry,* Vol. 197, 1952, p. 29.

16. S. L. Fitzgerald et al., "Trace Element Intakes and Dietary Phytat/Zn and Caz Phytate/Zn Millimolar Ratios in Periurban Guatemalan Women During the Third Trimester of Pregnancy," *American Journal of Clinical Nutrition,* Vol. 57, 1993, p. 725. See also J. W. Erdman and E. J. Fordyce, "Soy Products and the Human Diet," *American Journal of Clinical Nutrition,* Vol. 49, 1989, p. 725.

17. F. A. Kinil, "Hormone Toxicity in the Newborn," *Monographs on Endocrinology,* Vol. 31, 1990. See also R. J. Apfel and S. M. Fisher, *To Do No Harm: DES and the Dilemmas of Modern Medicine,* New Haven: Yale University Press, 1984.

18. A. Axelsol et al., "Soya—A Dietary Source of the Non-Steroidal Oestregen Equal in Man and Animals," *Journal of Endocrinology,* Vol. 102, 1984, p. 49. See also K. D. R. Setchell et al., "Non-Steroidal Estrogens of Dietary Origin: Possible Roles in Hormone-Dependent Disease," *American Journal of Clinical Nutrition,* Vol. 40, 1984, p. 569.

19. Richard James, "The Toxicity of Soy Beans and Their Related Products," unpublished manuscript, 1994, p. 1.

Understanding the Text

1. What does it mean to have access to "culturally appropriate food"?

2. What role does mustard—in its various manifestations—play in Indian culture? Why was the lack of mustard oil such a serious problem?

Reflection and Response

3. What does Shiva mean by "soy imperialism"? Does this term serve as a valid description of the dynamics she is describing? Why or why not?

4. What kinds of grassroots efforts are being made to protect India's edible-oil culture? Do you think they will succeed? Why or why not?

5. Why is Shiva critical of Monsanto's business practices? What evidence does she provide? Is her criticism justified? Why or why not?

Making Connections

6. Review Michael Pollan's argument "in defense of food" ("Eat Food: Food Defined," p. 9). What kinds of conclusions do you think he would he draw about Monsanto? In what ways would he agree with Shiva and the farmers? Do you consider theirs a compelling argument? Why or why not?

7. What goals and values do Shiva and Gary Paul Nabhan ("A Brief History of Cross-Border Food Trade," p. 156) share? What brings you to this conclusion? Use specific textual references to support your answer.

A Brief History of Cross-Border Food Trade

Gary Paul Nabhan

Gary Paul Nabhan is a research scientist, award-winning nature writer, and farming activist who has dedicated himself to the local food movement and community seed-saving projects. He holds the W. K. Kellogg Endowed Chair in Sustainable Food Systems at the University of Arizona Southwest Center, where he conducts research and works to conserve links between biodiversity and cultural diversity. He also works as a food justice activist and serves as an Ecumenical Franciscan brother. Also known as an Arab American essayist and poet, he has published several books and won many literary awards, including a MacArthur Foundation "genius" award. In this essay, originally published in the collection *Hungry for Change: Borderlands Food and Water in the Balance* (2012) by the Southwest Center's Kellogg Program in Sustainable Food Systems, Nabhan describes the complex history of the U.S.-Mexico food trade.

Many U.S. residents are amazed when they learn that three-fifths of the fresh produce they buy and eat was harvested from the West Coast of Mexico. It comes as further surprise that much of the saltwater fish and shrimp they eat comes from Mexico's reaches of the Gulf of Mexico, Pacific Ocean, and Gulf of California. However, we should not belittle New Yorkers or Minnesotans for this lack of knowledge, since few of us who live much closer to the U.S./Mexico border have an accurate sense of how much of our food comes from "el otro lado"—the lands and waters on the other side. Despite having lived much of my life in Arizona, and within sight of Mexican farms and ranches, I have, until recently, hardly fathomed the extent that I've been nourished by the foods produced in Sonora and surrounding states. As a means to overcome this shortsightedness, I have asked farmers, fishers, historians, and border brokers to explain to me just how our food system became so binational.°

Among my friends are a few archaeologists of desert foodways. They have reminded me that trade between farmers, foragers, and fishers has gone on in the Sonoran Desert for millennia, long before an international boundary split the region in half. Salt, corn, beans, turkeys, wild chiles, acorns, agaves, and other foods have been part of extra-local trade in the region for at least 4,000 years. Pochtecan traders may have taken Mayan chocolate as far north as Chaco Can-

binational: Of or relating to two nations.

yon, long before Spanish soldiers, miners, and priests arrived in the region. Of course, the Valley of Mexico became the prehistoric hub for food trade in Mesoamerica, while the lands we now know as the Southwestern United States were considered on the fringe of the Aztec empire, a barely developed frontier.

Historians have told me how Padre Kino and other Jesuit missionaries changed the diets of people in this region when they arrived here around 1687, bringing with them many seeds, fruit tree cuttings, and livestock and poultry breeds. These propagation materials were taken and traded from one watershed to the next, across the arid region now straddled by the border. Some items from the Sea of Cortes—like salted fish and the jerked meat of sea turtle—may have been transported many miles inland, while other items, like olive oil and altar wine from Mission grapes, were traded to missions that still lacked orchards and vineyards on the coast.

In New Mexico, Churro sheep, Corriente cattle, cultivated chiles, and grafted fruit trees were brought north along the Camino de Real from Veracruz, Mexico City, Durango, and Parral. This trade route remained essential to agricultural development in the border region, even after the Santa Fe Trail opened access to goods brought from steamboats along the Mississippi River.

> Despite having lived much of my life in Arizona, and within sight of Mexican farms and ranches, I have, until recently, hardly fathomed the extent that I've been nourished by the foods produced in Sonora and surrounding states.

It was not until the 1850s—immediately following the Treaty of Guadalupe Hidalgo and the so-called Gadsden "Purchase"—that there was enough pretense of a border to begin true "binational commerce." In 1851, boundary surveyors Emory and Bartlett headed south from Tucson and Calabasas to assist the commissary of their expedition by replenishing food and other supplies in Magdalena. But they found little more than fruits, tortillas, cakes, and mescal to keep their bellies full. And so they ventured as far south as Ures—Sonora's scrappy little capital at that time—to gather the rest of the foods they required for their journey across the Great American Desert to the California coast.

During the 1850s, Pima Indian farmers who irrigated crops along the Gila River floodplain began to produce enough surplus wheat to supply Gold Rush prospectors in northeastern Sonora and northern California. With the advent of the Civil War, Hispanic and Anglo commodity traders helped the Pima expand their market for White Sonora wheat flour to both Rebel and Yankee troops, so that these Pima farmers became Arizona's first to engage in "export agriculture."

Sonora, too, reshaped its production for export markets, developing trade in livestock, grain, and fruits through its port at Guaymas with the help of Wells Fargo's first brokerage banks in Mexico around 1860. By 1880, railroad lines up the west coast of Mexico started bringing live cattle to Tucson and El Paso in extraordinary volumes, consolidating the livestock industries of the borderlands into a single food production system. By World War II, American dependence on northern Mexican-born, grass-fed Corriente cattle was so large that virtually all the beef in K-rations came from this source. Even though post–World War II regulations and protocols for Hoof-and-Mouth disease outbreaks have made it more difficult to move cattle across the border, beef production remains a transborder business in many ways to this day.

It was not until 1906 that transborder trade accelerated, due to railroad tycoon Edward Harriman, who developed railcars with icehouses and refrigerators. Fresh produce from the west coast of Mexico could now enter the U.S. marketplace and arrive at its destination in a matter of days. As Harriman's Pacific Fruit Express became the largest operator of refrigerated railroad transporters in the world, fresh produce from the binational Southwest grew from a negligible portion of the U.S. grocery market share to 40 percent of the U.S. produce sales in 1929. (Some of my neighbors are the descendants of Nogales, Arizona's pioneering produce brokers, and they remain engaged in cross-border food trade to this day.)

At the same time, Harriman's railroad cars carried agricultural technologies south into Sonora and Sinaloa, ushering in the era of groundwater extraction and mechanized cultivation. Colonies of American and European entrepreneurs developed large-scale irrigated agriculture in southern Sonora and northern Sinaloa, usurping lands from both Yaqui and Mayo Indians.

In the late 19th century, U.S. citizens bought land for cultivation around the port town of Tapolobampo, in northern Sinaloa, to establish a socialist utopian community. Their project, called the Credit Foncier of Sinaloa, lasted only a few years in that hot and cactus-studded environment. But these efforts paved the way for larger-scale agricultural enterprises, which bought up the best farmland in the Fuerte river valley by the early 20th century, and had diverted most of the region's surface waters. The sugar plantations they developed later gave way to today's massive vegetable exportation operations. Today the area forms part of the larger northern Sinaloa ketchup and salsa belt, producing more tomatoes than any other region in Mexico.

Around the same time, and further north in the Mayo and Yaqui Valleys, another engineer, Carlos Conant, landed a concession from the Mexican government for close to 500,000 acres of coastal thorn-scrub.° In exchange, he was charged with platting,° subdividing, and spearheading agricultural development. The U.S.-based Richardson Construction Company (CCR) bought out Conant by the early 19th century, just before the 1910 revolution. However, the company had enough time before the war to start laying the infrastructural foun-dation for what would later become one of Mexico's premier grain-producing irrigation districts. Agricultural development came at a high price for the Yoemem (the Yaqui Indians) who had lived in the valley for thousands of years; to this day, they continue to struggle with state and federal officials to gain full recognition of their legal rights to ancestral lands, and to the waters of the Yaqui River.

Around present-day Hermosillo, near the coast, binational families—such as the Ronstadts—began to export wagons, tractors, and tillage equipment to the German, Dutch, French, and Italian agribusinessmen who developed large, irrigated land holdings in these southern reaches of the Sonoran Desert. This kind of exportation also occurred around the Port of Guaymas. Today, many of these families continue to play prominent roles in Sonora's agricultural production, as well as in indus-try and government.

While the Mexican Revolution led to repatriation of some of the lands that had been lost to smallholder farmers, it also fostered clan-destine trade in alcohol and firearms with businesses in Arizona and New Mexico. With Arizona's statehood and the Prohibition era, bar-rels of tequila and bacanora were bottled and shipped by Julius Rosenbaum out of Tucson, but these products were still grown and distilled on the west coast of Mexico. Guaymas harbor became the region's major, international shipping port for a variety of beverages, grains, fruits, and vegetables.

In the 1920s, the demand for air bladders of the totoaba—a pres-ently endangered fish in the Sea of Cortés—ushered in a new wave of marine resource exploitation. Motorized boats allowed the move-ment of fishermen back and forth across the sea, where they estab-lished new camps, depleted the local fisheries, and moved on. By 1935, Kino Bay had its first "collective" or ejido of Mexican fishermen. Ever since, most of Sonora's fish catch has been destined for Arizona and the broader United States. Around the same period, the Kino Bay

---

thornscrub: Land with a dry, warm climate, with mostly short, thorny trees and bushes.
platting: Mapping an area of land.

Club of American anglers had ramped up sports fishing along the coast, and in 1941 the United States government fostered its spread by helping Sonora build a paved 65-mile highway between Puerto Peñasco and Lukeville, then known as Kahlilville. During that time, sea turtles and lobsters were transported live, in tubs, up to Ajo and Phoenix.

Shrimp trawlers from Guaymas started raking the sea bottom clean 15 in the 1940s, taking and then discarding 10 to 40 pounds of live "by-catch" for every pound of saleable shrimp they caught in their nets. A combination of government subsidies and private investment had overcapitalized the open-sea shrimping sector, swelling the size of fleets, and dramatically increasing the scale of the assault on marine resources. By 1990, less than a half century later, trawlers had depleted the northern and central reaches of the sea it became impossible not to notice the many rusted-out hulls of bankrupt trawlers scattered around port towns like Yavaros, Guaymas, and Puerto Peñasco. The decline in the wild shrimp fishery inevitably led to efforts to farm shrimp (so-called "aquaculture") in confined areas along the coast—first accomplished in Guaymas by Monterrey Tech in the 1960s. The spread of shrimp farming along the Sonoran and Sinaloan coast caused the destruction of some mangrove lagoons—the natural nursery grounds for the wild-caught "Guaymas shrimp." Mostly, though, shrimp farming's most visible impact has been the fragmentation of delicate coastal landscapes. Today, shrimp monoculture all along Sonoran and Sinaloan shores is plagued with introduced diseases, though it still generates more products for export than Mexico's entire wild harvest shrimp sector. Despite prompting the loss of one fish stock after another, the 40–50,000 fishermen in the Sea of Cortés still haul in 60 percent of all seafood caught in Mexican waters. Roughly 150,000 to 170,000 tons of seafood are exported from Mexico to the U.S. each year, and three quarters of what is caught or cultured by Sonorans is served at American tables.

While the aquamarine (or "blue") revolution ramped up along the Sonoran coast in the 1960s, large-scale, hybrid grain production received a jumpstart in Ciudad Obregón with the Green Revolution, led by Minnesota-born plant breeder Norman Borlaug. The first releases of Borlaug's dwarf, fertilizer-responsive wheat—like Sonora 64—hit the marketplace in the early 1960s. It quickly drove the White Sonora heirloom bread wheat to near-extinction. The fertile floodplain soils of the Rio Yaqui, Mayo, and Fuerte valleys were suddenly transformed into a contiguous wheat belt; outside of the Bajío region, it is one of Mexico's most important granaries.

Ironically, just as irrigation infrastructure and chemical fertilizer plants began to dominate the Sonoran landscape—a massive federal investment intended to boost basic grain production—farmers suddenly converted to higher-value tomatoes, cucumbers, watermelons, and peppers, rather than staple crops like wheat. Much of the winter produce exported to the U.S. from Sonora and Sinaloa is now grown in these northern and northwestern irrigation districts that were originally developed to produce staple crops for Mexico's burgeoning population. In exchange for this nourishment provided by northern Mexican laborers, lands, and waters, Arizonans deliver $5 to $6 billion of goods and services to their neighbors south of the border each year in the form of farm equipment, computerized technologies, and vehicles, in addition to stone fruits, corn-fed feedlot beef and frozen processed foods. Metro areas near the border have become the staging areas for Walmarts and other food franchises that have now cropped up all over Mexico.

Several years ago, at a reception hosted by the Sonoran Department of Tourism in Kino Bay, I noticed a table filled with uniform mini-chimichangas—an offering to the snowbirds wintering along the coast.

"Did you have a woman here in the community who makes that many chimichangas for the reception?" I asked a state official.

"Oh, no, we buy them frozen from the Walmart in Hermosillo. By the time we drive them out to the coast here for receptions they're already thawed, so all we need to do is microwave them, and they're ready to serve. It really helps cut our costs by purchasing them in bulk." 20

I was speechless. My mind began wandering back and forth across the border, and through time as well. If alive today, what would the innovative woman who fashioned the very first *chivichanga*—made with hand-made tortilla from White Sonora wheat flour—think of these mass-produced facsimiles of her homegrown invention?

Understanding the Text

1. What is a "binational" food system? What is "binational commerce"?
2. What role did the railroad play in cross-border food trade between the United States and Mexico?

Reflection and Response

3. Where did the Sonoran Department of Tourism in Kino Bay, Mexico, get the chimichangas it served to U.S. tourists? Why do you think Nabhan includes

this story? What does it illustrate? Is it an effective illustration for his argument? Why or why not?

4. Does Nabhan think cross-border food trade is a positive thing for Mexico? For the United States? Why or why not?

Making Connections

5. Find at least three outside sources that discuss cross-border food trade. What role does cross-border food trade play in determining what is grown? What role does it play in what is eaten? Who does this help? Who does it hurt? How might these issues affect the food choices you make as a consumer? Use Nabhan's essay and your research to make an argument that responds to these questions.

6. Consider Nabhan's chimichanga story, Michael Idov's depiction of foodie culture ("When Did Young People Start Spending 25% of Their Paychecks on Pickled Lamb's Tongues?" p. 101), Amy Cyrex Sins's Doberge Cake ("Doberge Cake after Katrina," p. 45), and Lily Wong's dumplings ("Eating the Hyphen," p. 40). What makes food authentic? Is it something personal, cultural, geographical, political, ethical? Use the authors in this book or other outside sources to explore the authenticity of food.

7. Study your own food habits. Do you eat imported foods? Where do they come from? Who grows or produces them? Are your choices affected by cross-border trade? If you wanted to make choices that were informed by an understanding of cross-border trade and where your food came from, which authors in the collection would have advice for you? What would they say?

4

What Does It Mean to Eat Ethically?

W hile larger political, cultural, and socioeconomic factors may play a significant role in determining what we eat, we do make our own food choices. And thus, what we eat is at least partially a moral choice, whether we are cognizant of it or not. What are our ethical responsibilities when we make food choices? Does it matter *morally* what we choose to eat? What does it mean to eat ethically? What moral principles should guide our food choices and ways of eating?

In this section, various authors weigh in on what it means to eat ethically. They raise various issues that can play a role in the ethics of food: animal rights, environmental concerns, world hunger, farmer rights, and worker rights. These authors offer varied and sometimes conflicting views on the responsibilities and obligations we necessarily take on when we make dietary choices. They offer a range of potential responsibilities—social, political, personal, environmental, spiritual, global. And they make suggestions about what principles and priorities should affect our ethical obligations related to food.

Beginning with a focus on global hunger and its relation to food production, Margaret Mead encourages Americans to develop a "world conscience" and to think of the ways that our ability to produce enough food to feed the world changes the ethical position of those who can or do overconsume. Peter Singer, Gary Steiner, and Barbara Kingsolver offer a variety of moral perspectives on the ethics of eating meat, suggesting varying and complex views on human responsibility in animal consumption. Bill McKibben brings environmental factors into the equation. Blake Hurst takes issue with critiques of industrial farming by proponents of organic farming. On top of these concerns, Sally Kohn adds the moral imperative to consider worker rights. By making arguments in support of various ethical positions, the authors in this section argue for the moral principles they think should motivate our choices.

We do not eat in isolation. An ethics of eating, then, must take into account a variety of factors: what we eat, its ability to nourish us, how much we eat, where and how it is produced, who produces it, how they are compensated, and how food production and consumption affect our environment and natural resources. Moral obligations and responsibilities related to an ethics of food exist for consumers, producers, law and policy makers, regulators, and communities. They exist for the affluent and the poor. This chapter asks us to consider what it means to declare that eating is necessarily a moral act.

The Changing Significance of Food

Margaret Mead

Margaret Mead (1901–1978) was a highly respected, often controversial cultural anthropologist. She is best known for her book *Coming of Age in Samoa* (1928), which she wrote after conducting fieldwork there. She received her doctoral degree from Columbia University and served as curator of ethnology at the American Museum of Natural History in New York and executive secretary of the National Research Council's Committee on Food Habits. She popularized anthropological discoveries through her extensive writing and speaking engagements, in which she sometimes shared her view that small groups of committed individuals could, in fact, change the world. President Jimmy Carter awarded Mead the Presidential Medal of Freedom posthumously in 1979. In this essay, originally published in *American Scientist*, Mead provides a historical look at our relationship with food, examining how it has changed over time and been affected by economic, political, and cultural trends. She argues that Americans need to think about the relationship between the American diet and their capacity to feed the poor and the hungry both at home and abroad.

W e live in a world today where the state of nutrition in each country is relevant and important to each other country, and where the state of nutrition in the wealthy industrialized countries like the United States has profound significance for the role that such countries can play in eliminating famine and providing for adequate nutrition throughout the world. In a world in which each half knows what the other half does, we cannot live with hunger and malnutrition in one part of the world while people in another part are not only well nourished, but over-nourished. Any talk of one world, of brotherhood, rings hollow to those who have come face to face on the television screen with the emaciation° of starving children and to the people whose children are starving as they pore over month-old issues of glossy American and European magazines, where full color prints show people glowing with health, their plates piled high with food that glistens to match the shining textures of their clothes. Peoples who have resolutely tightened their belts and put up with going to bed hungry, peoples who have seen their children die because they did not have the strength to resist disease, and called it fate or the will of God,

---

emaciation: Extreme thinness.

can no longer do so, in the vivid visual realization of the amount and quality of food eaten—and wasted—by others.

Through human history there have been many stringent taboos on watching other people eat, or on eating in the presence of others. There have been attempts to explain this as a relationship between those who are involved and those who are not simultaneously involved in the satisfaction of a bodily need, and the inappropriateness of the already satiated watching others who appear—to the satisfied—to be shamelessly gorging. There is undoubtedly such an element in the taboos, but it seems more likely that they go back to the days when food was so scarce and the onlookers so hungry that not to offer them half of the little food one had was unthinkable, and every glance was a plea for at least a bite.

In the rural schools of America when my grandmother was a child, the better-off children took apples to school and, before they began to eat them, promised the poor children who had no apples that they might have the cores. The spectacle of the poor in rags at the rich man's gate and of hungry children pressing their noses against the glass window of the rich man's restaurant have long been invoked to arouse human compassion. But until the advent of the mass media and travel, the sensitive and sympathetic could protect themselves by shutting themselves away from the sight of the starving, by gifts of food to the poor on religious holidays, or perpetual bequests for the distribution of a piece of meat "the size of a child's head" annually. The starving in India and China saw only a few feasting foreigners and could not know how well or ill the poor were in countries from which they came. The proud poor hid their hunger behind a façade that often included insistent hospitality to the occasional visitor; the beggars flaunted their hunger and so, to a degree, discredited the hunger of their respectable compatriots.

> We cannot live with hunger and malnutrition in one part of the world while people in another part are not only well nourished, but over-nourished.

But today the articulate cries of the hungry fill the air channels and there is no escape from the knowledge of the hundreds of millions who are seriously malnourished, of the periodic famines that beset whole populations, or of the looming danger of famine in many other parts of the world. The age-old divisions between one part of the world and another, between one class and another, between the rich and the poor everywhere, have been broken down, and the tolerances and insensitivities of the past are no longer possible.

But it is not only the media of communication which can take a 5
man sitting at an overloaded breakfast table straight into a household
where some of the children are too weak to stand. Something else,
something even more significant, has happened. Today, for the first
time in the history of mankind, we have the productive capacity to
feed everyone in the world, and the technical knowledge to see that
their stomachs are not only filled but that their bodies are properly
nourished with the essential ingredients for growth and health. The
progress of agriculture—in all its complexities of improved seed, methods of cultivation, fertilizers and pesticides, methods of storage, preservation, and transportation—now make it possible for the food that is
needed for the whole world to be produced by fewer and fewer farmers, with greater and greater certainty. Drought and flood still threaten,
but we have the means to prepare for and deal with even mammoth
shortages—if we will. The progress of nutritional science has matched
the progress of agriculture; we have finer and finer-grained knowledge
of just which substances—vitamins, minerals, proteins—are essential,
especially to growth and full development, and increasing ability to
synthesize many of them on a massive scale.

These new twentieth-century potentialities have altered the ethical
position of the rich all over the world. In the past, there were so few
who lived well, and so many who lived on the edge of starvation, that
the well-to-do had a rationale and indeed almost a necessity to harden
their hearts and turn their eyes away. The jewels of the richest rajah°
could not have purchased enough food to feed his hungry subjects for
more than a few days; the food did not exist, and the knowledge of how
to use it was missing also. At the same time, however real the inability
of a war-torn and submarine-ringed Britain to respond to the famine
in Bengal, this inability was made bearable in Britain only by the extent to which the British were learning how to share what food they
had among all the citizens, old and young. "You do not know," the
American consul, who had come to Manchester from Spain, said to
me: "you do not know what it means to live in a country where no child
has to cry itself to sleep from hunger." But this was only achieved in
Britain in the early 1940s. Before, the well-fed turned away their eyes,
in the feeling that they were powerless to alleviate the perennial poverty and hunger of most of their own people and the peoples in their
far-flung commonwealth. And such turning away the eyes, in Britain
and in the United States and elsewhere, was accompanied by the ra-
tionalizations, not only of the inability of the well-to-do—had they

rajah: A ruler in India or the East Indies.

given all their wealth—to feed the poor, but of the undeservingness of the poor, who had they only been industrious and saving would have had enough, although of course of a lower quality, to keep "body and soul together."

When differences in race and in cultural levels complicated the situation, it was only too easy to insist that lesser breeds somehow, in some divinely correct scheme, would necessarily be less well fed, their alleged idleness and lack of frugality combining with such matters as sacred cows roaming over the landscapes—in India—or nights spent in the pub or the saloon—at home in Britain or America—while fathers drank up their meager pay checks and their children starved. So righteous was the assumed association between industriousness and food that, during the Irish famine, soup kitchens were set up out of town so that the starving could have the moral advantage of a long walk to receive the ration that stood between them and death. (The modern version of such ethical acrobatics can be found in the United States, in the mid-1960s, where food stamps were so expensive, since they had to be bought in large amounts, that only those who had been extraordinarily frugal, saving, and lucky could afford to buy them and obtain the benefits they were designed to give.)

The particular ways in which the well-to-do of different great civilizations have rationalized the contrast between rich and poor have differed dramatically, but ever since the agricultural revolution, we have been running a race between our capacity to produce enough food to make it possible to assemble great urban centers, outfit huge armies and armadas, and build and elaborate the institutions of civilization and our ability to feed and care for the burgeoning population which has always kept a little, often a great deal, ahead of the food supply.

In this, those societies which practiced agriculture contrasted with the earlier simpler societies in which the entire population was engaged in subsistence activities. Primitive peoples may be well or poorly fed, feasting seldom, or blessed with ample supplies of fish or fruit, but the relations between the haves and the have-nots were in many ways simpler. Methods by which men could obtain permanent supplies of food and withhold them from their fellows hardly existed. The sour, barely edible breadfruit mash which was stored in breadfruit pits against the ravages of hurricanes and famines in Polynesia was not a diet for the table of chiefs but a stern measure against the needs of entire communities. The chief might have a right to the first fruits, or to half the crop, but after he had claimed it, it was redistributed to his people. The germs of the kinds of inequities that later entered the world were present: there was occasional conspicuous destruction of food, piled up for prestige, oil poured on the flames of self-glorifying feasts, food left to rot after it was offered to the gods. People with very meager food resources might use phrases that made it seem that each man was the recipient of great generosity on the part of his fellows, or on the other hand always to be giving away a whole animal, and always receiving only small bits.

The fear of cannibalism that hovered over northern peoples might   10
be elaborated into cults of fear, or simply add to the concern that each member of a group had for all, against the terrible background that extremity might become so great that one of the group might in the end be sacrificed. But cannibalism could also be elaborated into a rite of vengeance or the celebration of victories in war, or even be used to provision an army in the field. Man's capacity to elaborate man's inhumanity to man existed before the beginning of civilization, which was made possible by the application of an increasingly productive technology to the production of food.

With the rise of civilizations, we also witness the growth of the great religions that made the brotherhood of all men part of their doctrine and the gift of alms or the life of voluntary poverty accepted religious practices. But the alms were never enough, and the life of individual poverty and abstinence was more efficacious for the individual's salvation than for the well-being of the poor and hungry, although both kept alive an ethic, as yet impossible of fulfillment, that it was right that all should be fed. The vision preceded the capability.

But today we have the capability. Whether that capability will be used or not becomes not a technical but an ethical question. It depends, in enormous measure, on the way in which the rich, industrialized countries handle the problems of distribution, of malnutrition and hunger, within their own borders. Failure to feed their own, with such high capabilities and such fully enunciated statements of responsibility and brotherhood, means that feeding the people of other countries is almost ruled out, except for sporadic escapist pieces of behavior where people who close their eyes to hunger in Mississippi can work hard to send food to a "Biafra." The development of the international instruments to meet food emergencies and to steadily improve the nutrition of the poorer countries will fail, unless there is greater consistency between ideal and practice at home.

And so, our present parlous° plight in the United States, with the many pockets of rural unemployment, city ghettos, ethnic enclaves,

---

parlous: Full of danger, perilous.

where Americans are starving and an estimated tenth of the population malnourished, must be viewed not only in its consequences for ourselves, as a viable political community, but also in its consequences for the world. We need to examine not only the conditions that make this possible, to have starving people in the richest country in the world, but also the repercussions of American conditions on the world scene.

Why, when twenty-five years ago we were well on the way to remedying the state of the American people who had been described by presidential announcement as "one third ill-housed, ill-clothed, and ill-fed," when the vitamin deficiency diseases had all but vanished, and a variety of instruments for better nutrition had been developed, did we find, just two short years ago, due to the urgent pleading of a few crusaders, that we had fallen so grievously behind? The situation is complex, closely related to a series of struggles for regional and racial justice, to the spread of automation and resulting unemployment, to changes in crop economies, as well as to population growth and the inadequacy of many of our institutions to deal with it. But I wish to single out here two conditions which have, I believe, seriously contributed to our blindness to what was happening: the increase in the diseases of affluence and the growth of commercial agriculture.

In a country pronounced only twenty years before to be one third 15 ill-fed, we suddenly began to have pronouncements from nutritional specialists that the major nutritional disease of the American people was overnutrition. If this had simply meant overeating, the old puritan ethics against greed and gluttony might have been more easily invoked, but it was over-nutrition that was at stake. And this in a country where our ideas of nutrition had been dominated by a dichotomy which distinguished food that was "good for you, but not good" from food that was "good, but not good for you." This split in man's needs, into our cultural conception of the need for nourishment and the search for pleasure, originally symbolized in the rewards for eating spinach or finishing what was on one's plate if one wanted to have a dessert, lay back of the movement to produce, commercially, nonnourishing foods. Beverages and snacks came in particularly for this demand, as it was the addition of between-meal eating to the three square, nutritionally adequate meals a day that was responsible for much of the trouble.

We began manufacturing, on a terrifying scale, foods and beverages that were guaranteed not to nourish. The resources and the ingenuity of industry were diverted from the preparation of foods necessary for life and growth to foods nonexpensive to prepare, expensive to buy.

And every label reassuring the buyer that the product was not nour-
ishing increased our sense that the trouble with Americans was that
they were too well nourished. The diseases of affluence, represented
by new forms of death in middle-age, had appeared before we had, in
the words of Jean Mayer, who has done so much to define the needs of
the country and of the world, conquered the diseases of poverty—the
ill-fed pregnant women and lactating women, sometimes resulting in
irreversible damage to the ill-weaned children, the school children so
poorly fed that they could not learn.

It was hard for the average American to believe that while he struggled, and paid, so as not to be over-nourished, other people, several
millions, right in this country, were hungry and near starvation. The
gross contradiction was too great. Furthermore, those who think of
their country as parental and caring find it hard to admit that this parental figure is starving their brothers and sisters. During the great
depression of the 1930s, when thousands of children came to school
desperately hungry, it was very difficult to wring from children the
admission that their parents had no food to give them. "Or what man
is there of you, whom, if his son ask bread, will he give a stone?"

So today we have in the United States a situation not unlike the
situation in Germany under Hitler, when a large proportion of the
decent and law-abiding simply refuse to believe that what is happening can be happening. "Look at the taxes we pay," they say, or they
point to the millions spent on welfare; surely with such quantities
assigned to the poor, people can't be really hungry, or if they are, it is
because they spend their money on TV sets and drink. How can the
country be overnourished and undernourished at the same time?

A second major shift, in the United States and in the world, is the
increasing magnitude of commercial agriculture, in which food is
seen not as food which nourishes men, women, and children, but as a
staple crop on which the prosperity of a country or region and the economic prosperity—as opposed to the simple livelihood—of the individual farmer depend. This is pointed up on a world scale in the report of
the Food and Agriculture Organization of the United Nations for 1969,
which states that there are two major problems in the world: food defi-
cits in the poor countries, which mean starvation, hunger, and malnutrition on an increasing scale, and food surpluses in the industrialized part of the world, serious food surpluses.

On the face of it, this sounds as foolish as the production of foods   20
guaranteed not to nourish, and the two are not unrelated. Surpluses,
in a world where people are hungry! Too much food, in a world where
children are starving! Yet we lump together all *agricultural* surpluses,

such as cotton and tobacco, along with food, and we see these surpluses as threatening the commercial prosperity of many countries, and farmers in many countries. And in a world politically organized on a vanishing agrarian basis, this represents a political threat to those in power. However much the original destruction of food, killing little pigs, may have been phrased as relieving the desperate situation of little farmers or poor countries dependent upon single crop exports, such situations could not exist if food as something which man needs to provide growth and maintenance had not been separated from food as a cash crop, a commercial as opposed to a basic maintenance enterprise. When it becomes the task of government to foster the economic prosperity of an increasingly small, but politically influential, sector of the electorate at the expense of the wellbeing of its own and other nations' citizens, we have reached an ethically dangerous position.

And this situation, in the United States, is in part responsible for the grievous state of our poor and hungry and for the paralysis that still prevents adequate political action. During the great depression, agriculture in this country was still a viable way of life for millions. The Department of Agriculture had responsibility, not only for food production and marketing, but also for the well-being from the cradle to the grave, in the simplest, most human sense, of every family who lived in communities under 2,500. Where the needs of urban man were parceled out among a number of agencies—Office of Education, Children's Bureau, Labor Department—there was still a considerable amount of integration possible in the Department of Agriculture, where theory and practices of farm wives, the education of children and youth, the question of small loans for small landowners, all could be considered together. It was in the Department of Agriculture that concerned persons found, during the depression, the kind of understanding of basic human needs which they sought.

There were indeed always conflicts between the needs of farmers to sell crops and the needs of children to be fed. School lunch schemes were tied to the disposal of surplus commodities. But the recognition of the wholeness of human needs was still there, firmly related to the breadth of the responsibilities of the different agencies within the Department of Agriculture. Today this is no longer so. Agriculture is big business in the United States. The subsidies used to persuade farmers to withdraw their impoverished land from production, like the terrible measures involving the slaughter of little pigs, are no longer ways of helping the small farmer on a family farm. The subsidies go to the rich commercial farmers, many of them the inheritors of

old exploitive plantation traditions, wasteful of manpower and land resources, often in the very counties where the farm workers, displaced
by machinery, are penniless, too poor to move away, starving. These
subsidies exceed the budget of the antipoverty administration.

So today, many of the reforms which are suggested, in the distribution of food or distribution of income from which food can be
bought, center on removing food relief programs from the Department of Agriculture and placing them under the Department of Health,
Education, and Welfare. In Britain, during World War II, it was necessary to have a Ministry of Food, concerned primarily in matching the
limited food supplies with basic needs.

At first sight, this proposal is sound enough. Let us remove from an
agency devoted to making a profit out of crops that are treated like any
other manufactured product the responsibility for seeing that food actually feeds people. After all, we do not ask clothing manufacturers to
take the responsibility for clothing people, or the house-building industry for housing them. To the extent that we recognize them at all,
these are the responsibilities of agencies of government which provide
the funds to supplement the activities of private industry. Why not also
in food? The Department of Health, Education, and Welfare is concerned with human beings; they have no food to sell on a domestic or
world market and no constituents to appease. And from this step it is
simply a second step to demand that the whole system of distribution
be re-oriented, that a basic guaranteed annual income be provided
each citizen, on the one hand, and that the government police standards, on behalf of the consumer, on the other.

But neither of these changes, shifting food relief programs from 25
Agriculture to Health, Education, and Welfare, or shifting the whole
welfare program into a guaranteed income, really meet the particular
difficulties that arise because we are putting food into two compart-
ments with disastrous effects; we are separating food that nourishes
people from food out of which some people, and some countries, derive
their incomes. It does not deal with the immediacy of the experience of
food by the well-fed, or with the irreparability of food deprivation during prenatal and postnatal growth, deprivation that can never be made
up. Human beings have maintained their dignity in incredibly bad conditions of housing and clothing, emerged triumphant from huts and log
cabins, gone from ill-shod childhood to Wall Street or the Kremlin. Poor
housing and poor clothing are demeaning to the human spirit when
they contrast sharply with the visible standards of the way others live.

But food affects not only man's diginity but the capacity of children
to reach their full potential, and the capacity of adults to act from day to

day. You can't eat either nutrition or part of a not yet realized guaranteed annual income, or political promises. You can't eat hope. We know that hope and faith have enormous effects in preventing illness and enabling people to put forth the last ounce of energy they have. But energy is ultimately dependent upon food. No amount of rearrangement of priorities in the future can provide food in the present. It is true that the starving adult, his efficiency enormously impaired by lack of food, may usually be brought back again to his previous state of efficiency. But this is not true of children. What they lose is lost for good.

What we do about food is therefore far more crucial, both for the quality of the next generation, our own American children, and children everywhere, and also for the quality of our responsible action in every field. It is intimately concerned with the whole problem of the pollution and exhaustion of our environment, with the danger that man may make this planet uninhabitable within a short century or so. If food is grown in strict relationship to the needs of those who will eat it, if every effort is made to reduce the costs of transportation, to improve storage, to conserve the land, and there, where it is needed, by recycling wastes and water, we will go a long way toward solving many of our environmental problems also. It is as a responsible gardener on a small, limited plot, aware of the community about him with whom he will face adequate food or famine, that man has developed what conserving agricultural techniques we have.

Divorced from its primary function of feeding people, treated simply as a commercial commodity, food loses this primary significance; the land is mined instead of replenished and conserved. The Food and Agriculture Organization, intent on food production, lays great stress on the increase in the use of artificial fertilizers, yet the use of such fertilizers with their diffuse runoffs may be a greater danger to our total ecology than the industrial wastes from other forms of manufacturing. The same thing is true of pesticides. With the marvels of miracle rice and miracle wheat, which have brought the resources of international effort and scientific resources together, go at present prescriptions for artificial fertilizer and pesticides. The innovative industrialized countries are exporting, with improved agricultural methods, new dangers to the environment of the importing countries. Only by treating food, unitarily, as a substance necessary to feed people, subject first to the needs of people and only second to the needs of commercial prosperity—whether they be the needs of private enterprise or of a developing socialist country short of foreign capital—can we hope to meet the ethical demands that our present situation makes on us. For the first time since the beginning of civilization, we can feed everyone, now. Those who are not fed will die or, in the case of children, be permanently damaged.

We are just beginning to develop a world conscience. Our present dilemma is due to previous humanitarian moves with unanticipated effects. Without the spread of public health measures, we would not have had the fall in infant death rates which has resulted in the population explosion. Without the spread of agricultural techniques, there would not have been the food to feed the children who survived. The old constraints upon population growth—famine, plague, and war— are no longer acceptable to a world whose conscience is just barely stirring on behalf of all mankind. As we are groping our way back to a new version of the full fellow-feeling and respect for the natural world which the primitive Eskimo felt when food was scarce, so we are trembling on the edge of a new version of the sacrifice to cannibalism of the weak, just as we have the technical means to implement visions of responsibility that were very recently only visions.

The temptation is to turn aside, to deny what is happening to the environment, to trust to the "green revolution" and boast of how much rice previously hungry countries will export, to argue about legalities while people starve and infants and children are irreparably damaged, to refuse to deal with the paradoxes of hunger in plenty, and the coincidences of starvation and overnutrition. The basic problem is an ethical one; the solution of ethical problems can be solved only with a full recognition of reality. The children of the agricultural workers of the rural South, displaced by the machine, are hungry; so are the children in the Northern cities to which black and white poor have fled in search of food. On our American Indian reservations, among the Chicanos of California and the Southwest, among the seasonally employed, there is hunger now. If this hunger is not met now, we disqualify ourselves, we cripple ourselves, to deal with world problems.

We must balance our population so that every child that is born can be well fed. We must cherish our land, instead of mining it, so that food produced is first related to those who need it; and we must not despoil the earth, contaminate, and pollute it in the interests of immediate gain. Behind us, just a few decades ago, lies the vision of André Mayer and John Orr, the concepts of a world food bank, the founding of the United Nations Food and Agriculture Organization; behind us lie imaginative vision and deep concern. In the present we have new and various tools to make that vision into concrete actuality. But we must resolve the complications of present practice and present conceptions if the very precision and efficiency of our new knowledge is not to provide a stumbling block to the exercise of fuller humanity.

Understanding the Text

1. Mead points out that though we now have the technical ability to produce enough food to feed everyone in the world, we still do not. Why not, according to Mead?

2. What are some ways that people in the past have justified the contrast between the rich's easy access to food and the poor's lack of access to proper nourishment?

Reflection and Response

3. How has the capacity to feed all peoples in the world "altered the ethical position of the rich all over the world," according to Mead? (para. 6). Do you agree? Why or why not?

4. What are some solutions to the world's hunger problem proposed by Mead? Do you think they would work if pursued today? Why or why not?

5. What is a "world conscience"? What does Mead's call for a "world conscience" tell us about the ethical position she adopts? Why does she think this is the only morally legitimate path to take?

Making Connections

6. How might Frances Moore Lappé's essay ("Biotechnology Isn't the Key to Feeding the World," p. 249) be said to "update" the argument Mead makes here? In what ways does Lappé pick up where Mead left off? What would Mead say about the state of affairs described by Lappé?

7. What is the changing significance of food? Mead wrote this essay over four decades ago. Do you think her conclusions are still useful for thinking about an ethics of eating? Why or why not? Locate two outside sources to help you support your response.

8. What is Mead's primary ethical concern? What other authors in this collection share this concern? Use textual examples from at least three other sources to support your response.

Equality for Animals?

Peter Singer

Peter Singer is widely considered one of the most influential—and widely read—philosophers of our time. Born in Australia to Jewish parents, he studied philosophy in college and received his master's degree for a thesis titled "Why Should I Be Moral?" He is widely known for his writing about animal equality, most notably in *Animal Liberation* (1975). Other books he has written include *Practical Ethics* (third edition published in 2011) and *The Life You Can Save: Acting Now to End World Poverty* (2009). Singer is currently the Ira W. DeCamp Professor of Bioethics at Princeton University and a Laureate Professor at the Centre for Applied Philosophy and Public Ethics at the University of Melbourne. Singer's utilitarian philosophy guides his worldview. In the excerpt from *Practical Ethics* included here, he makes a utilitarian ethical argument against eating meat as part of a longer argument in favor of equality for animals.

Animals as Food

For most people in modern, urbanized societies, the principal form of contact with nonhuman animals is at meal times. The use of animals for food is probably the oldest and the most widespread form of animal use. There is also a sense in which it is the most basic form of animal use, the foundation stone of an ethic that sees animals as things for us to use to meet our needs and interests.

If animals count in their own right, our use of animals for food becomes questionable. Inuit living a traditional lifestyle in the far north where they must eat animals or starve can reasonably claim that their interest in surviving overrides that of the animals they kill. Most of us cannot defend our diet in this way. People living in industrialized societies can easily obtain an adequate diet without the use of animal flesh. Meat is not necessary for good health or longevity. Indeed, humans can live healthy lives without eating any animal products at all, although a vegan diet requires greater care, especially for young children, and a B12 vitamin supplement should be taken. Nor is animal production in industrialized societies an efficient way of producing food, because most of the animals consumed have been fattened on grains and other foods that we could have eaten directly. When we feed these grains to animals, only about one-quarter—and in some cases, as little as one-tenth—of the nutritional value remains as meat for human consumption. So, with the exception of animals raised entirely on grazing land unsuitable for crops, animals are eaten neither for health nor to increase our food supply. Their flesh is a luxury, consumed because people like its taste. (The livestock industry also contributes more to global warming than the entire transport sector.)

In considering the ethics of the use of animal products for human food in industrialized societies, we are considering a situation in which a relatively minor human interest must be balanced against the lives and welfare of the animals involved. The principle of equal consideration of interests does not allow major interests to be sacrificed for minor interests.

The case against using animals for food is at its strongest when animals are made to lead miserable lives so that their flesh can be made available to humans at the lowest possible cost. Modern forms of intensive farming apply science and technology to the attitude that animals are objects for us to use. Competition in the marketplace forces meat producers to copy rivals who are prepared to cut costs by giving animals more miserable lives. In buying the meat, eggs, or milk produced in these ways, we tolerate methods of meat production that confine sentient animals in cramped, unsuitable conditions for the entire duration of their lives. They are treated like machines that convert fodder° into flesh, and any innovation that results in a higher "conversion ratio" is liable to be adopted. As one authority on the subject has said, "cruelty is acknowledged only when profitability ceases." To avoid speciesism, we must stop these practices. Our custom is all the support that factory farmers need. The decision to cease giving them that support may be difficult, but it is less difficult than it would have been for a white Southerner to go against the values of his community and free his slaves. If we do not change our dietary habits, how can we censure those slave holders who would not change their own way of living?

These arguments apply to animals reared in factory farms—which 5 means that we should not eat chicken, pork, or veal unless we know that the meat we are eating was not produced by factory farm methods. The same is true of beef that has come from cattle kept in crowded feedlots (as most beef does in the United States). Eggs come from hens kept in small wire cages, too small even to allow them to stretch their wings, unless the eggs are specifically sold as "cage-free" or "free range." (At the time of writing, Switzerland has banned the

---

fodder: Food for livestock, especially coarse hay or straw.

battery cage, and the European Union is in the process of phasing it out. In the United States, California voted in 2008 to ban it, and that ban will come into effect in 2015. A law passed in Michigan in 2009 requires battery cages to be phased out over 10 years.) Dairy products also often come from cows confined to a barn, unable to go out to pasture. Moreover, to continue to give milk, dairy cows have to be made pregnant every year, and their calf then taken away from them shortly after birth, so we can have the milk. This causes distress to both the cow and the calf.

Concern about the suffering of animals in factory farms does not take us all the way to a vegan diet, because it is possible to buy animal products from animals allowed to graze outside. (When animal products are labeled "organic," this should mean that the animals have access to the outdoors, but the interpretation of this rule is sometimes loose.) The lives of free-ranging animals are undoubtedly better than those of animals reared in factory farms. It is still doubtful if using them for food is compatible with equal consideration of interests. One problem is, of course, that using them for food involves killing them (even laying hens and dairy cows are killed when their productivity starts to drop, which is far short of their natural life span). . . . Apart from killing them, there are also many other things done to animals in order to bring them cheaply to our dinner table. Castration, the separation of mother and young, the breaking up of herds, branding, transporting, slaughterhouse handling, and finally the moment of slaughter itself—all of these are likely to involve suffering and do not take the animals' interests into account. Perhaps animals can be reared on a small scale without suffering in these ways. Some farmers take pride in producing "humanely raised" animal products, but the standards of what is regarded as "humane" vary widely. Any shift toward more humane treatment of animals is welcome, but it seems unlikely that these methods could produce the vast quantity of animal products now consumed by our large urban populations. At the very least, we would have to considerably reduce the amount of meat, eggs, and dairy products that we consume. In any case, the important question is not whether animal products *could* be produced without suffering, but whether those we are considering buying *were* produced without suffering. Unless we can be confident that they were, the principle of equal consideration of interests implies that their production wrongly sacrificed important interests of the animals to satisfy less important interests of our own. To buy the results of this process of production is to support it and encourage producers to continue to do it. Because those of us living in developed societies have a wide range of food choices and do not need to eat these products, encouraging the continuation of a cruel system of producing animal products is wrong.

For those of us living in cities where it is difficult to know how the animals we might eat have lived and died, this conclusion brings us very close to a vegan way of life. . . .

Animals Eat Each Other, So Why Shouldn't We Eat Them?

This might be called the Benjamin Franklin Objection because Franklin recounts in his *Autobiography* that he was for a time a vegetarian, but his abstinence from animal flesh came to an end when he was watching some friends prepare to fry a fish they had just caught. When the fish was cut open, it was found to have a smaller fish in its stomach. "Well," Franklin said to himself, "if you eat one another, I don't see why we may not eat you," and he proceeded to do so.

Franklin was at least honest. In telling this story, he confesses that he convinced himself of the validity of the objection only after the fish was already in the frying pan and smelling "admirably well"; and he remarks that one of the advantages of being a "reasonable creature" is that one can find a reason for whatever one wants to do. The replies that can be made to this objection are so obvious that Franklin's acceptance of it does testify more to his hunger on that occasion than to his powers of reason. For a start, most animals who kill for food would not be able to survive if they did not, whereas we have no need to eat animal flesh. Next, it is odd that humans, who normally think of the behavior of animals as "beastly" should, when it suits them, use an argument that implies that we ought to look to animals for moral guidance. The most decisive point, however, is that nonhuman animals are not capable of considering the alternatives open to them or of reflecting on the ethics of their diet. Hence, it is impossible to hold the animals responsible for what they do or to judge that because of their killing they "deserve" to be treated in a similar way. Those who read these lines, on the other hand, must consider the justifiability of their dietary habits. You cannot evade responsibility by imitating beings who are incapable of making this choice.

Sometimes people draw a slightly different conclusion from the fact that animals eat each other. This suggests, they think, not that animals deserve to be eaten, but rather that there is a natural law according to which the stronger prey on the weaker, a kind of Darwinian "survival of the fittest" in which by eating animals we are merely playing our part.

This interpretation of the objection makes two basic mistakes, one of fact and the other of reasoning. The factual mistake lies in the assumption that our own consumption of animals is part of some natural evolutionary process. This might be true of those who still hunt for food, but it has nothing to do with the mass production of domestic animals in factory farms.

Suppose that we did hunt for our food, though, and this was part of some natural evolutionary process. There would still be an error of reasoning in the assumption that because this process is natural it is right. It is, no doubt, "natural" for women to produce an infant every year or two from puberty to menopause, but this does not mean that it is wrong to interfere with this process. We need to understand nature and develop the best theories we can to explain why things are as they are, because only in that way can we work out what the consequences of our actions are likely to be; but it would be a serious mistake to assume that natural ways of doing things are incapable of improvements. . . .

Understanding the Text

1. According to Singer, what might be an ethically sound reason for killing animals to eat them?

2. What is a factory farm? What role do factory farms play in the industrial food chain?

Reflection and Response

3. What is the "Benjamin Franklin Objection"? How does Singer counter it? Does he make a good case for his position? Explain your answer with textual analysis.

4. What is the "principle of equal consideration of interests"? How does Singer use it to make his case against using animals as food? Is his use of this principle rhetorically effective? Why or why not?

Making Connections

5. Would Margaret Mead ("The Changing Significance of Food," p. 166) agree with Singer's critique of factory farms? Why or why not?

6. Singer is known for being a utilitarian. What type of philosophical approach is this? How does it lead him to the position that a vegan diet is the most ethical one? Use outside research to explain utilitarianism and support your response.

7. Singer and Gary Steiner ("Animal, Vegetable, Miserable," p. 195) both argue against eating animals. Compare their rhetorical approaches. How does each build a case? What kinds of evidence does each use? How do they appeal to emotions, logic, and ethical considerations? Whose approach do you think is more effective and why?

8. List all of the reasons Singer gives to support his argument that we should not eat animals. Explain which authors in this chapter agree with him and to what extent. Then analyze what their points of agreement and disagreement say about their ethical positions.

You Can't Run Away on Harvest Day

Barbara Kingsolver

Barbara Kingsolver studied biology before becoming a prolific and award-winning author. Her books have been translated into more than twenty languages, and her stories and essays have been published in major literary anthologies and most major U.S. newspapers and magazines. Best known for her novels and short stories, including *The Bean Trees* (1988), *Animal Dreams* (1990), *The Poisonwood Bible* (1998), and *Prodigal Summer* (2000), she has more recently written about her experiences raising and harvesting her own food. Her 2007 memoir *Animal, Vegetable, Miracle: A Year of Food Life* chronicles her family's year devoted to eating locally—to eating food produced on their family farm or in their southern Appalachian community. In this essay excerpt from *Animal, Vegetable, Miracle*, Kingsolver provides an introspective and moving account of her experience slaughtering chickens and turkeys—and the moral principles that guide her ethics of eating.

The Saturday of Labor Day weekend dawned with a sweet, translucent bite, like a Golden Delicious apple. I always seem to harbor a childlike hope through the berry-stained months of June and July that summer will be for keeps. But then a day comes in early fall to remind me why it should end, after all. In September the quality of daylight shifts toward flirtation. The green berries on the spicebush shrubs along our lane begin to blink red, first one and then another, like faltering but resolute holiday lights. The woods fill with the restless singing of migrant birds warming up to the proposition of flying south. The cool air makes us restless too: jeans and sweater weather, perfect for a hike. Steven and I rose early that morning, looked out the window, looked at each other, and started in on the time-honored marital grumble: Was this *your* idea?

We weren't going on a hike today. Nor would we have the postsummer Saturday luxury of sitting on the porch with a cup of coffee and watching the farm wake up. On the docket instead was a hard day of work we could not postpone. The previous morning we'd sequestered half a dozen roosters and as many torn turkeys in a room of the barn we call "death row." We hold poultry there, clean and comfortable with water but no food, for a twenty-four-hour fast prior to harvest. It makes the processing cleaner and seems to calm the animals also. I could tell you it gives them time to get their emotional affairs in order, if that helps. But they have limited emotional affairs, and no idea what's coming.

We had a lot more of both. Our plan for this gorgeous day was the removal of some of our animals from the world of the living into the realm of food. At five months of age our roosters had put on a good harvest weight, and had lately opened rounds of cockfighting, venting their rising hormonal angst against any moving target, including us. When a rooster flies up at you with his spurs, he leaves marks. Lily now had to arm herself with a length of pipe in order to gather the eggs. Our barnyard wasn't big enough for this much machismo. We would certainly take no pleasure in the chore, but it was high time for the testosterone-reduction program. We sighed at the lovely weather and pulled out our old, bloody sneakers for harvest day.

There was probably a time when I thought it euphemistic to speak of "harvesting" animals. Now I don't. We calculate "months to harvest" when planning for the right time to start poultry. We invite friends to "harvest parties," whether we'll be gleaning° vegetable or animal. A harvest implies planning, respect, and effort. With animals, both the planning and physical effort are often greater, and respect for the enterprise is substantially more complex. It's a lot less fun than spending an autumn day picking apples off trees, but it's a similar operation on principle and the same word.

Killing is a culturally loaded term, for most of us inextricably tied 5 up with some version of a command that begins, "Thou shalt not." Every faith has it. And for all but perhaps the Jainists of India, that command is absolutely conditional. We know it does not refer to mosquitoes. Who among us has never killed living creatures on purpose? When a child is sick with an infection we rush for the medicine spoon, committing an eager and purposeful streptococcus massacre. We sprinkle boric acid or grab a spray can to rid our kitchens of cockroaches. What we mean by "killing" is to take a life cruelly, as in murder—or else more accidentally, as in "Oops, looks like I killed my African violet." Though the results are incomparable, what these different "killings" have in common is needless waste and some presumed measure of regret.

Most of us, if we know even a little about where our food comes from, understand that every bite put into our mouths since infancy (barring the odd rock or marble) was formerly alive. The blunt biological truth is that we animals can only remain alive by eating other life. Plants are inherently more blameless, having been born with the talent of whipping up their own food, peacefully and without noise,

gleaning: Gathering, collecting.

out of sunshine, water, and the odd mineral ingredient sucked up through their toes. Strangely enough, it's the animals to which we've assigned some rights, while the saintly plants we maim and behead with moral impunity. Who thinks to beg forgiveness while mowing the lawn?

The moral rules of destroying our fellow biota° get even more tangled, the deeper we go. If we draw the okay-to-kill line between "animal" and "plant," and thus exclude meat, fowl, and fish from our diet on moral grounds, we still must live with the fact that every sack of flour and every soybean-based block of tofu came from a field where countless winged and furry lives were extinguished in the plowing, cultivating, and harvest. An estimated 67 million birds die each year from pesticide exposure on U.S. farms. Butterflies, too, are universally killed on contact in larval form by the genetically modified pollen contained in most U.S. corn. Foxes, rabbits, and bobolinks are starved out of their homes or dismembered by the sickle mower. Insects are "controlled" even by organic pesticides; earthworms are cut in half by the plow. Contrary to lore, they won't grow into two; both halves die.

> I find myself fundamentally allied with a vegetarian position in every way except one: however selectively, I eat meat.

To believe we can live without taking life is delusional. Humans may only cultivate nonviolence in our diets by degree. I've heard a Buddhist monk suggest the *number* of food-caused deaths is minimized in steak dinners, which share one death over many meals, whereas the equation is reversed for a bowl of clams. Others of us have lost heart for eating any steak dinner that's been shoved through the assembly line of feedlot life—however broadly we might share that responsibility. I take my gospel from Wendell Berry, who writes in *What Are People For*, "I dislike the thought that some animal has been made miserable in order to feed me. If I am going to eat meat, I want it to be from an animal that has lived a pleasant, uncrowded life outdoors, on bountiful pasture, with good water nearby and trees for shade. And I am getting almost as fussy about food plants."

I find myself fundamentally allied with a vegetarian position in every way except one: however selectively, I eat meat. I'm unimpressed by arguments that condemn animal harvest while ignoring, wholesale, the animal killing that underwrites vegetal foods. Uncountable deaths by pesticide and habitat removal—the beetles and

---

biota: Living things, both plant and animal.

bunnies that die collaterally for our bread and veggie-burgers—are lives plumb wasted. Animal harvest is at least not gratuitous, as part of a plan involving labor and recompense. We raise these creatures for a reason. Such premeditation may be presumed unkind, but without it our gentle domestic beasts in their picturesque shapes, colors, and finely tuned purposes would never have had the distinction of existing. To envision a vegan version of civilization, start by erasing from all time the Three Little Pigs, the boy who cried wolf, *Charlotte's Web*, the golden calf, *Tess of the d'Urbervilles*. Next, erase civilization, brought to you by the people who learned to domesticate animals. Finally, rewrite our evolutionary history, since *Homo sapiens* became the species we are by means of regular binges of carnivory.

Most confounding of all, in the vegan revision, are the chapters ad- 10 dressing the future. If farm animals have civil rights, what aspect of their bondage to humans shall they overcome? Most wouldn't last two days without it. Recently while I was cooking eggs, my kids sat at the kitchen table entertaining me with readings from a magazine profile of a famous, rather young vegan movie star. Her dream was to create a safe-haven ranch where the cows and chickens could live free, happy lives and die natural deaths. "Wait till those cows start bawling to be milked," I warned. Having nursed and weaned my own young, I can tell you there is no pain to compare with an overfilled udder. We wondered what the starlet might do for those bursting Jerseys, not to mention the eggs the chickens would keep dropping everywhere. What a life's work for that poor gal: traipsing about the farm in her strappy heels, weaving among the cow flops, bending gracefully to pick up eggs and stick them in an incubator where they would maddeningly *hatch*, and grow up bent on laying *more* eggs. It's dirty work, trying to save an endless chain of uneaten lives. Realistically, my kids observed, she'd hire somebody.

Forgive us. We know she meant well, and as fantasies of the super-rich go, it's more inspired than most. It's just the high-mindedness that rankles; when moral superiority combines with billowing ignorance, they fill up a hot-air balloon that's awfully hard not to poke. The farm-liberation fantasy simply reflects a modern cultural confusion about farm animals. They're human property, not just legally but biologically. Over the millennia of our clever history, we created from wild progenitors° whole new classes of beasts whose sole purpose was to feed us. If turned loose in the wild, they would haplessly starve, succumb to predation, and destroy the habitats and lives of most or all

progenitor: Ancestor.

natural things. If housed at the public expense they would pose a more immense civic burden than our public schools and prisons combined. No thoughtful person really wants those things to happen. But living at a remove from the actual workings of a farm, most humans no longer learn appropriate modes of thinking about animal harvest. Knowing that our family raises meat animals, many friends have told us—not judgmentally, just confessionally—"I don't think I could kill an animal myself." I find myself explaining: It's not what you think. It's nothing like putting down your dog.

Most nonfarmers are intimate with animal life in only three categories: people; pets (i.e., junior people); and wildlife (as seen on nature shows, presumed beautiful and rare). Purposely beheading any of the above is unthinkable, for obvious reasons. No other categories present themselves at close range for consideration. So I understand why it's hard to think about harvest, a categorical act that includes cutting the heads off living lettuces, extended to crops that blink their beady eyes. On our farm we don't especially enjoy processing our animals, but we do value it, as an important ritual for ourselves and any friends adventurous enough to come and help, because of what we learn from it. We reconnect with the purpose for which these animals were bred. We dispense with all delusions about who put the *live* in livestock, and who must take it away.

A friend from whom we buy pasture-grazed lamb and poultry has concurred with us on this point. Kirsty Zahnke grew up in the U.K., and observes that American attitudes toward life and death probably add to the misgivings. "People in this country do everything to cheat death, it seems. Instead of being happy with each moment, they worry so much about what comes next. I think this gets transposed to animals—the preoccupation with 'taking a life.' My animals have all had a good life, with death as its natural end. It's not without thought and gratitude that I slaughter my animals, it is a hard thing to do. It's taken me time to be able to eat my own lambs that I had played with. But I always think of Kahlil Gibran's words:

> When you kill a beast, say to him in your heart:
>
> By the same power that slays you, I too am slain, and I too shall be consumed.
>
> For the law that delivers you into my hand shall deliver me into a mightier hand.
>
> Your blood and my blood is naught but the sap that feeds the tree of heaven."

Kirsty works with a local environmental organization and frequently hosts its out-of-town volunteers, who camp at her farm while working in the area. Many of these activists had not eaten meat for many years before arriving on the Zahnkes' meat farm—a formula not for disaster, she notes, but for education. "If one gets to know the mantras of the farm owners, it can change one's viewpoint. I would venture to say that seventy-five percent of the vegans and vegetarians who stayed at least a week here began to eat our meat or animal products, simply because they see what I am doing as right—for the animals, for the environment, for humans."

I respect every diner who makes morally motivated choices about 15 consumption. And I stand with nonviolence, as one of those extremist moms who doesn't let kids at her house pretend to shoot each other, *ever*, or make any game out of human murder. But I've come to different conclusions about livestock. The ve-vangelical pamphlets showing jam-packed chickens and sick downer-cows usually declare, as their first principle, that all meat is factory-farmed. That is false, and an affront to those of us who work to raise animals humanely, or who support such practices with our buying power. I don't want to cause any creature misery, so I won't knowingly eat anything that has stood belly deep in its own poop wishing it was dead until *bam*, one day it was. (In restaurants I go for the fish, or the vegetarian option.)

But meat, poultry, and eggs from animals raised on open pasture are the traditional winter fare of my grandparents, and they serve us well here in the months when it would cost a lot of fossil fuels to keep us in tofu. Should I overlook the suffering of victims of hurricanes, famines, and wars brought on this world by profligate fuel consumption? Bananas that cost a rain forest, refrigerator-trucked soy milk, and pre-washed spinach shipped two thousand miles in plastic containers do not seem cruelty-free, in this context. A hundred different paths may lighten the world's load of suffering. Giving up meat is one path; giving up bananas is another. The more we know about our food system, the more we are called into complex choices. It seems facile to declare one single forbidden fruit, when humans live under so many different kinds of trees.

To breed fewer meat animals in the future is possible; phasing out those types destined for confinement lots is a plan I'm assisting myself, by raising heirloom breeds. Most humans could well consume more vegetable foods, and less meat. But globally speaking, the vegetarian option is a luxury. The oft-cited energetic argument for vegetarianism, that it takes ten times as much land to make a pound of meat as a pound of grain, only applies to the kind of land where rain falls abundantly on rich topsoil. Many of the world's poor live in marginal lands that can't support plant-based agriculture. Those not blessed with the fruited plain and amber waves of grain must make do with woody tree pods, tough-leaved shrubs, or sparse grasses. Camels, reindeer, sheep, goats, cattle, and other ruminants are uniquely adapted to transform all those types of indigestible cellulose into edible milk and meat. The fringes of desert, tundra, and marginal grasslands on every continent—coastal Peru, the southwestern United States, the Kalahari, the Gobi, the Australian outback, northern Scandinavia—are inhabited by herders. The Navajo, Mongols, Lapps, Masai, and countless other resourceful tribes would starve without their animals. . . .

After many meatless years it felt strange to us to break the taboo, but over time our family has come back to carnivory. I like listening to a roasting bird in the oven on a Sunday afternoon, following Julia Child's advice to "regulate the chicken so it makes quiet cooking noises" as its schmaltzy aroma fills the house. When a friend began raising beef cattle entirely on pasture (rather than sending them to a CAFO° as six-month-olds, as most cattle farmers do), we were born again to the idea of hamburger. We can go visit his animals if we need to be reassured of the merciful cowness of their lives.

As meat farmers ourselves we are learning as we go, raising heritage breeds: the thrifty antiques that know how to stand in the sunshine, gaze upon a meadow, and munch. (Even mate without help!) We're grateful these old breeds weren't consigned to extinction during the past century, though it nearly did happen. Were it not for these animals that can thrive outdoors, and the healthy farms that maintain them, I would have stuck with tofu-burgers indefinitely. That wasn't a bad life, but we're also enjoying this one.

Believing in the righteousness of a piece of work, alas, is not what 20 gets it done. On harvest day we pulled on our stained shoes, sharpened our knives, lit a fire under the big kettle, and set ourselves to the whole show: mud, blood, and lots of little feathers. There are some things about a chicken harvest that are irrepressibly funny, and one of them is the feathers; in your hair, on the backs of your hands, dangling behind your left shoe the way toilet paper does in slapstick movies. Feathery little white tags end up stuck all over the chopping block and the butchering table like Post-it notes from the chicken hereafter. Sometimes we get through the awful parts on the strength

CAFO: Concentrated Animal Feed Operation.

of black comedy, joking about the feathers or our barn's death row and the "dead roosters walking."

But today was not one of those times. Some friends had come over to help us, including a family that had recently lost their teenage son in a drowning accident. Their surviving younger children, Abby and Eli, were among Lily's closest friends. The kids were understandably solemn and the adults measured all our words under the immense weight of grief as we set to work. Lily and Abby went to get the first rooster from the barn while I laid out the knives and spread plastic sheets over our butchering table on the back patio. The guys stoked a fire under our 50-gallon kettle, an antique brass instrument Steven and I scored at a farm auction.

The girls returned carrying Rooster #1 upside down, by the legs. Inversion has the immediate effect of lulling a chicken to sleep, or something near to it. What comes next is quick and final. We set the rooster gently across our big chopping block (a legendary fixture of our backyard, whose bloodstains hold visiting children in thrall), and down comes the ax. All sensation ends with that quick stroke. He must then be held by the legs over a large plastic bucket until all the blood has run out. Farmers who regularly process poultry have more equipment, including banks of "killing cones" or inverted funnels that contain the birds while the processor pierces each neck with a sharp knife, cutting two major arteries and ending brain function. We're not pros, so we have a more rudimentary setup. By lulling and swiftly decapitating my animal, I can make sure my relatively unpracticed handling won't draw out the procedure or cause pain.

What you've heard is true: the rooster will flap his wings hard during this part. If you drop him he'll thrash right across the yard, unpleasantly spewing blood all around, though the body doesn't *run*—it's nothing that well coordinated. His newly detached head silently opens and closes its mouth, down in the bottom of the gut bucket, a world apart from the ruckus. The cause of all these actions is an explosion of massively firing neurons without a brain to supervise them. Most people who claim to be running around like a chicken with its head cut off, really, are not even close. The nearest thing might be the final convulsive seconds of an All-Star wrestling match.

For Rooster #1 it was over, and into the big kettle for a quick scald. After a one-minute immersion in 145-degree water, the muscle tissue releases the feathers so they're easier to pluck. "Easier" is relative— every last feather still has to be pulled, carefully enough to avoid tearing the skin. The downy breast feathers come out by handfuls, while the long wing and tail feathers sometimes must be removed individually with pliers. If we were pros we would have an electric scalder and automatic plucker, a fascinating bucket full of rotating rubber fingers that does the job in no time flat. For future harvests we might borrow a friend's equipment, but for today we had a pulley on a tree limb so we could hoist the scalded carcass to shoulder level, suspending it there from a rope so several of us could pluck at once. Lily, Abby, and Eli pulled neck and breast feathers, making necessary observations such as "Gag, look where his head came off," and "Wonder which one of these tube thingies was his windpipe." Most kids need only about ninety seconds to get from *eeew gross* to solid science. A few weeks later Abby would give an award-winning, fully illustrated 4-H presentation entitled "You Can't Run Away on Harvest Day."

Laura and Becky and I answered the kids' questions, and also 25 talked about Mom things while working on back and wing feathers. (Our husbands were on to the next beheading.) Laura and I compared notes on our teenage daughters—relatively new drivers on the narrow country roads between their jobs, friends, and home—and the worries that come with that territory. I was painfully conscious of Becky's quiet, her ache for a teenage son who never even got to acquire a driver's license. The accident that killed Larry could not have been avoided through any amount of worry. We all cultivate illusions of safety that could fall away in the knife edge of one second.

I wondered how we would get through this afternoon, how *she* would get through months and years of living with impossible loss. I wondered if I'd been tactless, inviting these dear friends to an afternoon of ending lives. And then felt stupid for that thought. People who are grieving walk with death, every waking moment. When the rest of us dread that we'll somehow remind them of death's existence, we are missing their reality. Harvesting turkeys—which this family would soon do on their own farm—was just another kind of work. A rendezvous with death, for them, was waking up each morning without their brother and son.

By early afternoon six roosters had lost their heads, feathers, and viscera, and were chilling on ice. We had six turkeys to go, the hardest piece of our work simply because the animals are larger and heavier. Some of these birds were close to twenty pounds. They would take center stage on our holiday table and those of some of our friends. At least one would be charcuterie—in the garden I had sage, rosemary, garlic, onions, everything we needed for turkey sausage. And the first two roosters we'd harvested would be going on the rotisserie later that afternoon.

We allowed ourselves a break before the challenge of hoisting, plucking, and dressing the turkeys. While Lily and her friends constructed feather crowns and ran for the poultry house to check in with the living, the adults cracked open beers and stretched out in lawn chairs in the September sun.

Our conversation turned quickly to the national preoccupation of that autumn: Katrina, the hurricane that had just hit southern Louisiana and Mississippi. We were horrified by the news that was beginning to filter out of that flooded darkness, the children stranded on rooftops, the bereaved and bewildered families slogging through streets waist-deep in water, breaking plate glass windows to get bottles of water. People drowning and dying of thirst at the same time.

It was already clear this would be an epic disaster. New Orleans and 30 countless other towns across southern Louisiana and Mississippi were being evacuated and left for dead. The news cameras had focused solely on urban losses, sending images of flooded streets, people on rooftops, broken storefronts, and the desperate crises of people in the city with no resources for relocating or evacuating. I had not seen one photograph from the countryside—a wrecked golf course was the closest thing to it. I wondered about the farmers whose year of work still lay in the fields, just weeks or days away from harvest, when the flood took it all. I still can't say whether the rural victims of Katrina found their support systems more resilient, or if their hardships simply went unreported.

The disaster reached into the rest of the country with unexpected tentacles. Our town and schools were already taking in people who had lost everything. The office where I'd just sent my passport for renewal was now underwater. Gasoline had passed $3 a gallon, here and elsewhere, leaving our nation in sticker shock. U.S. citizens were making outlandish declarations about staying home. Climate scientists were saying, "If you warm up the globe, you eventually pay for it." Economists were eyeing our budget deficits and predicting collapse, mayhem, infrastructure breakdown. In so many ways, disaster makes us take stock. For me it had inspired powerful cravings about living within our means. I wasn't thinking so much of my household budget or the national one but the *big* budget, the one that involves consuming approximately the same things we produce. Taking a symbolic cue from my presumed-soggy passport, I suddenly felt like sticking very close to home, with a hand on my family's production, even when it wasn't all that easy or fun—like today.

Analysts of current events were mostly looking to blame administrators. Fair enough, but there were also, it seemed, obvious vulnerabilities here—whole populations, depending on everyday, long-distance lifelines, supplies of food and water and fuel and everything else that are acutely centralized. That's what we consider normal life. Now nature had written a hugely abnormal question across the bottom of our map. I wondered what our answers might be. . . .

Understanding the Text

1. What influences Kingsolver's decision to eat meat? What makes her see this as a morally defensible position?

2. What is animal harvest, and why does Kingsolver think it is important for her family to participate in it?

Reflection and Response

3. Describe your own reactions to the events described by Kingsolver. Why do you think she depicts "harvest day" the way she does? What images does she want us to come away with? What emotional reaction do you think she hopes to elicit?

4. Kingsolver argues that "*Killing* is a culturally loaded term" and that "To believe we can live without taking life is delusional" (para. 5; para. 8). How and why does she draw these conclusions? Do you agree with her? Why or why not?

Making Connections

5. Imagine growing up in Barbara Kingsolver's household. How would daily life resemble or differ from your own upbringing? Consider her essay in relation to the essay by her daughter Camille, included in the first section of this collection ("Taking Local on the Road," p. 37). Compare the relationship between Camille's upbringing and food values to the relationship between your own upbringing and food values. What, if anything, does your upbringing reveal about your own ethics of eating?

6. Reflect on Kingsolver's, Gary Steiner's ("Animal, Vegetable, Miserable," p. 195), and Peter Singer's ("Equality for Animals," p. 178) arguments regarding the ethics of meat eating in relation to your own life experiences and moral choices. Do you eat meat? Have you harvested it? Worked with farm animals? Hunted? If you eat meat, does it matter to you if the animals you eat roam freely? Were treated humanely? Lived a good life? Do you think it is wrong to kill animals for consumption? What moral principles guide your thinking? How do the views of Singer, Kingsolver, and Steiner inform your position? Describe what influences your own position on eating meat. Which authors speak to your concerns or moral principles? How?

7. Kingsolver claims that she follows Wendell Berry's beliefs about human responsibility in animal consumption. Analyze Berry's essay "The Pleasures of Eating" (p. 64). What principles do Kingsolver and Berry share? Do you find potential points of disagreement? Locate textual examples to support your analysis.

Animal, Vegetable, Miserable

Gary Steiner

Gary Steiner is a moral philosopher and John Howard Harris Professor of Philosophy at Bucknell University. His areas of interest include modern philosophy, Descartes, and the moral status of animals. He is widely published in academic journals and popular media, and has written several books, including *Animals and the Limits of Postmodernism* (2013) and *Animals and the Moral Community: Mental Life, Moral Status, and Kinship* (2008). Much of his writing is dedicated to making a case for his view that animals deserve a moral status comparable to that of human beings, and that it is our moral obligation to grant animals this status. In this essay, originally published in the *New York Times* in 2009, Steiner examines the challenges faced by people who adopt a vegan diet.

Lately more people have begun to express an interest in where the meat they eat comes from and how it was raised. Were the animals humanely treated? Did they have a good quality of life before the death that turned them into someone's dinner?

Some of these questions, which reach a fever pitch in the days leading up to Thanksgiving, pertain to the ways in which animals are treated. (Did your turkey get to live outdoors?) Others focus on the question of how eating the animals in question will affect the consumer's health and well-being. (Was it given hormones and antibiotics?)

None of these questions, however, make any consideration of whether it is wrong to kill animals for human consumption. And even when people ask this question, they almost always find a variety of resourceful answers that purport to justify the killing and consumption of animals in the name of human welfare. Strict ethical vegans, of which I am one, are customarily excoriated for equating our society's treatment of animals with mass murder. Can anyone seriously consider animal suffering even remotely comparable to human suffering? Those who answer with a resounding no typically argue in one of two ways.

Some suggest that human beings but not animals are made in God's image and hence stand in much closer proximity to the divine than any non-human animal; according to this line of thought, animals were made expressly for the sake of humans and may be used without scruple to satisfy their needs and desires. There is ample support in the Bible and in the writings of Christian thinkers like

Some say that animals are made to make us eat it

Augustine and Thomas Aquinas for this pointedly anthropocentric way of devaluing animals.

Others argue that the human capacity for abstract thought makes 5 us capable of suffering that both qualitatively and quantitatively exceeds the suffering of any non-human animal. Philosophers like Jeremy Bentham, who is famous for having based moral status not on linguistic or rational capacities but rather on the capacity to suffer, argue that because animals are incapable of abstract thought, they are imprisoned in an eternal present, have no sense of the extended future, and hence cannot be said to have an interest in continued existence.

The most penetrating and iconoclastic response to this sort of reasoning came from the writer Isaac Bashevis Singer in his story "The Letter Writer," in which he called the slaughter of animals the "eternal Treblinka."

The story depicts an encounter between a man and a mouse. The man, Herman Gombiner, contemplates his place in the cosmic scheme of things and concludes that there is an essential connection between his own existence as "a child of God" and the "holy creature" scuffling about on the floor in front of him.

Surely, he reflects, the mouse has some capacity for thought; Gombiner even thinks that the mouse has the capacity to share love and gratitude with him. Not merely a means for the satisfaction of human desires, nor a mere nuisance to be exterminated, this tiny creature possesses the same dignity that any conscious being possesses. In the face of that inherent dignity, Gombiner concludes, the human practice of delivering animals to the table in the form of food is abhorrent and inexcusable.

question about animal feelings

Many of the people who denounce the ways in which we treat animals in the course of raising them for human consumption never stop to think about this profound contradiction. Instead, they make impassioned calls for more "humanely" raised meat. Many people soothe their consciences by purchasing only free-range fowl and eggs, blissfully ignorant that "free range" has very little if any practical significance. Chickens may be labeled free-range even if they've never been outside or seen a speck of daylight in their entire lives. And that Thanksgiving turkey? Even if it is raised "free range," it still lives a life of pain and confinement that ends with the butcher's knife.

Help them

question

How can intelligent people who purport to be deeply concerned 10 with animal welfare and respectful of life turn a blind eye to such practices? And how can people continue to eat meat when they become aware that nearly 53 billion land animals are slaughtered every year for human consumption? The simple answer is that most people just don't care about the lives or fortunes of animals. If they did care, they would learn as much as possible about the ways in which our society systematically abuses animals, and they would make what is at once a very simple and a very difficult choice: to forswear the consumption of animal products of all kinds.

The easy part of this consists in seeing clearly what ethics requires and then just plain doing it. The difficult part: You just haven't lived until you've tried to function as a strict vegan in a meat-crazed society.

> You just haven't lived until you've tried to function as a strict vegan in a meat-crazed society.

What were once the most straightforward activities become a constant ordeal. You might think that it's as simple as just removing meat, eggs, and dairy products from your diet, but it goes a lot deeper than that.

To be a really strict vegan is to strive to avoid all animal products, and this includes materials like leather, silk, and wool, as well as a panoply of cosmetics and medications. The more you dig, the more you learn about products you would never stop to think might contain or involve animal products in their production—like wine and beer (isinglass, a kind of gelatin derived from fish bladders, is often used to "fine," or purify, these beverages), refined sugar (bone char is sometimes used to bleach it), or Band-Aids (animal products in the adhesive). Just last week I was told that those little comfort strips on most razor blades contain animal fat.

To go down this road is to stare headlong into an abyss that, to paraphrase Nietzsche, will ultimately stare back at you.

The challenges faced by a vegan don't end with the nuts and bolts 15 of material existence. You face quite a few social difficulties as well, perhaps the chief one being how one should feel about spending time with people who are not vegans.

Is it O.K. to eat dinner with people who are eating meat? What do you say when a dining companion says, "I'm really a vegetarian—I don't eat red meat at home." (I've heard it lots of times, always without any prompting from me.) What do you do when someone starts to grill you (so to speak) about your vegan ethics during dinner? (Wise vegans always defer until food isn't around.) Or when someone starts to lodge accusations to the effect that you consider yourself morally superior to others, or that it is ridiculous to worry so much about animals when there is so much human suffering in the world? (Smile politely and ask them to pass the seitan.)

Let me be candid: By and large, meat-eaters are a self-righteous bunch. The number of vegans I know personally is . . . five. And I have been a vegan for almost 15 years, having been a vegetarian for almost 15 before that.

Five. I have lost more friends than this over arguments about animal ethics. One lapidary conclusion to be drawn here is that people take deadly seriously the prerogative to use animals as sources of satisfaction. Not only for food, but as beasts of burden, as raw materials, and as sources of captive entertainment—which is the way animals are used in zoos, circuses, and the like.

These uses of animals are so institutionalized, so normalized, in our society that it is difficult to find the critical distance needed to see them as the horrors that they are: so many forms of subjection, servitude, and—in the case of killing animals for human consumption and other purposes—outright murder.

People who are ethical vegans believe that differences in intelli- 20 gence between human and non-human animals have no moral significance whatsoever. The fact that my cat can't appreciate Schubert's late symphonies and can't perform syllogistic logic does not mean that I am entitled to use him as an organic toy, as if I were somehow not only morally superior to him but virtually entitled to treat him as a commodity with minuscule market value.

We have been trained by a history of thinking of which we are scarcely aware to view non-human animals as resources we are entitled to employ in whatever ways we see fit in order to satisfy our needs and desires. Yes, there are animal welfare laws. But these laws have been formulated by, and are enforced by, people who proceed from the proposition that animals are fundamentally inferior to human beings. At best, these laws make living conditions for animals marginally better than they would be otherwise—right up to the point when we send them to the slaughterhouse.

Think about that when you're picking out your free-range turkey, which has absolutely nothing to be thankful for on Thanksgiving. All it ever had was a short and miserable life, thanks to us intelligent, compassionate humans.

Understanding the Text

1. What is a "strict ethical vegan"? What beliefs must someone adopt to become an ethical vegan? What would someone be required to do to live as an ethical vegan?

2. Why is Steiner a strict ethical vegan? What challenges does he face? How does it affect his day-to-day life and his social relationships?

Reflection and Response

3. How do Jeremy Bentham and Isaac Bashevis Singer figure in Steiner's essay? What points does he use them to make?

4. Why does Steiner conclude that it is ethically untenable even to eat "humanely" treated or free-range animals? What moral principle warrants his position?

Making Connections

5. Imagine how Steiner would respond to Barbara Kingsolver's argument ("You Can't Run Away on Harvest Day," p. 184). How might he argue against her position? What flaws would he find in her line of reasoning and in the moral principles she purports to follow? How might she respond to his critique?

6. Steiner titled his 2009 essay "Animal, Vegetable, Miserable," clearly alluding to Barbara Kingsolver's book titled *Animal, Vegetable, Miracle* published one year earlier. What does each title suggest? Why do you think Kingsolver considered this a good title for her book? Why might Steiner have alluded to it in the negative way that he did? Do you think these titles are effective? Why or why not?

7. Steiner describes the difficulties he faces as he lives as a vegan in a meat-eating world. Compare his dilemma to Dhruv Khullar's description of how difficult it is to eat a healthy diet in an unhealthy culture ("Why Shame Won't Stop Obesity," p. 127). What similarities do you notice? Together, what do these arguments teach us about the process of making personal food choices?

Shouldn't eat meat because it is bad for the environment

The Only Way to Have a Cow

Bill McKibben

Bill McKibben wrote *The End of Nature* in 1989, a book often described as the first book on climate change written for a popular audience. McKibben is an environmentalist and widely published author and journalist who writes extensively on the environment, nature, food policy, economic policy, and the impact of climate change. In his book *Deep Economy: The Wealth of Communities and the Durable Future* (2007), he argues for the value of local economies and documents his year of eating locally in Middlebury, Vermont. He is a frequent contributor to various publications, including the *New York Times*, the *Atlantic Monthly*, *Mother Jones*, and *Rolling Stone*. He has received many awards, fellowships, and honorary degrees and is the Schumann Distinguished Scholar at Middlebury College. In this essay, originally published in *Orion* in 2010, McKibben calls on his readers to take environmental factors into account when deciding on the ethics of eating meat.

May I say—somewhat defensively—that I haven't cooked red meat in many years? That I haven't visited a McDonald's since college? That if you asked me how I like my steak, I'd say I don't really remember? I'm not a moral abstainer—I'll eat meat when poor people in distant places offer it to me, especially when they're proud to do so and I'd be an ass to say no. But in everyday life, for a series of reasons that began with the dietary scruples of the woman I chose to marry, hamburgers just don't come into play.

I begin this way because I plan to wade into one of the most impassioned fracases now underway on the planet—to meat or not to meat—and I want to establish that I Do Not Have A Cow In This Fight. In recent years vegetarians and vegans have upped their attack on the consumption of animal flesh, pointing out not only that it's disgusting (read Jonathan Safran Foer's new book) but also a major cause of climate change. The numbers range from 18 percent of the world's greenhouse gas emissions to—in one recent study that was quickly discredited—51 percent. Whatever the exact figure, suffice it to say it's high: there's the carbon that comes from cutting down the forest to start the farm, and from the fertilizer and diesel fuel it takes to grow the corn, there's the truck exhaust from shipping cows hither and yon, and most of all the methane that emanates from the cows themselves (95 percent of it from the front end, not the hind, and these millions of feedlot cows would prefer if you used the word *eructate* in place of *belch*). This news has led to an almost endless series of statistical calculations: going vegan is 50 percent more effective in reducing greenhouse gas emissions than switching to a hybrid car according to a University of Chicago study; the UN Food and Agriculture Organization finds that a half pound of ground beef has the same effect on climate change as driving an SUV 10 miles. It has led to a lot of political statements: the British health secretary last fall called on Englishmen to cut their beefeating by dropping at least a sausage a week from their diets, and Paul McCartney has declared that "the biggest change anyone could make in their own lifestyle to help the environment would be to become vegetarian." It has even led to the marketing of a men's flip-flop called the Stop Global Warming Toepeeka that's made along entirely vegan lines.

Industrial livestock production is essentially indefensible—ethically, ecologically, and otherwise. We now use an enormous percentage of our arable land to grow corn that we feed to cows who stand in feedlots and eructate until they are slaughtered in a variety of gross ways and lodge in our ever-larger abdomens. And the fact that the product of this exercise "tastes good" sounds pretty lame as an excuse. There are technofixes—engineering the corn feed so it produces less methane, or giving the cows shots so they eructate less violently. But this type of tailpipe fix only works around the edges, and with the planet warming fast that's not enough. We should simply stop eating factory-farmed meat, and the effects on climate change would be but one of the many benefits.

> We should simply stop eating factory-farmed meat, and the effects on climate change would be but one of the many benefits.

Still, even once you've made that commitment, there's a nagging ecological question that's just now being raised. It goes like this: long before humans had figured out the whole cow thing, nature had its own herds of hoofed ungulates. Big herds of big animals—perhaps 60 million bison ranging across North America, and maybe 100 million antelope. That's considerably more than the number of cows now resident in these United States. These were noble creatures, but uncouth—*eructate* hadn't been coined yet. They really did just belch. So why weren't they filling the atmosphere with methane? Why wasn't their manure giving off great quantities of atmosphere-altering gas?

The answer, so far as we can tell, is both interesting and potentially radical in its implications. These old-school ungulates weren't all that different in their plumbing—they were methane factories with legs too. But they used those legs for something. They didn't stand 5 still in feedlots waiting for corn, and they didn't stand still in big western federal allotments overgrazing the same tender grass. They didn't stand still at all. Maybe they would have enjoyed stationary life, but like teenagers in a small town, they were continually moved along by their own version of the police: wolves. And big cats. And eventually Indians. By predators.

As they moved, they kept eating grass and dropping manure. Or, as soil scientists would put it, they grazed the same perennials once or twice a year to "convert aboveground biomass to dung and urine." Then dung beetles buried the results in the soil, nurturing the grass to grow back. These grasslands covered places that don't get much rain—the Southwest and the Plains, Australia, Africa, much of Asia. And all that grassland sequestered stupendous amounts of carbon and methane from out of the atmosphere—recent preliminary research indicates that methane-loving bacteria in healthy soils will sequester more of the gas in a day than cows supported by the same area will emit in a year.

We're flat out of predators in most parts of the world, and it's hard to imagine, in the short time that we have to deal with climate change, ending the eating of meat and returning the herds of buffalo and packs of wolves to all the necessary spots. It's marginally easier to imagine mimicking those systems with cows. The key technology here is the single-strand electric fence—you move your herd or your flock once or twice a day from one small pasture to the next, forcing them to eat everything that's growing there but moving them along before they graze all the good stuff down to bare ground. Now their manure isn't a problem that fills a cesspool, but a key part of making the system work. Done right, some studies suggest, this method of raising cattle could put much of the atmosphere's oversupply of greenhouse gases back in the soil inside half a century. That means shifting from feedlot farming to rotational grazing is one of the few changes we could make that's on the same scale as the problem of global warming. It won't do away with the need for radically cutting emissions, but it could help get the car exhaust you emitted back in high school out of the atmosphere.

Oh, and grass-fed beef is apparently much better for you—full of Omega 3s, like sardines that moo. Better yet, it's going to be more expensive, because you can't automate the process the same way you can feedlot agriculture. You need the guy to move the fence every afternoon. (That's why about a billion of our fellow humans currently make their livings as herders of one kind or another—some of them use slingshots, or dogs, or shepherd's crooks, or horses instead of electric fence, but the principle is the same.) More expensive, in this case, as in many others, is good; we'd end up eating meat the way most of the world does—as a condiment, a flavor, an ingredient, not an entrée.

I doubt McDonald's will be in favor. I doubt Paul McCartney will be in favor. It doesn't get rid of the essential dilemma of killing something and then putting it in your mouth. But it's possible that the atmosphere would be in favor, and that's worth putting down your fork and thinking about.

Understanding the Text

1. Why does McKibben conclude that it is impossible to defend industrial livestock production?

2. What is the relationship between factory farming and climate change?

3. What is rotational grazing, and why does McKibben advocate a return to it?

4. Why does McKibben almost never eat meat? When does he eat meat, and why?

Reflection and Response

5. What is the significance of the title? Why do you think McKibben selected it?

6. Why does McKibben think that it is good that grass-fed beef will be or is more expensive?

Making Connections

7. McKibben concludes that neither extreme (not McDonald's and not Paul McCartney's) will favor his position. Why not? How does McKibben position himself in relation to various other positions in this debate? How would Margaret Mead ("The Changing Significance of Food," p. 166), David Biello ("Will Organic Food Fail to Feed the World?" p. 232), and Masanobu Fukuoka ("Living by Bread Alone," p. 87) evaluate his position? Use textual evidence to support your answer.

8. McKibben suggests that an ethics of eating must concern itself with environmental factors. Does he make a good case for why this particular issue should take the forefront? Who in this collection might disagree with his position, and on what grounds? What do their positions tells us about their ethical concerns?

The Omnivore's Delusion: Against the Agri-intellectuals

Blake Hurst

Blake Hurst has farmed for more than 30 years, first as a hog farmer and now growing corn, soybeans, and flowers on his family farm in northwest Missouri. He also serves as president of the Missouri Farm Bureau. As a freelance writer, Hurst has published many articles on food and farming, including in the *Wall Street Journal*, the *New York Times*, *Wilson Quarterly*, and the *American*, among other periodicals. In this often-quoted essay, originally published in 2009 in the *American* (the online magazine of the American Enterprise Institute), Hurst questions various ethical arguments against farming practices. He blasts the way intellectuals criticize industrial farming, arguing that their critiques are unfair and reliant on ignorance.

I'm dozing, as I often do on airplanes, but the guy behind me has been broadcasting nonstop for nearly three hours. I finally admit defeat and start some serious eavesdropping. He's talking about food, damning farming, particularly livestock farming, compensating for his lack of knowledge with volume.

I'm so tired of people who wouldn't visit a doctor who used a stethoscope instead of an MRI demanding that farmers like me use 1930s technology to raise food. Farming has always been messy and painful, and bloody and dirty. It still is.

But now we have to listen to self-appointed experts on airplanes frightening their seatmates about the profession I have practiced for more than 30 years. I'd had enough. I turned around and politely told the lecturer that he ought not believe everything he reads. He quieted and asked me what kind of farming I do. I told him, and when he asked if I used organic farming, I said no, and left it at that. I didn't answer with the first thought that came to mind, which is simply this: I deal in the real world, not superstitions, and unless the consumer absolutely forces my hand, I am about as likely to adopt organic methods as the *Wall Street Journal* is to publish their next edition by setting the type by hand.

He was a businessman, and I'm sure spends his days with spreadsheets, projections, and marketing studies. He hasn't used a slide rule in his career and wouldn't make projections with tea leaves or soothsayers. He does not blame witchcraft for a bad quarter, or expect the factory that makes his product to use steam power instead of electricity, or horses and wagons to deliver his products instead of trucks and trains. But he expects me to farm like my grandfather, and not incidentally, I suppose, to live like him as well. He thinks farmers are too stupid to farm sustainably, too cruel to treat their animals well, and too careless to worry about their communities, their health, and their families. I would not presume to criticize his car, or the size of his house, or the way he runs his business. But he is an expert about me, on the strength of one book, and is sharing that expertise with captive audiences every time he gets the chance. Enough, enough, enough.

Industrial Farming and Its Critics

Critics of "industrial farming" spend most of their time concerned 5 with the processes by which food is raised. This is because the results of organic production are so, well, troublesome. With the subtraction of every "unnatural" additive, molds, fungus, and bugs increase. Since it is difficult to sell a religion with so many readily quantifiable bad results, the trusty family farmer has to be thrown into the breach, saving the whole organic movement by his saintly presence, chewing on his straw, plodding along, at one with his environment, his community, his neighborhood. Except that some of the largest farms in the country are organic—and are giant organizations dependent upon lots of hired stoop labor doing the most backbreaking of tasks in order to save the sensitive conscience of my fellow passenger the merest whiff of pesticide contamination. They do not spend much time talking about that at the Whole Foods store.

The most delicious irony is this: the parts of farming that are the most "industrial" are the most likely to be owned by the kind of family farmers that elicit such a positive response from the consumer. Corn farms are almost all owned and managed by small family farmers. But corn farmers salivate at the thought of one more biotech breakthrough, use vast amounts of energy to increase production, and raise large quantities of an indistinguishable commodity to sell to huge corporations that turn that corn into thousands of industrial products.

Most livestock is produced by family farms, and even the poultry industry, with its contracts and vertical integration,° relies on family farms to contract for the production of the birds. Despite the obvious change in scale over time, family farms, like ours, still meet around the kitchen table, send their kids to the same small schools, sit in the

---

vertical integration: A style of management where different companies working on different parts of a process all have the same owner.

same church pew, and belong to the same civic organizations our parents and grandparents did. We may be industrial by some definition, but not our own. Reality is messier than it appears in the book my tormentor was reading, and farming more complicated than a simple morality play.

On the desk in front of me are a dozen books, all hugely critical of present-day farming. Farmers are often given a pass in these books, painted as either naïve tools of corporate greed, or economic nullities° forced into their present circumstances by the unrelenting forces of the twin grindstones of corporate greed and unfeeling markets. To the farmer on the ground, though, a farmer blessed with free choice and hard-won experience, the moral choices aren't quite so easy. Biotech crops actually cut the use of chemicals, and increase food safety. Are people who refuse to use them my moral superiors? Herbicides cut the need for tillage, which decreases soil erosion by millions of tons. The biggest environmental harm I have done as a farmer is the topsoil

> Farming [is] more complicated than a simple morality play.

(and nutrients) I used to send down the Missouri River to the Gulf of Mexico before we began to practice no-till farming, made possible only by the use of herbicides. The combination of herbicides and genetically modified seed has made my farm more sustainable, not less, and actually reduces the pollution I send down the river.

Finally, consumers benefit from cheap food. If you think they don't, just remember the headlines after food prices began increasing in 2007 and 2008, including the study by the Food and Agriculture Organization of the United Nations announcing that 50 million additional people are now hungry because of increasing food prices. Only "industrial farming" can possibly meet the demands of an increasing population and increased demand for food as a result of growing incomes.

So the stakes in this argument are even higher. Farmers can raise 10 food in different ways if that is what the market wants. It is important, though, that even people riding in airplanes know that there are environmental and food safety costs to whatever kind of farming we choose.

Pigs in a Pen

In his book *Dominion*, author Mathew Scully calls "factory farming" an "obvious moral evil so sickening and horrendous it would leave us ashen." Scully, a speechwriter for the second President Bush, can

nullity: Nothingness, nonentity.

hardly be called a man of the left. Just to make sure the point is not lost, he quotes the conservative historian Paul Johnson a page later:

> The rise of factory farming, whereby food producers cannot remain competitive except by subjecting animals to unspeakable deprivation, has hastened this process. The human spirit revolts at what we have been doing.

Arizona and Florida have outlawed pig gestation crates, and California recently passed, overwhelmingly, a ballot initiative doing the same. There is no doubt that Scully and Johnson have the wind at their backs, and confinement raising of livestock may well be outlawed everywhere. And only a person so callous as to have a spirit that cannot be revolted, or so hardened to any kind of morality that he could countenance an obvious moral evil, could say a word in defense of caging animals during their production. In the quote above, Paul Johnson is forecasting a move toward vegetarianism. But if we assume, at least for the present, that most of us will continue to eat meat, let me dive in where most fear to tread.

Lynn Niemann was a neighbor of my family's, a farmer with a vision. He began raising turkeys on a field near his house around 1956. They were, I suppose, what we would now call "free range" turkeys. Turkeys raised in a natural manner, with no roof over their heads, just gamboling around in the pasture, as God surely intended. Free to eat grasshoppers, and grass, and scratch for grubs and worms. And also free to serve as prey for weasels, who kill turkeys by slitting their necks and practicing exsanguination. Weasels were a problem, but not as much a threat as one of our typically violent early summer thunderstorms. It seems that turkeys, at least young ones, are not smart enough to come in out of the rain, and will stand outside in a downpour, with beaks open and eyes skyward, until they drown. One night Niemann lost 4,000 turkeys to drowning, along with his dream, and his farm.

Now, turkeys are raised in large open sheds. Chickens and turkeys raised for meat are not grown in cages. As the critics of "industrial farming" like to point out, the sheds get quite crowded by the time Thanksgiving rolls around and the turkeys are fully grown. And yes, the birds are bedded in sawdust, so the turkeys do walk around in their own waste. Although the turkeys don't seem to mind, this quite clearly disgusts the various authors I've read who have actually visited a turkey farm. But none of those authors, whose descriptions of the horrors of modern poultry production have a certain sameness, were there when Niemann picked up those 4,000 dead turkeys. Sheds are expensive, and it was easier to raise turkeys in open, inexpensive pastures. But that type of production really was hard on the turkeys. Protected from the weather and predators, today's turkeys may not be aware that they are a part of a morally reprehensible system.

Like most young people in my part of the world, I was a 4-H member. Raising cattle and hogs, showing them at the county fair, and then sending to slaughter those animals that we had spent the summer feeding, washing, and training. We would then tour the packing house, where our friend was hung on a rail, with his loin eye measured and his carcass evaluated. We farm kids got an early start on dulling our moral sensibilities. I'm still proud of my win in the Atchison County Carcass competition of 1969, as it is the only trophy I have ever received. We raised the hogs in a shed, or farrowing (birthing) house. On one side were eight crates of the kind that the good citizens of California have outlawed. On the other were the kind of wooden pens that our critics would have us use, where the sow could turn around, lie down, and presumably act in a natural way. Which included lying down on my 4-H project, killing several piglets, and forcing me to clean up the mess when I did my chores before school. The crates protect the piglets from their mothers. Farmers do not cage their hogs because of sadism, but because dead pigs are a drag on the profit margin, and because being crushed by your mother really is an awful way to go. As is being eaten by your mother, which I've seen sows do to newborn pigs as well.

I warned you that farming is still dirty and bloody, and I wasn't kidding. So let's talk about manure. It is an article of faith amongst the agri-intellectuals that we no longer use manure as fertilizer. To quote Dr. Michael Fox in his book *Eating with a Conscience*, "The animal waste is not going back to the land from which the animal feed originated." Or Bill McKibben, in his book *Deep Economy*, writing about modern livestock production: "But this concentrates the waste in one place, where instead of being useful fertilizer to spread on crop fields it becomes a toxic threat."

In my inbox is an email from our farm's neighbor, who raises thousands of hogs in close proximity to our farm, and several of my family members' houses as well. The email outlines the amount and chemical analysis of the manure that will be spread on our fields this fall, manure that will replace dozens of tons of commercial fertilizer. The manure is captured underneath the hog houses in cement pits, and is knifed into the soil after the crops are harvested. At no time is it exposed to erosion, and it is an extremely valuable resource, one which farmers use to its fullest extent, just as they have since agriculture began.

In the southern part of Missouri, there is an extensive poultry industry in areas of the state where the soil is poor. The farmers there spread the poultry litter on pasture, and the advent of poultry barns made cattle production possible in areas that used to be waste ground. The "industrial" poultry houses are owned by family farmers, who have then used the byproducts to produce beef in areas where cattle couldn't survive before. McKibben is certain that the contracts these farmers sign with companies like Tyson are unfair, and the farmers might agree. But they like those cows, so there is a waiting list for new chicken barns. In some areas, there is indeed more manure than available cropland. But the trend in the industry, thankfully, is toward a dispersion of animals and manure, as the value of the manure increases, and the cost of transporting the manure becomes prohibitive.

We Can't Change Nature

The largest producer of pigs in the United States has promised to gradually end the use of hog crates. The Humane Society promises to take their initiative drive to outlaw farrowing crates and poultry cages to more states. Many of the counties in my own state of Missouri have chosen to outlaw the building of confinement facilities. Barack Obama has been harshly critical of animal agriculture. We are clearly in the process of deciding that we will not continue to raise animals the way we do now. Because other countries may not share our sensibilities, we'll have to withdraw or amend free trade agreements to keep any semblance of a livestock industry.

We can do that, and we may be a better society for it, but we can't 20 change nature. Pigs will be allowed to "return to their mire," as Kipling had it, but they'll also be crushed and eaten by their mothers. Chickens will provide lunch to any number of predators, and some number of chickens will die as flocks establish their pecking order.

In recent years, the cost of producing pork dropped as farmers increased feed efficiency (the amount of feed needed to produce a pound of pork) by 20 percent. Free-range chickens and pigs will increase the price of food, using more energy and water to produce the extra grain required for the same amount of meat, and some people will go hungry. It is also instructive that the first company to move away from farrowing crates is the largest producer of pigs. Changing the way we raise animals will not necessarily change the scale of the companies involved in the industry. If we are about to require more expensive ways of producing food, the largest and most well-capitalized farms will have the least trouble adapting.

The Omnivores' Delusions

Michael Pollan, in an 8,000-word essay in the *New York Times Magazine*, took the expected swipes at animal agriculture. But his truly radical prescriptions had to do with raising of crops. Pollan, who seemed to be aware of the nitrogen problem in his book *The Omnivore's Dilemma*, left nuance behind, as well as the laws of chemistry, in his recommendations. The nitrogen problem is this: without nitrogen, we do not have life. Until we learned to produce nitrogen from natural gas early in the last century, the only way to get nitrogen was through nitrogen produced by plants called legumes, or from small amounts of nitrogen that are produced by lightning strikes. The amount of life the earth could support was limited by the amount of nitrogen available for crop production.

In his book, Pollan quotes geographer Vaclav Smil to the effect that 40 percent of the people alive today would not be alive without the ability to artificially synthesize nitrogen. But in his directive on food policy, Pollan damns agriculture's dependence on fossil fuels, and urges the president to encourage agriculture to move away from expensive and declining supplies of natural gas toward the unlimited sunshine that supported life, and agriculture, as recently as the 1940s. Now, why didn't I think of that?

Well, I did. I've raised clover and alfalfa for the nitrogen they produce, and half the time my land is planted to soybeans, another nitrogen-producing legume. Pollan writes as if all of his ideas are new, but my father tells of agriculture extension meetings in the late 1950s entitled "Clover and Corn, the Road to Profitability." Farmers know that organic farming was the default position of agriculture for thousands of years, years when hunger was just around the corner for even advanced societies. I use all the animal manure available to me, and do everything I can to reduce the amount of commercial fertilizers I use. When corn genetically modified to use nitrogen more efficiently enters the market, as it soon will, I will use it as well. But none of those things will completely replace commercial fertilizer.

Norman Borlaug, founder of the green revolution, estimates that the amount of nitrogen available naturally would only support a worldwide population of 4 billion souls or so. He further remarks that we would need another 5 billion cows to produce enough manure to fertilize our present crops with "natural" fertilizer. That would play havoc with global warming. And cows do not produce nitrogen from the air, but only from the forages they eat, so to produce more manure we will have to plant more forages. Most of the critics of industrial farming maintain the contradictory positions that we should increase the use of manure as a fertilizer, and decrease our consumption of meat. Pollan would solve the problem with cover crops, planted after the corn crop is harvested, and with mandatory composting. Pollan should talk to some actual farmers before he presumes to advise a president.

Pollan tells of flying over the upper Midwest in the winter, and seeing the black, fallow soil. I suppose one sees what one wants to see, but we have not had the kind of tillage implement on our farm that would produce black soil in nearly 20 years. Pollan would provide our nitrogen by planting those black fields to nitrogen-producing cover crops after the cash crops are harvested. This is a fine plan, one that farmers have known about for generations. And sometimes it would even work. But not last year, as we finished harvest in November in a freezing rain. It is hard to think of a legume that would have done its thing between then and corn planting time. Plants do not grow very well in freezing weather, a fact that would evidently surprise Pollan.

And even if we could have gotten a legume established last fall, it would not have fixed any nitrogen before planting time. We used to plant corn in late May, plowing down our green manure and killing the first flush of weeds. But that meant the corn would enter its crucial growing period during the hottest, driest parts of the summer, and that soil erosion would be increased because the land was bare during drenching spring rains. Now we plant in early April, best utilizing our spring rains, and ensuring that pollination occurs before the dog days of August.

A few other problems come to mind. The last time I planted a cover crop, the clover provided a perfect habitat in early spring for bugs, bugs that I had to kill with an insecticide. We do not normally apply insecticides, but we did that year. Of course, you can provide nitrogen with legumes by using a longer crop rotation, growing clover one year and corn the next. But that uses twice as much water to produce a corn crop, and takes twice as much land to produce the same number of bushels. We are producing twice the food we did in 1960 on less land, and commercial nitrogen is one of the main reasons why. It may be that we decide we would rather spend land and water than energy, but Pollan never mentions that we are faced with that choice.

His other grand idea is mandatory household composting, with the compost delivered to farmers free of charge. Why not? Compost is a valuable soil amendment, and if somebody else is paying to deliver it to my farm, then bring it on. But it will not do much to solve the nitrogen problem. Household compost has somewhere between 1 and 5 percent nitrogen, and not all that nitrogen is available to crops the first year. Presently, we are applying about 150 pounds of nitrogen per acre to corn, and crediting about 40 pounds per acre from the preceding year's soybean crop. Let's assume a 5 percent nitrogen rate, or about 100 pounds of nitrogen per ton of compost. That would require 3,000 pounds of compost per acre. Or about 150,000 tons for the corn raised in our county. The average truck carries about 20 tons. Picture 7,500 trucks traveling from New York City to our small county here in the Midwest, delivering compost. Five million truckloads to fertilize the country's corn crop. Now, that would be a carbon footprint!

Pollan thinks farmers use commercial fertilizer because it is easier, and because it is cheap. Pollan is right. But those are perfectly defensible reasons. Nitrogen quadrupled in price over the last several years, and farmers are still using it, albeit more cautiously. We are using GPS monitors on all of our equipment to ensure that we do not use too much, and our production of corn per pound of nitrogen is rapidly increasing. On our farm, we have increased yields about 50 percent during my career, while applying about the same amount of nitrogen we did when I began farming. That fortunate trend will increase even faster with the advent of new GMO hybrids. But as much as Pollan might desire it, even President Obama cannot reshuffle the chemical deck that nature has dealt. Energy may well get much more expensive, and peak oil production may have been reached. But food production will have a claim on fossil fuels long after we have learned how to use renewables and nuclear power to handle many of our other energy needs.

Farming and Connectedness

Much of farming is more "industrial," more technical, and more complex than it used to be. Farmers farm more acres, and are less close to the ground and their animals than they were in the past. Almost all critics of industrial agriculture bemoan this loss of closeness, this "connectedness," to use author Rod Dreher's term. It is a given in most of the writing about agriculture that the knowledge and experience of the organic farmer is what makes him so unique and so important. The "industrial farmer," on the other hand, is a mere pawn of Cargill, backed into his ignorant way of life by forces too large, too far from the farm, and too powerful to resist. Concern about this alienation, both between farmers and the land, and between consumers and their food supply, is what drives much of the literature about agriculture.

The distance between the farmer and what he grows has certainly increased, but, believe me, if we weren't closely connected, we wouldn't still be farming. It's important to our critics that they emphasize this alienation, because they have to ignore the "industrial" farmer's experience and knowledge to say the things they do about farming.

But farmers have reasons for their actions, and society should listen to them as we embark upon this reappraisal of our agricultural system. I use chemicals and diesel fuel to accomplish the tasks my grandfather used to do with sweat, and I use a computer instead of a lined notebook and a pencil, but I'm still farming the same land he did 80 years ago, and the fund of knowledge that our family has accumulated about our small part of Missouri is valuable. And everything I know and I have learned tells me this: we have to farm "industrially" to feed the world, and by using those "industrial" tools sensibly, we can accomplish that task and leave my grandchildren a prosperous and productive farm, while protecting the land, water, and air around us.

Understanding the Text

1. Why does Hurst think it is a bad idea to allow pigs free range to wander as they please?
2. What is the nitrogen problem?
3. Why does Hurst object to the way critics of industrial farming make their cases?

Reflection and Response

4. What is Hurst so angry about? How does he communicate this emotion in writing?
5. Hurst suggests that critics of "industrial farming" do not realize that they cannot have it "both ways"—organic and local. What evidence does he use to support his position? Does he make a good case?

Making Connections

6. How does Hurst position his argument in relation to ones made by Michael Pollan ("Eat Food: Food Defined," p. 9) and Bill McKibben ("The Only Way to Have a Cow," p. 200)? What are the fundamental differences in how they view the environmental impact of "industrial farming"? What moral principles do they each privilege? Is there any shared terrain?

7. Consider the arguments made by Hurst, David Biello ("Will Organic Food Fail to Feed the World?" p. 232), and Eliot Coleman ("Real Food, Real Farming," p. 236) and analyze the positions they take on the impact of organic farming. Explain the debate over organic vs. commercially grown food. Why do organic proponents support it? How does Hurst argue against their position? Which argument makes the most sense to you? Why? What does your position say about your values?

Do Foodies Care about Workers?

Sally Kohn

Sally Kohn was introduced to community organizing when she was 12 by her mother. She has worked for social justice in a variety of roles and continues to help grassroots organizations develop effective ways of communicating their messages to others. She has fought for domestic partnership benefits, organized a project on health-care reform in rural communities, and published a report on the experiences of gay youth in New York's juvenile justice system. She is the founder of the grassroots think tank Movement Vision Lab. Currently, she continues to work as an activist, television commentator, and writer. She is a columnist for *Salon* and a progressive contributor to *Fox News.* Her writing has appeared in the *Washington Post*, *Politico*, *Time*, and *USA Today.* According to Mediaite's Power Grid influence index, Kohn is ranked as one of the top 100 most influential television pundits in America. In this essay, originally published by *Salon* in 2012, Kohn argues that people who care about food should focus not just on "organic" and "local" labels but also on worker justice.

In a scene from the hit show *Portlandia,* Fred Armisen and Carrie Brownstein play hipsters at a local restaurant. They ask about the chicken on the menu.

"The chicken is a heritage breed—woodland-raised chicken that's been fed a diet of sheep's milk, soy, and hazelnuts."

"Is it local?" asks Armisen.

Yes, replies the waitress.

Then the questions get outlandish. Are the hazelnuts the chicken 5 ate organic? USDA organic or some other standard of organic? How big is the area where the chickens are able to roam free?

Like a lot of great satire, the scene is funny because it so painfully reflects reality. And as in reality, the characters in the sketch never ask, "Does the poultry worker who killed the chicken get paid sick days?"

In fact, so-called foodies who are outraged at the idea of inhumanely raised pigs are remarkably uninterested in the inhumane work conditions of those who help get their pork to the table. Stopped at a farmers' market or in line at a top restaurant, foodies are definitely concerned when told about the dismal treatment of food workers. But does it shape their buying habits? Not really. Responses range from "I've never really thought about it" to "At least they have jobs."

Yes, and those jobs are bad jobs and getting worse. The food industry employs one in five private-sector workers. Yet only an estimated

13 percent of those workers make a living wage. Thanks to lobbying by the National Restaurant Association (once led by Herman Cain°), the national minimum wage for tipped workers is $2.13 per hour. Many warehouse and farm workers are paid by the piece, which can amount to even less. And so, in a situation riddled with irony, food-system workers rely on food stamps at double the rate of the rest of the U.S. workforce.

That's right: That $22 dish of line-caught halibut with organic pea shoots and avocado gelée? The worker who washed the plate it's on can't afford to feed his family.

"We've always assumed that when we support organic farmers, 10 we're supporting people—not only taking care of the land but also taking care of the people who work the land," says Alice Waters, the chef-owner of Chez Panisse restaurant in Berkeley, California, considered the fairy godmother of the foodie universe. But more and more, we're seeing the fallacy of that assumption.

For some time, the organic giant Whole Foods has been under scrutiny for labor abuses and union busting. In 2005, the Coalition of Immokalee Workers won an agreement from Taco Bell to pay 1 cent more per pound of tomatoes, resulting in a 75 percent increase in wages for tomato pickers. And just this year, 3,000 diners at an Olive Garden in Fayetteville, North Carolina, had to be tested for hepatitis C because the company doesn't provide paid sick days, and so an employee came to work ill. These and other horror stories are just the tip of the iceberg, according to "The Hands That Feed Us," a recent report by the Food Chain Workers Alliance.

> The next time you order that hormone-free hamburger on a stone-ground bun with organic ketchup, ask for a side of worker justice.

Slowly, food-sperts like Eric Schlosser and Mark Bittman are speaking up for food-worker justice, but consumers don't seem to care much. Jessamyn Rodriguez founded Hot Bread Kitchen, a nonprofit bakery whose mission is to train and employ immigrant women. Rodriguez says customers are compelled by the workers'-rights pedigree of her products, but they don't demand it the same way they demand pure ingredients. "It's one step further from self-interest," says Rodriguez. Of course, points out New York restaurateur and organic pioneer Peter Hoffman, the hipsters who drove the organic

Herman Cain: Businessman, CEO of Godfather's Pizza, and briefly a Republican candidate for president in 2011.

movement to prominence don't care only about keeping their bodies clean. If that were the case, they'd drink substantially less beer and have fewer tattoos. Rather, the organic movement is as political as it is personal, a practical way to manifest environmental awareness in daily life. Your politics are what you eat. So why not eat what's good for workers? There are even guidebooks to help.

It would be nice to think that, just as elite chefs and advocates had to lay the groundwork for the mass organic movement, so too will worker justice eventually make it onto the foodie table. Which sounds good, especially if you'd like to go back to that restaurant with the halibut that you love and not think about this anymore.

But if it disturbs you that an estimated 79 percent of food-service workers don't have paid sick days, 52 percent don't receive health and safety training from their employers, 35 percent experience wage theft on a weekly basis, and 75 percent have never had an opportunity to apply for a better position, maybe it's time to put down your fork and open your mouth. After all, these food-service workers are disproportionately black and Latino. Many are undocumented immigrants. It's optimistic at best to think the traditionally elite, environmentally driven food movement will inevitably embrace the concerns of these workers and be the driving force for change.

In the food industry, as in America overall, the concerns of low- 15 wage workers tend to get swept under the table. A generation of hipsters has built its identity around sustainable food. Maybe it's time to start a new trend. The next time you order that hormone-free hamburger on a stone-ground bun with organic ketchup, ask for a side of worker justice.

Understanding the Text

1. According to Kohn, what is the painful reality for food industry workers?
2. What do we learn from this article about the typical treatment of food workers?

Reflection and Response

3. Kohn suggests that "foodies" may have their priorities wrong. What does she say they prioritize? Why does she object?
4. How does Kohn describe the current relationship between the sustainable food movement and worker justice? What changes does she suggest?

Making Connections

5. Kohn implies that any food movement that aims for moral integrity necessarily must consider food worker rights. Michael Idov ("When Did Young People

Start Spending 25% of Their Paychecks on Pickled Lamb's Tongues?," p. 101) describes "foodie" culture as focused purely on pleasure and consumption for consumption's sake. Is there a way to reconcile the two positions? Should social justice play a role in our food choices, or is eating for sheer pleasure morally justifiable? As you take a position in this debate, anticipate potential objections and carefully think through how you will argue against them.

6. According to Kohn, "Your politics are what you eat" (para. 12). Select three authors whose food preferences, food choices, or food values tell us something about their food politics. Compare their food politics to your own.

7. Which authors in this collection express a concern for workers' rights? Which ones imply a concern even if they don't explicitly discuss it? What does this concern tell us about their moral principles?

5

What Is the Future of Food?

We never know what the future will bring, but we do know that we will need food. In this last chapter, authors weigh in on what they think will influence the future of food. They identify problems that will remain at the forefront—climate change, global hunger, and labor injustice, to name a few. They also discuss potential changes that might lessen the negative impact of food production on the environment and that might bring food production to the urban centers where food is in short supply. Still, even as we think of solutions to existing concerns, new problems will inevitably emerge.

Prince Charles of Wales offers a complex look at the future of food in his analysis of the complex relationships among food production, global food supply, environmental sustainability, and health. While David Biello and Eliot Coleman largely agree with many of Prince Charles's assertions, Robert Paarlberg complicates their views with his critique of the organic food movement and argues for a different kind of emphasis on solving world hunger. As a set, they reveal the crisis of values that underlies much of the debate over organic versus conventional farming and the related environmental and health impacts. Frances Moore Lappé adds to this debate by suggesting that a "scarcity of democracy"—and not food—is the real culprit behind world hunger. While Lappé focuses on the politics of food production and distribution, Natasha Bowens looks at the economic, social, and political impact of food injustice on peoples of color. Finally, Jennifer Cockrall-King offers a ray of hope for urban agriculture in her portrait of Chicago's vertical farm known as The Plant. Taken together, these selections suggest that the future of food will be no less complex than the present. They also reveal that the ways we define food and determine its purpose will continue to change as other aspects of culture, business, politics, and society change. The factors that help determine what foods are available and what foods we choose to eat will continue to evolve, too.

The readings in this chapter, then, suggest as many questions as they answer. Here are some to consider: Is the future of food going to be organic? Will it rely on conventional, industrial approaches? Or will we adopt hybrid approaches? What ethical principles will guide food policy in the future? What kinds of moral choices will individuals make? Will they see food choices as moral choices more or less than they do now? What roles will innovative approaches and new technologies play in feeding the population? Should we focus on futuristic, potentially expensive, inventions or return to the basics? What roles will corporations and industrial farming play in the future of food? What roles will small-scale farming and local businesses play? Will worker justice and the impacts of food production on historically oppressed groups be considered? Will democracy emerge as a positive force in bringing about food equity? Will people care more or less about global hunger in the future than they do now? Will the global hunger crisis ever become a thing of the past? While these questions have yet to be answered, the readings in this chapter offer food for thought, and ways for us to think critically about the future of food.

On the Future of Food

Prince Charles of Wales

Prince Charles of Wales is the eldest child of Queen Elizabeth II and her heir apparent. He has many humanitarian and social concerns, and he is especially focused on promoting environmental awareness. A strong proponent of organic farming, he launched his own organic food brand, Duchy Originals, in 1990; it sells sustainably produced goods, including many food products. He also wrote *Highgrove: An Experiment in Organic Gardening and Farming* (1993; with the *Daily Telegraph*'s environment editor, Charles Clover) and *The Elements of Organic Gardening* (2007; with Stephanie Donaldson). He has tried to reduce his own household's carbon footprint with various measures, including more environmentally friendly travel arrangements. While his efforts are not without critics, he is recognized as a leading voice in the fight for sustainable agriculture. In his keynote speech (excerpted here) at the Future of Food conference at Georgetown University in Washington, D.C., on May 4, 2011, he argued that feeding the world's population using sustainable methods is one of our most important challenges.

Over the past 30 years I have been venturing into extremely dangerous territory by speaking about the future of food. I have all the scars to prove it . . . ! Questioning the conventional world view is a risky business. And the only reason I have done so is for the sake of your generation and for the integrity of Nature herself. It is your future that concerns me and that of your grandchildren, and theirs too. That is how far we should be looking ahead. I have no intention of being confronted by my grandchildren, demanding to know why on Earth we didn't do something about the many problems that existed, when we knew what was going wrong. The threat of that question, the responsibility of it, is precisely why I have gone on challenging the assumptions of our day. And I would urge you to do the same, because we need to face up to asking whether how we produce our food is actually fit for purpose in the very challenging circumstances of the twenty-first century. We simply cannot ignore that question any longer.

Very nearly 30 years ago I began by talking about the issue, but I realized in the end I had to go further. I had to put my concern into action, to demonstrate how else we might do things so that we secure food production for the future, but also, crucially, to take care of the Earth that sustains us. Because if we don't do that, if we do not work within Nature's system, then Nature will fail to be the durable, continuously sustaining force she has always been. Only by safeguarding Nature's resilience can we hope to have a resilient form of food production and ensure food security in the long term.

This is the challenge facing us. We have to maintain a supply of healthy food at affordable prices when there is mounting pressure on nearly every element affecting the process. In some cases we are pushing Nature's life-support systems so far, they are struggling to cope with what we ask of them. Soils are being depleted, demand for water is growing ever more voracious, and the entire system is at the mercy of an increasingly fluctuating price of oil.

Remember that when we talk about agriculture and food production, we are talking about a complex and interrelated system and it is simply not possible to single out just one objective, like maximizing production, without also ensuring that the system which delivers those increased yields meets society's other needs. As Eric° has highlighted, these should include the maintenance of public health, the safeguarding of rural employment, the protection of the environment, and contributing to overall quality of life.

So I trust that this conference will not shy away from the big 5 questions. Chiefly, how can we create a more sustainable approach to agriculture while recognizing those wider and important social and economic parameters—an approach that is capable of feeding the world with a global population rapidly heading for nine billion? And can we do so amid so many competing demands on land, in an increasingly volatile climate, and when levels of the planet's biodiversity are under such threat or in serious decline?

As I see it, these pressures mean we haven't much choice in the matter. We are going to have to take some very brave steps. We will have to develop much more sustainable, or durable forms of food production because the way we have done things up to now are no longer as viable as they once appeared to be. The more I talk with people about this issue, the more I realize how vague the general picture remains of the perilous state we are in. So, just to be absolutely clear, I feel I should offer you a quick pen sketch of just some of the evidence that this is so.

Certainly, internationally, food insecurity is a growing problem. There are also many now who consider that global food systems are well on the way to being in crisis. Yield increases for staple food crops are declining. They have dropped from 3 percent in the 1960s to 1 percent today—and that is really worrying because, for the first time, that rate is less than the rate of population growth. And all of this, of

Eric: Eric Schlosser also spoke at the conference (see p. 20), http://www.georgetown.edu/story/futureoffoodgallery.html.

course, has to be set against the ravages caused by climate change. Already yields are suffering in Africa and India where crops are failing to cope with ever-increasing temperatures and fluctuating rainfall. We all remember the failure of last year's wheat harvest in Russia and droughts in China. They have caused the cost of food to rocket and, with it, inflation around the world, stoking social discontent in many countries, notably in the Middle East. It is a situation I fear will only become more volatile as we suffer yet more natural disasters. . . .

Set against these threats to yields is the ever-growing demand for food. The United Nations Food and Agriculture Organization estimates that the demand will rise by 70 percent between now and 2050. The curve is quite astonishing. The world somehow has to find the means of feeding a staggering 219,000 new mouths every day. That's about 450 since I started talking! What is more, with incomes rising in places like China and India, there will also be more people wealthy enough to consume more, so the demand for meat and dairy products may well increase yet further. And all that extra livestock will compete for feed more and more with an energy sector that has massively expanded its demand for biofuels. Here in the U.S., I am told, four out of every ten bushels of corn are now grown to fuel motor vehicles.

This is the context we find ourselves in and it is set against the backdrop of a system heavily dependent upon fossil fuels and other forms of diminishing natural capital—mineral fertilizers and so on. Most forms of industrialized agriculture now have an umbilical dependency on oil, natural gas, and other non-renewable resources. One study I have read estimates that a person today on a typical Western diet is, in effect, consuming nearly a U.S. gallon of diesel every day! And when you consider that in the past decade the cost of artificial nitrogen fertilizers has gone up fourfold and the cost of potash three times, you start to see how uncomfortable the future could become if we do not wean ourselves off our dependency. And that's not even counting the impact of higher fuel prices on the other costs of production—transport and processing—all of which are passed on to the consumer. It is indeed a vicious circle.

Then add the supply of land into the equation—where do we grow   10
all of the extra plants or graze all that extra stock when urban expansion is such a pressure? Here in the United States I am told that one acre is lost to development every minute of every day—which means that since 1982 an area the size of Indiana has been built over—though that is small fry compared with what is happening in places like India where, somehow, they have to find a way of housing another 300 million people in the next 30 years. But on top of this is the very real problem of soil erosion.

Again, in the U.S., soil is being washed away 10 times faster than the Earth can replenish it, and it is happening 40 times faster in China and India. Twenty-two thousand square miles of arable land is turning into desert every year and, all told, it appears a quarter of the world's farmland, two billion acres, is degraded.

Given these pressures, it seems likely we will have to grow plants in more difficult terrain. But the only sustainable way to do that will be by increasing the long-term fertility of the soil, because, as I say, achieving increased production using imported, non-renewable inputs is simply not sustainable.

There are many other pressures on the way we produce our food, but I just need to highlight one more, if I may, before I move on to the possible solutions, because it is so important. It is that magical substance we have taken for granted for so long—water.

In a country like the United States a fifth of all your grain production is dependent upon irrigation. For every pound of beef produced in the industrial system, it takes 2,000 gallons of water. That is a lot of water and there is plenty of evidence that the Earth cannot keep up with the demand. The Ogallala Aquifer on the Great Plains, for instance, is depleting by 1.3 trillion gallons faster than rainfall can replenish it. And when you consider that of all the water in the world, only 5 percent of it is fresh and a quarter of that sits in Lake Baikal in Siberia, there is not a lot left. Of the remaining 4 percent, nearly three quarters of it is used in agriculture, but 30 percent of that water is wasted. If you set that figure against future predictions, then the picture gets even worse. By 2030 it is estimated that the world's farmers will need 45 percent more water than today. And yet already, because of irrigation, many of the world's largest rivers no longer reach the sea for part of the year—including, I am afraid, the Colorado and Rio Grande.

Forgive me for laboring these points, but the impact of all of this has already been immense. Over a billion people—one-seventh of the world's population—are hungry and another billion suffer from what is called "hidden hunger," which is the lack of essential vitamins and nutrients in their diets. And on the reverse side of the coin, let us not forget the other tragic fact—that over a billion people in the world are now considered overweight or obese. It is an increasingly insane picture. In one way or another, half the world finds itself on the wrong side of the food equation.

You can see, I hope, that in a global ecosystem that is, to say the least, under stress, our apparently unbridled demands for energy, land, and water put overwhelming pressure on our food systems. I am not alone in thinking that the current model is simply not durable in the long term. It is not "keeping everything going continuously" and it is, therefore, not sustainable.

So what is a "sustainable food production" system? We should be very clear about it, or else we will end up with the same system that we have now, but dipped in "green wash." For me, it has to be a form of agriculture that does not exceed the carrying capacity of its local eco-system and which recognizes that the soil is the planet's most vital renewable resource. Topsoil is the cornerstone of the prosperity of nations. It acts as a buffer against drought and as a carbon sink and it is the primary source of the health of all animals, plants, and people. If we degrade it, as we are doing, then Nature's capital will lose its innate resilience and it won't be very long, believe you me, before our human economic capital and economic systems also begin to lose their resilience.

Let's, then, try and look for a moment at what very probably is not a genuinely sustainable form of agriculture—for the long term, and by that I mean generations as yet unborn. In my own view it is surely not dependent upon the use of chemical pesticides, fungicides, and insecticides; nor, for that matter, upon artificial fertilizers and growth-promoters or G.M. You would have perhaps thought it unlikely to create vast monocultures and to treat animals like machines by using industrial rearing systems. Nor would you expect it to drink the Earth dry, deplete the soil, clog streams with nutrient-rich run-off and create, out of sight and out of mind, enormous dead zones in the oceans. You would also think, wouldn't you, that it might not lead to the destruction of whole cultures or the removal of many of the remaining small farmers around the world? Nor, presumably, would it destroy biodiversity at the same time as cultural and social diversity.

On the contrary, genuinely sustainable farming maintains the resilience of the entire ecosystem by encouraging a rich level of bio-diversity in the soil, in its water supply, and in the wildlife—the birds, insects, and bees that maintain the health of the whole system. Sustainable farming also recognizes the importance to the soil of planting trees; of protecting and enhancing water-catchment systems; of mitigating, rather than adding to, climate change. To do this it must be a mixed approach. One where animal waste is recycled and organic waste is composted to build the soil's fertility. One where antibiotics are only used on animals to treat illnesses, not deployed in prophylactic doses to prevent them; and where those animals are fed on grass-based regimes as Nature intended.

You may think this an idealized definition—that it isn't possible in "the real world"—but if you consider this the gold standard, then for 20 food production to become more "sustainable" it has to reduce the use of those substances that are dangerous and harmful not only to human health, but also to the health of those natural systems, such as the oceans, forests, and wetlands, that provide us with the services essential to life on this planet—but which we rashly take for granted. At the same time, it has to minimize the use of non-renewable external inputs. Fertilizers that do not come from renewable sources do not enable a sustainable approach which, ultimately, comes down to giving back to Nature as much as it takes out and recognizing that there are necessary limits to what the Earth can do. Equally, it includes the need for producers to receive a reasonable price for their labors above the price of production. And that, ladies and gentlemen, leads me to the nub of what I would like you to consider.

Having myself tried to farm as sustainably as possible for some 26 years in England, which is not as long as other people here I know, I certainly know of plenty of current evidence that adopting an approach which mirrors the miraculous ingenuity of Nature can produce surprisingly high yields of a wide range of vegetables, arable crops, beef, lamb, and milk. And yet we are told ceaselessly that sustainable or organic agriculture cannot feed the world. I find this claim very hard to understand. Especially when you consider the findings of an impeccably well-researched International Assessment of Agricultural Knowledge, Science and Technology for Development, conducted in 2008 by the U.N. I am very pleased, by the way, to see that the co-chair of that report, Professor Hans Herren, will be taking part in the International Panel discussion towards the end of the conference. His report drew on evidence from more than 400 scientists worldwide and concluded that small-scale, family-based farming systems, adopting so-called agro-ecological approaches, were among the most productive systems in developing countries. This was a major study and a very explicit statement. And yet, for some strange reason, the conclusions of this exhaustive report seem to have vanished without trace.

> This is the heart of the problem, it seems to me—why it is that an industrialized system, deeply dependent on fossil fuels and chemical treatments, is promoted as viable, while a much less damaging one is rubbished and condemned as unfit for purpose.

This is the heart of the problem, it seems to me—why it is that an industrialized system, deeply dependent on fossil fuels and chemical treatments, is promoted as viable, while a much less damaging one is rubbished and condemned as unfit for purpose. The reasons lie in the anomalies that exist behind the scenes.

I would certainly urge you, first, to look at the slack in the system. Under the current, inherently unsustainable system, in the developed world we actually throw away approximately 40 percent of the food we have bought.

Food is now much cheaper than it was and one of the unexpected consequences of this is, perhaps, that we do not value it as once we did. I cannot help feeling some of this problem could be avoided with better food education. You only have to consider the progress your First Lady, Mrs. Obama, has achieved lately by launching her "Let's Move" campaign—a wonderful initiative, if I may say so. With manufacturers making their "Healthy Weight Commitment" and pledging to cut 1.5 trillion calories a year from their products; with Walmart promising to sell products with less sugar, salt, and trans-fats, and to reduce their prices on healthy items like fresh fruits and vegetables; and with the first lady's big drive to improve healthy eating in schools and the excellent thought of urging doctors to write out prescriptions for exercise; these are marvellous ideas that I am sure will make a major difference.

Alas, in developing countries approximately 40 percent of food is 25 lost between farm and market. Could that be remedied too, this time by better on-farm storage? And we should also remember that many, if not most, of the farmers in the developing world are achieving a fraction of the yields they might do if the soil was nurtured more with an eye to organic matter content and improved water management.

However, the really big issue we need to consider is how conventional, agri-industrial techniques are able to achieve the success they do, and how we measure that success. And here I come to the aspect of food production that troubles me most.

The well-known commentator in this country on food matters, Michael Pollan, pointed out recently that, so far, the combined market for local and organic food, both in the U.S. and Europe, has only reached around 2 or 3 percent of total sales. And the reason, he says, is quite simple. It is the difficulty in making sustainable farming more profitable for producers and sustainable food more affordable for consumers. With so much growing concern about this, my International Sustainability Unit carried out a study into why sustainable food production systems struggle to make a profit, and how it is that intensively produced food costs less. The answer to that last question may seem obvious, but my I.S.U. study reveals a less apparent reason.

It looked at five case studies and discovered two things: firstly, that the system of farm subsidies is geared in such a way that it favors overwhelmingly those kinds of agricultural techniques that are responsible for the many problems I have just outlined. And secondly, that the cost of that damage is not factored into the price of food production. Consider, for example, what happens when pesticides get into the water supply. At the moment, the water has to be cleaned up at enormous cost to consumer water bills; the primary polluter is not charged. Or take the emissions from the manufacture and application of nitrogen fertilizer, which are potent greenhouse gases. They, too, are not costed at source into the equation.

This has led to a situation where farmers are better off using intensive methods and where consumers who would prefer to buy sustainably produced food are unable to do so because of the price. There are many producers and consumers who want to do the right thing but, as things stand, "doing the right thing" is penalized. And so this raises an admittedly difficult question—has the time arrived when a long, hard look is needed at the way public subsidies are generally geared? And should the recalibration of that gearing be considered so that it helps healthier approaches and "techniques"? Could there be benefits if public finance were redirected so that subsidies are linked specifically to farming practices that are more sustainable, less polluting, and of wide benefit to the public interest, rather than what many environmental experts have called the curiously "perverse" economic incentive system that too frequently directs food production?

The point, surely, is to achieve a situation where the production of 30 healthier food is rewarded and becomes more affordable and that the Earth's capital is not so eroded. Nobody wants food prices to go up, but if it is the case that the present low price of intensively produced food in developed countries is actually an illusion, only made possible by transferring the costs of cleaning up pollution or dealing with human health problems onto other agencies, then could correcting these anomalies result in a more beneficial arena where nobody is actually worse off in net terms? It would simply be a more honest form of accounting that may make it more desirable for producers to operate more sustainably— particularly if subsidies were redirected to benefit sustainable systems of production. It is a question worth considering, and I only ask it because my concern is simply that we seek to produce the healthiest food possible from the healthiest environment possible—for the long term— and to ensure that it is affordable for ordinary consumers. . . .

I am a historian, not an economist, but what I am hinting at here is that it is surely time to grasp one of the biggest nettles of all and re-assess what has become a fundamental aspect of our entire economic model.

As far as I can see, responding to the problems we have with a "business as usual" approach towards the way in which we measure G.D.P. offers us only short-term relief. It does not promise a long-term cure. Why? Because we cannot possibly maintain the approach in the long term if we continue to consume our planet as rapaciously as we are doing. Capitalism depends upon capital, but our capital ultimately depends upon the health of Nature's capital. Whether we like it or not, the two are in fact inseparable.

There are alternative ways to growing our food which, if used with new technology—things like precision irrigation, for instance—would go a very long way to resolving some of the problems we face. If they are underpinned by smarter financial ways of supporting them, they could strengthen the resilience of our agriculture, marine, and energy systems. We could ensure a means of supply that is capable of withstanding the sorts of sudden fluctuations on international markets which are bound to come our way, as the price of oil goes up and the impact of our accelerating disruption of entire natural systems becomes greater.

In essence what I am suggesting here is something very simple. We need to include in the bottom line the true costs of food production—the true financial costs and the true costs to the Earth. It is what I suppose you could call "Accounting for Sustainability," a name I gave to a project I set up six years ago, initially to encourage businesses to expand their accounting process so that it incorporates the interconnected impact of financial, environmental, and social elements on their long-term performance. What if Accounting for Sustainability was applied to the agricultural sector? This was certainly the implicit suggestion in a recent and very important study by the U.N. The Economics of Ecosystems and Biodiversity, or T.E.E.B., assessed the multitrillion-dollar importance to the world's economy of the natural world and concluded that the present system of national accounts needs to be upgraded rapidly so they include the health of natural capital, and thereby accurately reflect how the services offered by natural ecosystems are performing—let alone are paid for. Incidentally, to create a genuine market for such services—in the same way as a carbon market has been created—could conceivably make a substantial contribution to reducing poverty in the developing world.

This is very important. If we hope to redress the market failure that will otherwise blight the lives of future generations, we have to see that there is a direct relationship between the resilience of the planet's ecosystems and the resilience of our national economies. . . .

It is, I feel, our apparent reluctance to recognize the interrelated na- 35
ture of the problems and therefore the solutions, that lies at the heart of

our predicament and certainly of our ability to determine the future of food. How we deal with this systemic failure in our thinking will define us as a civilization and determine our survival. Ladies and gentlemen, let me end by reminding you of the words of one of your own founding fathers and visionaries. It was George Washington who entreated your forebears to "Raise a standard to which the wise and honest can repair; the rest is in the hands of God"—and, indeed, as so often in the past, in the hands of your great country, the United States of America.

Understanding the Text

1. According to Prince Charles, what issues will affect the future of food?

2. Why is he committed to making positive impacts on the future of food? What impact does he hope to make?

Reflection and Response

3. Prince Charles argues that the central problem with industrialized food production is a failure of values, which he blames on "anomalies that exist behind the scenes" (para. 22). What does he mean by "anomalies"? What anomalies is he talking about?

4. What was the International Assessment of Agricultural Knowledge, Science and Technology for Development study conducted by the United Nations in 2008? What were its findings? Why is Prince Charles so pleased with them?

Making Connections

5. What does Prince Charles say about Michelle Obama's program Let's Move!? Why does he think ideas like hers are sure to make a difference? What kind of difference? Do you agree? Why or why not?

6. Prince Charles critiques some of Blake Hurst's conclusions ("The Omnivore's Delusion," p. 204) about the difference between the industrialized food system and sustainable food systems. What arguments made by Hurst does Prince Charles reject? How? What counterevidence does he offer? Which position do you find more compelling? Why?

7. Prince Charles asserts that his main hope is that "we seek to produce the healthiest food possible from the healthiest environment possible—for the long term—and to ensure that it is affordable for ordinary consumers" (para. 30). Which authors in this chapter make suggestions for the future of food that would help him achieve his goals? Describe how their suggestions would help make his desired end a reality.

8. "Nature" plays an important role in Prince Charles's conception of the future of food. How does he depict Nature? Compare his depiction of Nature to the one offered by at least two other authors.

Will Organic Food Fail to Feed the World?

David Biello

David Biello is a journalist and the associate editor of *Scientific American*. He also writes for *Yale Environment 360* and hosts the podcast *60-Second Earth*. He covers environmental issues in the United States and internationally.

In 2009 he won the Internews Earth Journalism Award for his series *A Guide to Carbon Capture and Storage*, published in *Scientific American*. He continues to cover international climate negotiations and is working on a documentary on the future of electricity with Detroit Public Television. In this article, first published in *Scientific American* in 2012, Biello suggests a hybrid approach to food production that takes environmental impact and yield into account.

Food for hungry mouths, feed for animals headed to the slaughterhouse, fiber for clothing, and even, in some cases, fuel for vehicles— all derive from global agriculture. As a result, in the world's temperate climes human agriculture has supplanted 70 percent of grasslands, 50 percent of savannas, and 45 percent of temperate forests. Farming is also the leading cause of deforestation in the tropics and one of the *largest sources of greenhouse gas emissions*, a major contributor to the ongoing maul of species known as the sixth extinction, and a perennial source of nonrenewable groundwater mining and water pollution.

To restrain the environmental impact of agriculture as well as produce more wholesome foods, some farmers have turned to so-called organic techniques. This type of farming is meant to minimize environmental and human health impacts by avoiding the use of synthetic fertilizers, chemical pesticides, and hormones or antibiotic treatments for livestock, among other tactics. But the use of industrial technologies, particularly synthetic nitrogen fertilizer, has fed the swelling human population during the last century. Can organic agriculture feed a world of nine billion people?

In a bid to bring clarity to what has too often been an emotional debate, environmental scientists at McGill University in Montreal and the University of Minnesota performed an analysis of 66 studies comparing conventional and organic methods across 34 different crop species. "We found that, overall, organic yields are considerably lower than conventional yields," explains McGill's Verena Seufert, lead author of the study to be published in *Nature* on April 26. (*Scientific American* is part of Nature Publishing Group.) "But, this yield difference varies across different conditions. When farmers apply best

232

management practices, organic systems, for example, perform relatively better."

In particular, organic agriculture delivers just 5 percent less yield in rain-watered legume crops, such as alfalfa or beans, and in perennial crops, such as fruit trees. But when it comes to major cereal crops, such as corn or wheat, and vegetables, such as broccoli, conventional methods delivered more than 25 percent more yield.

The key limit to further yield increases via organic methods appears to be nitrogen—large doses of synthetic fertilizer can keep up with high demand from crops during the growing season better than the slow release from compost, manure, or nitrogen-fixing cover crops. Of course, the cost of using 171 million metric tons of synthetic nitrogen fertilizer is paid in dead zones at the mouths of many of the world's rivers. These anoxic zones result from nitrogen-rich runoff promoting algal blooms that then die and, in decomposing, suck all the oxygen out of surrounding waters. "To address the problem of [nitrogen] limitation and to produce high yields, organic farmers should use best management practices, supply more organic fertilizers, or grow legumes or perennial crops," Seufert says.

In fact, more knowledge would be key to any effort to boost organic farming or its yields. Conventional farming requires knowledge of how to manage what farmers know as inputs—synthetic fertilizer, chemical pesticides, and the like—as well as fields laid out precisely via global-positioning systems. Organic farmers, on the other hand, must learn to manage an entire ecosystem geared to producing food—controlling pests through biological means, using the waste from animals to fertilize fields, and even growing one crop amidst another. "Organic farming is a very knowledge-intensive farming system," Seufert notes. An organic farmer "needs to create a fertile soil that provides sufficient nutrients at the right time when the crops need them. The same is true for pest management."

But the end result is a healthier soil, which may prove vital in efforts to make it more resilient in the face of climate change as well as conserve it. Organic soils, for example, retain water better than those farms that employ conventional methods. "You use a lot more water [in irrigation] because the soil doesn't have the capacity to retain the water you use," noted farmer Fred Kirschenmann, president of Stone Barns Center for Food and Agriculture at the "Feeding the World While the Earth Cooks" event at the New America Foundation in Washington, D.C., on April 12 [, 2012].

At the same time, a still-growing human population requires more food, which has led some to propose further intensifying conventional methods of applying fertilizer and pesticides to specially bred crops, enabling either a second Green Revolution or improved yields from farmlands currently under cultivation. Crops genetically modified to endure drought may also play a role as well as efforts to develop perennial versions of annual staple crops, such as wheat, which could help reduce environmental impacts and improve soil. "Increasing salt, drought, or heat tolerance of our existing crops can move them a little but not a lot," said biologist Nina Fedoroff of Pennsylvania State University at the New America event. "That won't be enough."

And breeding new perennial versions of staple crops would require compressing millennia of crop improvements that resulted in the high-yielding wheat varieties of today, such as the dwarf wheat created by breeder Norman Borlaug and his colleagues in the 1950s, into a span of years while changing the fundamental character of wheat from an annual crop to a perennial one. Then there is the profit motive. "The private sector is not likely to embrace an idea like perennial crop seeds, which do not require the continued purchase of seeds and thus do not provide a very good source of profit," Seufert notes.

> The world already produces 22 trillion calories annually via agriculture, enough to provide more than 3,000 calories to every person on the planet. The food problem is one of distribution and waste.

Regardless, the world already produces 22 trillion calories annually via agriculture, enough to provide more than 3,000 calories to every person on the planet. The food problem is one of distribution and waste—whether the latter is food spoilage during harvest, in storage, or even after purchase. According to the Grocery Manufacturers Association, in the U.S. alone, 215 meals per person go to waste annually. 10

"Since the world already produces more than enough food to feed everyone well, there are other important considerations" besides yield, argues ecologist Catherine Badgley of the University of Michigan, who also compared yields from organic and conventional methods in a 2006 study that found similar results. Those range from environmental impacts of various practices to the number of people employed in farming. As it stands, conventional agriculture relies on cheap energy, cheap labor, and other unsustainable practices. "Anyone who thinks we will be using Roundup [a herbicide] in eight [thousand] to 10,000 years is foolish," argued organic evangelist Jeff Moyer, farm director of the Rodale Institute, at the New America Foundation event.

But there is unlikely to be a simple solution. Instead the best farming practices will vary from crop to crop and place to place. Building healthier soils, however, will be key everywhere. "Current conventional agriculture is one of the major threats to the environment and degrades the very natural resources it depends on. We thus need to change the way we produce our food," Seufert argues. "Given the current precarious situation of agriculture, we should assess many alternative management systems, including conventional, organic, other agro-ecological, and possibly hybrid systems to identify the best options to improve the way we produce our food."

Understanding the Text

1. What are some of the negative impacts of conventional farming methods that Biello names?

2. What did environment scientists at McGill University and the University of Minnesota find in their comparison study of conventional and organic farming methods?

Reflection and Response

3. What makes organic farming a "very knowledge-intensive" system? What are the benefits of this? What are its drawbacks?

4. What kind of hybrid approach to food production is suggested by Biello? What evidence does he present to support his argument in favor of this approach?

Making Connections

5. Biello and Margaret Mead ("The Changing Significance of Food," p. 166) both argue that we produce enough food to feed the world, but we fail to do so. Compare the evidence they each present and the solutions they recommend. Taken together, what do they suggest about the future of food?

6. What concrete ways does Biello suggest we use to fight global hunger problems? Which authors in this collection would applaud his approach? Which would critique it? Where do you stand? Which positions do you find more compelling? Why? Use textual evidence to support your response.

Real Food, Real Farming

Eliot Coleman

Eliot Coleman is a farmer, author, and longtime proponent of organic farming. He has written extensively about it, publishing many articles and book chapters and the books *The New Organic Grower* (1989), *Four Season Harvest* (1992), and *Winter Harvest Handbook* (2009). He and his wife maintain an experimental market garden called Four Season Farm in Maine that is recognized internationally as a model of small-scale sustainable agriculture. Coleman first opened the original incarnation of this experimental farm in 1970, and he continues to create new innovations and redesign his tools and methods. While he writes and lectures on the subject of organic farming and sustainable agriculture, he continues to improve and refine his craft. In the selection here, he posits that as the term "organic" has become big business and is regulated by the United States Department of Agriculture, it has lost its meaning. He argues that we need to think beyond "organic" and demand "real" food.

N ew ideas, especially those that directly challenge an established orthodoxy,° follow a similar path. First, the orthodoxy says the new idea is rubbish. Then the orthodoxy attempts to minimize the new idea's increasing appeal. Finally, when the new idea proves unstoppable, the orthodoxy tries to claim the idea as its own. This is precisely the path organic food production has followed. First, the organic pioneers were ridiculed. Then, as evidence of the benefits of organic farming became more obvious to more people, mainstream chemical agriculture actively condemned organic ideas as not feasible. Now that the food-buying public has become increasingly enthusiastic about organically grown foods, the food industry has moved to take it over. Toward that end the U.S. Department of Agriculture–controlled national definition of "organic" is tailored to meet the marketing needs of organizations that have no connection to the agricultural integrity organic once represented. We now need to ask whether we want to be content with an "organic" food option that places the marketing concerns of corporate America ahead of nutrition, flavor, and social benefits to consumers.

When I started as an organic grower 45 years ago, organic was a way of thinking rather than a "profit center." The decision to farm organically was a statement of faith in the wisdom of the natural

orthodoxy: Generally accepted belief.

world and the nutritional superiority of properly cultivated food. It was obvious that good farming and exceptional food only resulted from the care and nurturing practiced by the good farmer.

The initial development of organic farming during the first half of the twentieth century arose from the gut feelings of farmers who were trying to reconcile the biological truths they saw in their own fields with the chemical dogma the agricultural science-of-the-moment was preaching. The farmers came to very different conclusions from those of the academic agronomists. The farmers worked on developing agricultural techniques that harmonized with the direction in which their "unscientific" conclusions were leading them. Their goals were to grow the most nutritious food possible while, simultaneously, protecting the soil for future generations.

> "Organic" is now dead as a meaningful synonym for the highest quality food.

The development and refinement of those biologically based agricultural practices continues today. It's what makes this farming adventure so compelling. Each year I hope to do things better than I did last year because I will know Nature's systems better. But my delight in the intricacies of the natural world—my adventure into an ever-deeper appreciation of the soil-plant-animal nutrition cycle and how to optimize it—is not acceptable to the homogenized mentality of mass marketing. The food giants that have taken over "organic" want a simplistic list of ingredients so they can do organic-by-the-numbers. They are derisive about what they label "belief systems," and they are loath to acknowledge that more farmer commitment is involved in producing real food than any number of approved inputs can encompass.

The transition of "organic" from small farm to big business is now 5 upon us. Although getting toxic chemicals out of agriculture is an improvement we can all applaud, it only removes the negatives. The government standards are based on what not to do rather than on what to do. The positive focus, enhancing the biological quality of the food produced, is nowhere to be seen. The government standards are administered through the USDA, whose director said when introducing them, "Organic food does not mean it is superior, safer or more healthy than conventional food." Well, I still agree with the old-time organic pioneers. I believe that properly grown food is superior, safer, and healthier. I also believe national certification bureaucracies are only necessary when food is grown by strangers in faraway places rather than by neighbors you know. I further believe good, fresh food, grown locally by committed growers, is the very best to be found.

In my opinion, "organic" is now dead as a meaningful synonym for the highest quality food. Those of us who still care need to identify not only that our food is grown to higher, more considered standards but also that it is much fresher because it is grown right where it is sold. On our farm we now sell our produce as "RealFood." The sign at the entrance to our farm says "REAL FOOD—REAL FARMING." Real-Food is defined to mean locally grown and unprocessed, in addition to exceptional quality. It identifies fresh foods produced by local growers who want to emphasize the beneficial soil-improving practices they do use, rather than just being content with rejecting the poisonous practices they don't use. It's a term we think defines our intentions, as "organic" did when we began years ago.

"RealFood" Standards

All foods are produced by the growers who sell them. Fresh fruits and vegetables, milk, eggs, and meat products are produced within a 50-mile radius of the place of their final sale. The seed and storage crops (grains, beans, nuts, potatoes, etc.) are produced within a 300-mile radius of their final sale. The growers' fields, barns, and greenhouses are open for inspection at any time, so customers themselves can be the certifiers of their food.

All agricultural practices used on farms selling under the "RealFood" label are chosen to produce foods of the highest nutritional quality. Soils are nourished, as in the natural world, with farm-derived organic matter and mineral particles from ground rock. Green manures and cover crops are included within broadly based crop rotations to maintain biological diversity. A "plant-positive" rather than "pest-negative" philosophy is followed, focusing on correcting the cause of problems (strengthening the plant through optimum growing conditions to prevent pests) rather than treating symptoms (killing the pests that prey on weak plants). Livestock are raised outdoors on grass-based pasture systems to the fullest extent possible. The goal is vigorous, healthy crops and livestock endowed with their inherent powers of vitality and resistance.

Understanding the Text

1. What is "organic" food? How does the USDA define it? How would Coleman define it?
2. Why does Coleman argue that we need to go beyond "organic"?

Reflection and Response

3. What are the benefits of seeing "organic" as a way of thinking? What do we lose when we regulate it? Are there potential gains that Coleman does not consider? Explain?

4. Does Coleman seem optimistic about the future of food? Explain your answer using specific textual evidence.

5. What does Coleman mean by "RealFood"? Does demanding "RealFood," as he defines the term, seem like a realistic goal? Consider your own food choices and food options in your response. Is it in your reach to make such demands?

Making Connections

6. How does Coleman describe the relationship between scientific knowledge and the experiences of real farmers? What conflicts does he describe? How does his representation of this relationship differ from the one offered by Blake Hurst ("The Omnivore's Delusion," p. 204)? Explain using specific textual evidence from both essays.

7. What does Coleman suggest as priorities for the future of food production? What significant values and beliefs does he share with Prince Charles ("On the Future of Food," p. 222) and with Barbara Kingsolver ("You Can't Run Away on Harvest Day," p. 184)? How might these beliefs be used to develop new practices and/or concrete policy changes?

Attention Whole Foods Shoppers

Robert Paarlberg

Robert Paarlberg is a professor of political science at Wellesley College and an adjunct professor of public policy at the Harvard Kennedy School. He conducts research on public policy, with a specific interest in international food and agriculture policy. His current research examines national policy responses to obesity and climate change, and he is particularly interested in the relationship between the failure of democratic governments to take action on such issues in the face of modern views of personal freedom and material abundance. He is the author of many scholarly articles and books, including *Food Politics: What Everyone Needs to Know* (2010). In this essay published in *Foreign Policy* in 2010, he draws connections between personal ideals about food and larger global realities of world hunger. He argues that we should prioritize finding effective ways to address world hunger over ideals that emphasize eating "organic, local, and slow" food.

From Whole Foods recyclable cloth bags to Michelle Obama's organic White House garden, modern eco-foodies are full of good intentions. We want to save the planet. Help local farmers. Fight climate change—and childhood obesity, too. But though it's certainly a good thing to be thinking about global welfare while chopping our certified organic onions, the hope that we can help others by changing our shopping and eating habits is being wildly oversold to Western consumers. Food has become an elite preoccupation in the West, ironically, just as the most effective ways to address hunger in poor countries have fallen out of fashion.

Helping the world's poor feed themselves is no longer the rallying cry it once was. Food may be today's cause célèbre, but in the pampered West, that means trendy causes like making food "sustainable"—in other words, organic, local, and slow. Appealing as that might sound, it is the wrong recipe for helping those who need it the most. Even our understanding of the global food problem is wrong these days, driven too much by the single issue of international prices. In April 2008, when the cost of rice for export had tripled in just six months and wheat reached its highest price in 28 years, a *New York Times* editorial branded this a "World Food Crisis." World Bank president Robert Zoellick warned that high food prices would be particularly damaging in poor countries, where "there is no margin for survival." Now that international rice prices are down 40 percent from their peak and wheat prices have fallen by more than half, we too quickly conclude that the crisis is over. Yet 850 million people in poor countries were chronically undernourished before the 2008 price spike, and the number is even larger now, thanks in part to last year's global recession. This is the real food crisis we face.

It turns out that food prices on the world market tell us very little about global hunger. International markets for food, like most other international markets, are used most heavily by the well-to-do, who are far from hungry. The majority of truly undernourished people—62 percent, according to the U.N. Food and Agriculture Organization— live in either Africa or South Asia, and most are small farmers or rural landless laborers living in the countryside of Africa and South Asia. They are significantly shielded from global price fluctuations both by the trade policies of their own governments and by poor roads and infrastructure. In Africa, more than 70 percent of rural households are cut off from the closest urban markets because, for instance, they live more than a 30-minute walk from the nearest all-weather road.

Poverty—caused by the low income productivity of farmers' labor— is the primary source of hunger in Africa, and the problem is only getting worse. The number of "food insecure" people in Africa (those consuming less than 2,100 calories a day) will increase 30 percent over the next decade without significant reforms, to 645 million, the U.S. Agriculture Department projects.

> If we are going to get serious about solving global hunger, we need to de-romanticize our view of preindustrial food and farming.

What's so tragic about this is that we know from experience how to 5 fix the problem. Wherever the rural poor have gained access to improved roads, modern seeds, less expensive fertilizer, electrical power, and better schools and clinics, their productivity and their income have increased. But recent efforts to deliver such essentials have been undercut by deeply misguided (if sometimes well-meaning) advocacy against agricultural modernization and foreign aid.

In Europe and the United States, a new line of thinking has emerged in elite circles that opposes bringing improved seeds and fertilizers to traditional farmers and opposes linking those farmers more closely to international markets. Influential food writers, advocates, and celebrity restaurant owners are repeating the mantra that "sustainable food" in the future must be organic, local, and slow. But guess what: Rural Africa already has such a system, and it doesn't work. Few smallholder farmers in Africa use any synthetic chemicals, so their food is de facto organic. High transportation costs force them to purchase and sell almost all of their food locally. And food preparation is painfully slow. The result is nothing to celebrate: average income levels of only $1 a day and a one-in-three chance of being malnourished.

If we are going to get serious about solving global hunger, we need to de-romanticize our view of preindustrial food and farming. And that means learning to appreciate the modern, science-intensive, and highly capitalized agricultural system we've developed in the West. Without it, our food would be more expensive and less safe. In other words, a lot like the hunger-plagued rest of the world.

Original Sins

Thirty years ago, had someone asserted in a prominent journal or newspaper that the Green Revolution was a failure, he or she would have been quickly dismissed. Today the charge is surprisingly common. Celebrity author and eco-activist Vandana Shiva claims the Green Revolution has brought nothing to India except "indebted and discontented farmers." A 2002 meeting in Rome of 500 prominent international NGOs, including Friends of the Earth and Greenpeace, even blamed the Green Revolution for the rise in world hunger. Let's set the record straight.

The development and introduction of high-yielding wheat and rice seeds into poor countries, led by American scientist Norman Borlaug and others in the 1960s and 1970s, paid huge dividends. In Asia these new seeds lifted tens of millions of small farmers out of desperate poverty and finally ended the threat of periodic famine. India, for instance, doubled its wheat production between 1964 and 1970 and was able to terminate all dependence on international food aid by 1975. As for indebted and discontented farmers, India's rural poverty rate fell from 60 percent to just 27 percent today. Dismissing these great achievements as a "myth" (the official view of Food First, a California-based organization that campaigns globally against agricultural modernization) is just silly.

It's true that the story of the Green Revolution is not everywhere a   10 happy one. When powerful new farming technologies are introduced into deeply unjust rural social systems, the poor tend to lose out. In Latin America, where access to good agricultural land and credit has been narrowly controlled by traditional elites, the improved seeds made available by the Green Revolution *increased* income gaps. Absentee landlords in Central America, who previously allowed peasants to plant subsistence crops on underutilized land, pushed them off to sell or rent the land to commercial growers who could turn a profit using the new seeds. Many of the displaced rural poor became slum dwellers. Yet even in Latin America, the prevalence of hunger declined more than 50 percent between 1980 and 2005.

In Asia, the Green Revolution seeds performed just as well on small nonmechanized farms as on larger farms. Wherever small farmers had sufficient access to credit, they took up the new technology just as quickly as big farmers, which led to dramatic income gains and no increase in inequality or social friction. Even poor landless laborers gained, because more abundant crops meant more work at harvest time, increasing rural wages. In Asia, the Green Revolution was good for both agriculture and social justice.

And Africa? Africa has a relatively equitable and secure distribution of land, making it more like Asia than Latin America and increasing the chances that improvements in farm technology will help the poor. If Africa were to put greater resources into farm technology, irrigation, and rural roads, small farmers would benefit.

Organic Myths

There are other common objections to doing what is necessary to solve the real hunger crisis. Most revolve around caveats° that purist critics raise regarding food systems in the United States and western Europe. Yet such concerns, though well-intentioned, are often misinformed and counterproductive—especially when applied to the developing world.

Take industrial food systems, the current bugaboo of American food writers. Yes, they have many unappealing aspects, but without them food would be not only less abundant but also less safe. Traditional food systems lacking in reliable refrigeration and sanitary packaging are dangerous vectors for diseases. Surveys over the past several decades by the Centers for Disease Control and Prevention have found that the U.S. food supply became steadily safer over time, thanks in part to the introduction of industrial-scale technical improvements. Since 2000, the incidence of *E. coli* contamination in beef has fallen 45 percent. Today in the United States, most hospitalizations and fatalities from unsafe food come not from sales of contaminated products at supermarkets, but from the mishandling or improper preparation of food inside the home. Illness outbreaks from contaminated foods sold in stores still occur, but the fatalities are typically quite limited. A nationwide scare over unsafe spinach in 2006 triggered the

caveat: Warning, caution.

virtual suspension of all fresh and bagged spinach sales, but only three known deaths were recorded. Incidents such as these command attention in part because they are now so rare. Food Inc. should be criticized for filling our plates with too many foods that are unhealthy, but not foods that are unsafe.

Where industrial-scale food technologies have not yet reached into the developing world, contaminated food remains a major risk. In Africa, where many foods are still purchased in open-air markets (often uninspected, unpackaged, unlabeled, unrefrigerated, unpasteurized, and unwashed), an estimated 700,000 people die every year from food- and water-borne diseases, compared with an estimated 5,000 in the United States. 15

Food grown organically—that is, without any synthetic nitrogen fertilizers or pesticides—is not an answer to the health and safety issues. The *American Journal of Clinical Nutrition* last year published a study of 162 scientific papers from the past 50 years on the health benefits of organically grown foods and found no nutritional advantage over conventionally grown foods. According to the Mayo Clinic, "No conclusive evidence shows that organic food is more nutritious than is conventionally grown food."

Health professionals also reject the claim that organic food is safer to eat due to lower pesticide residues. Food and Drug Administration surveys have revealed that the highest dietary exposures to pesticide residues on foods in the United States are so trivial (less than one one-thousandth of a level that would cause toxicity) that the safety gains from buying organic are insignificant. Pesticide exposures remain a serious problem in the developing world, where farm chemical use is not as well regulated, yet even there they are more an occupational risk for unprotected farmworkers than a residue risk for food consumers.

When it comes to protecting the environment, assessments of organic farming become more complex. Excess nitrogen fertilizer use on conventional farms in the United States has polluted rivers and created a "dead zone" in the Gulf of Mexico, but halting synthetic nitrogen fertilizer use entirely (as farmers must do in the United States to get organic certification from the Agriculture Department) would cause environmental problems far worse.

Here's why: Less than 1 percent of American cropland is under certified organic production. If the other 99 percent were to switch to organic and had to fertilize crops without any synthetic nitrogen fertilizer, that would require a lot more composted animal manure. To supply enough organic fertilizer, the U.S. cattle population would have to increase roughly fivefold. And because those animals would have to be raised organically on forage crops, much of the land in the lower 48 states would need to be converted to pasture. Organic field crops also have lower yields per hectare. If Europe tried to feed itself organically, it would need an additional 28 million hectares of cropland, equal to all of the remaining forest cover in France, Germany, Britain, and Denmark combined.

Mass deforestation probably isn't what organic advocates intend. 20 The smart way to protect against nitrogen runoff is to reduce synthetic fertilizer applications with taxes, regulations, and cuts in farm subsidies, but not try to go all the way to zero as required by the official organic standard. Scaling up registered organic farming would be on balance harmful, not helpful, to the natural environment.

Not only is organic farming less friendly to the environment than assumed, but modern conventional farming is becoming significantly more sustainable. High-tech farming in rich countries today is far safer for the environment, per bushel of production, than it was in the 1960s, when Rachel Carson criticized the indiscriminate farm use of DDT in her environmental classic *Silent Spring*. Thanks in part to Carson's devastating critique, that era's most damaging insecticides were banned and replaced by chemicals that could be applied in lower volume and were less persistent in the environment. Chemical use in American agriculture peaked soon thereafter, in 1973. This was a major victory for environmental advocacy.

And it was just the beginning of what has continued as a significant greening of modern farming in the United States. Soil erosion on farms dropped sharply in the 1970s with the introduction of "no-till" seed planting, an innovation that also reduced dependence on diesel fuel because fields no longer had to be plowed every spring. Farmers then began conserving water by moving to drip irrigation and by leveling their fields with lasers to minimize wasteful runoff. In the 1990s, GPS equipment was added to tractors, autosteering the machines in straighter paths and telling farmers exactly where they were in the field to within one square meter, allowing precise adjustments in chemical use. Infrared sensors were brought in to detect the greenness of the crop, telling a farmer exactly how much more (or less) nitrogen might be needed as the growing season went forward. To reduce wasteful nitrogen use, equipment was developed that can insert fertilizers into the ground at exactly the depth needed and in perfect rows, only where it will be taken up by the plant roots.

These "precision farming" techniques have significantly reduced the environmental footprint of modern agriculture relative to the quantity of food being produced. In 2008, the Organization for Economic Cooperation and Development published a review of the "environmental performance of agriculture" in the world's 30 most advanced industrial countries—those with the most highly capitalized and science-intensive farming systems. The results showed that between 1990 and 2004, food production in these countries continued to increase (by 5 percent in volume), yet adverse environmental impacts were reduced in every category. The land area taken up by farming declined 4 percent, soil erosion from both wind and water fell, gross greenhouse gas emissions from farming declined 3 percent, and excessive nitrogen fertilizer use fell 17 percent. Biodiversity also improved, as increased numbers of crop varieties and livestock breeds came into use.

Seeding the Future

Africa faces a food crisis, but it's not because the continent's population is growing faster than its potential to produce food, as vintage Malthusians such as environmental advocate Lester Brown and advocacy organizations such as Population Action International would have it. Food production in Africa is vastly less than the region's known potential, and that is why so many millions are going hungry there. African farmers still use almost no fertilizer; only 4 percent of cropland has been improved with irrigation; and most of the continent's cropped area is not planted with seeds improved through scientific plant breeding, so cereal yields are only a fraction of what they could be. Africa is failing to keep up with population growth not because it has exhausted its potential, but instead because too little has been invested in reaching that potential.

One reason for this failure has been sharply diminished assistance from international donors. When agricultural modernization went out of fashion among elites in the developed world beginning in the 1980s, development assistance to farming in poor countries collapsed. Per capita food production in Africa was declining during the 1980s and 1990s and the number of hungry people on the continent was doubling, but the U.S. response was to withdraw development assistance and simply ship more food aid to Africa. Food aid doesn't help farmers become more productive—and it can create long-term dependency. But in recent years, the dollar value of U.S. food aid to Africa has reached 20 times the dollar value of agricultural development assistance.

The alternative is right in front of us. Foreign assistance to support agricultural improvements has a strong record of success, when undertaken with purpose. In the 1960s, international assistance from the Rockefeller Foundation, the Ford Foundation, and donor governments led by the United States made Asia's original Green Revolution possible. U.S. assistance to India provided critical help in improving agricultural education, launching a successful agricultural extension service, and funding advanced degrees for Indian agricultural specialists at universities in the United States. The U.S. Agency for International Development, with the World Bank, helped finance fertilizer plants and infrastructure projects, including rural roads and irrigation. India could not have done this on its own—the country was on the brink of famine at the time and dangerously dependent on food aid. But instead of suffering a famine in 1975, as some naysayers had predicted, India that year celebrated a final and permanent end to its need for food aid.

Foreign assistance to farming has been a high-payoff investment everywhere, including Africa. The World Bank has documented average rates of return on investments in agricultural research in Africa of 35 percent a year, accompanied by significant reductions in poverty. Some research investments in African agriculture have brought rates of return estimated at 68 percent. Blind to these realities, the United States cut its assistance to agricultural research in Africa 77 percent between 1980 and 2006.

When it comes to Africa's growing hunger, governments in rich countries face a stark choice: They can decide to support a steady new infusion of financial and technical assistance to help local governments and farmers become more productive, or they can take a "worry later" approach and be forced to address hunger problems with increasingly expensive shipments of food aid. Development skeptics and farm modernization critics keep pushing us toward this unappealing second path. It's time for leaders with vision and political courage to push back.

Understanding the Text

1. What is a crisis of values?
2. What do global food prices reveal about food availability and food production?
3. What is food security?

Reflection and Response

4. What does Paarlberg suggest about the future of the politics of food? What are at least two ways to respond to his position? What do you think is the best way? Explain your response.

5. Why do you think Paarlberg titles his essay "Attention Whole Foods Shoppers"? Why does Paarlberg single out this particular demographic? How does he characterize them? What do people who shop at Whole Foods represent for him?

Making Connections

6. Paarlberg criticizes Vandana Shiva's critique ("Soy Imperialism and the Destruction of Local Food Cultures," p. 143) of the Green Revolution. What's at stake in this debate? And for whom? Compare their positions, and describe the differences in their fundamental assumptions.

7. Paarlberg criticizes organic food advocates, arguing that they romanticize preindustrial food and farming. How might he critique Eliot Coleman's position that we need to demand "real food" ("Real Food, Real Farming," p. 236)? Who makes a more compelling case? Explain your response with evidence from the texts.

8. Margaret Mead ("The Changing Significance of Food," p. 166), Prince Charles ("On the Future of Food," p. 222), and Paarlberg all say they want to reduce world hunger. What values and ideas for doing so do they share? Where do they diverge? Whose approach to solving world hunger seems more realistic? Whose approach seems more ethical? Whose approach do you think has the potential to actually succeed? What role should moral considerations play in the solution?

Biotechnology Isn't the Key to Feeding the World

Frances Moore Lappé

Frances Moore Lappé is an environmental activist and author who has written 18 books, including *Diet for a Small Planet* (1971) and *EcoMind: Changing the Way We Think, to Create the World We Want* (2011). The winner of many awards and the recipient of many honorary degrees, Lappé is known for her tireless dedication to democratic social movements and the fight against world hunger. Her extensive writings aim to change the way we think about agriculture, nutrition, and food production and consumption. In this essay, she argues that democracy—not biotechnology—is the key to finding a solution to the problem of world hunger. It is not that we do not have enough food, she explains; it is that we do not have a successful democratic process.

Biotechnology companies and even some scientists argue that we need genetically modified seeds to feed the world and to protect the Earth from chemicals. Their arguments feel eerily familiar.

Thirty years ago, I wrote *Diet for a Small Planet* for one reason. As a researcher buried in the agricultural library at the University of California, Berkeley, I was stunned to learn that the experts—equivalent to the biotech proponents of today—were wrong. They were telling us that we had reached the Earth's limits to feed ourselves, but in fact there was more than enough food for us all.

Hunger, I learned, is the result of economic "givens" that we have created, assumptions and structures that actively generate scarcity from plenty. Today this is more, not less, true.

Throughout history, ruminants had served humans by turning grasses and other "inedibles" into high-grade protein. They were our four-legged protein factories. But once we began feeding livestock from cropland that could grow edible food, we began to convert ruminants into our protein disposals.

Only a small fraction of the nutrients fed to animals return to us in 5 meat; the rest animals use largely for energy or they excrete. Thirty years ago, one-third of the world's grain was going to livestock; today it is closer to one-half. And now we are mastering the same disappearing trick with the world's fish supply. By feeding fish to fish, again, we are reducing the potential supply.

We are shrinking the world's food supply for one reason: The hundreds of millions of people who go hungry cannot create a sufficient "market demand" for the fruits of the Earth. So more and more of it flows into the mouths of livestock, which convert it into what the better-off can afford. Corn becomes filet mignon. Sardines become salmon.

Enter biotechnology. While its supporters claim that seed biotechnology methods are "safe" and "precise," other scientists strongly refute that, as they do claims that biotech crops have actually reduced pesticide use.

But this very debate is in some ways part of the problem. It is a tragic distraction our planet cannot afford.

We are still asking the wrong question. Not only is there already enough food in the world, but as long as we are only talking about food—how best to produce it—we will never end hunger or create the communities and food safety we want.

We must ask instead: How do we build communities in tune with   10 nature's wisdom in which no one, anywhere, has to worry about putting food—safe, healthy food—on the table? Asking this question takes us far beyond food. It takes us to the heart of democracy itself, to whose voices are heard in matters of land, seeds, credit, employment, trade, and food safety.

Hunger is not caused by a scarcity of food but by a scarcity of democracy.

The problem is, this question cannot be addressed by scientists or by any private entity, including even the most high-minded corporation. Only citizens can answer it, through public debate and the resulting accountable institutions that come from our engagement.

Where are the channels for public discussion and where are the accountable polities?

Increasingly, public discussion about food and hunger is framed by advertising by multinational corporations that control not only food processing and distribution but farm inputs and seed patents.

Two years ago, the seven leading biotech companies, including Monsanto, teamed up under the neutral-sounding Council for Biotechnology Information and are spending millions to, for example, blanket us with full-page newspaper ads about biotech's virtues.

Government institutions are becoming ever more beholden to   15 these corporations than to their citizens. Nowhere is this more obvious than in decisions regarding biotechnology—whether it is the approval or patenting of biotech seeds and foods without public input or the rejection of mandatory labeling of biotech foods despite broad public demand for it.

The absence of genuine democratic dialogue and accountable government is a prime reason most people remain blind to the many breakthroughs in the last 30 years that demonstrate we can grow abundant, healthy food and also protect the Earth.

Hunger is not caused by a scarcity of food but by a scarcity of democracy. Thus it can never be solved by new technologies, even if they were to be proved "safe." It can be solved only as citizens build democracies in which government is accountable to them, not to private corporate entities.

Understanding the Text

1. To what is Lappé referring when she writes about "our four-legged protein factories"?

2. What does she mean by "protein disposals"?

3. On what does Lappé blame world hunger? What does she think is the best way to decrease or eliminate it?

Reflection and Response

4. Lappé argues that proponents and opponents of biotechnology are distracted and thus not focused on the right issue. What is the right issue for Lappé, and how does she make and support her position on the issue? Do you agree with her? Why or why not?

5. What connections does Lappé argue exist among food availability, hunger, farming practices, biotechnology, and democracy? How does she describe their current relationships? How would she change them if she could?

Making Connections

6. Identify the other selections in this reader that discuss biotechnology. Try to place them on a continuum. Who agrees with Lappé? Who does not? And to what extent?

7. In what ways does Lappé's argument about the future of food complement the argument made by Prince Charles ("On the Future of Food," p. 222)? In what ways does it complicate Robert Paarlberg's position ("Attention Whole Foods Shoppers," p. 240)? Who makes the best case? Whose evidence seems the strongest? Explain your response using textual references.

Brightening Up the Dark Farming History of the Sunshine State

Natasha Bowens

Natasha Bowens describes herself as a "young, brown, female farmer" who advocates for food sovereignty for people of color and historically oppressed groups. She quit her job at a Washington, D.C., think tank to devote herself to learning about farming and advocating for food justice, especially in communities of color. A writer and photographer, she documents her farming journey and her explorations of agriculture, race, and class on her blog *Brown.Girl.Farming* (browngirlfarming.com). She also wrote the series *The Color of Food* for Grist.org in which she explores farming and food justice in a variety of locations. In this piece, the last installment of *The Color of Food* in 2011, Bowens analyzes the complex relationships among farming, race, and class through her observations of food and labor injustice in Florida.

I eagerly wandered up and down the streets of Miami's Little Haiti looking for any sign of a farm. If you're familiar with Little Haiti—or any neighborhood in Miami, really—you're probably thinking that a farm is the last thing I was going to find. Then I knocked on the door of a typical Miami home, painted a sandy yellow with a red-tiled roof, walked through the sun room and the kitchen and ended up in a not-so-typical backyard. It was like climbing through the wardrobe into Narnia.

Three turkeys were strutting around to Beethoven playing on a stereo, followed by an angry goose with his neck outstretched. Two large emus flashed their long eyelashes as they stared at me, the intruder.

I had been transported to an urban paradise, designed to grow food by mimicking the natural ecologies of south Florida . . . OK, maybe minus the emu.

Earth 'n' Us is a permaculture farm that has been in this North Miami neighborhood for 33 years. When it began, Little Haiti was one of the poorest areas of the city and well known for its crime and drug trade. Now Ray, the owner, is growing and expanding the farm to neighboring lots with help from members of the community.

Ray has already acquired an acre of land behind his house, on 5 which you can find an abundance of fruit trees, like mangoes, avocados, bananas, and papayas, as well as two gardens growing everything from okra to beets and cabbage. The land also supports chickens, ducks, geese, goats, pigs, emus, turkeys, a python, and an iguana.

(It's just not Florida without snakes and lizards.) Tree houses for residents, renters, and WWOOF° volunteers overlook the gardens.

"Ray's been here for so long, and he created this urban paradise just because he's that kind of guy. But now he sees the need to expand and educate the kids in the neighborhood, and to produce more food for the community," Matrice, a WWOOF volunteer who's been studying permaculture at Earth 'n' Us for six months, told me. (Ray and Matrice wished to be known by first name only.)

Earth 'n' Us hosts workshops on various topics including permaculture design and home brewing, as well as movie nights and tours for the local kids. Its neighbor, Community Food Works, also offers courses on beekeeping and alternative energy solutions and runs a permaculture certificate program.

'Ponics Scheme

About 30 minutes north, another urban grower is trying to offer healthy food for the community and provide courses on how people can grow their own food using hydroponics.

Jessica Padron started The Urban Farmer when she had her daughter Bella. "I wasn't happy about the idea of not knowing for sure if our food was safe," she told me. "So I researched a way to grow our own food that would require little maintenance and be easy for me as a working mom."

The hydroponics farm is built on an industrial site in Pompano 10
Beach that was formerly an auto shop. Padron and her partners had to remove 300 [cubic] yards of material out of the site to begin constructing the farm. They chose an outdoor hydroponics system because the soil at the site was so contaminated.

The system includes towers tiered with polystyrene containers that hold coconut husks for the plants to grow in. All that's needed is a daily feed of water and a 16-nutrient solution, and they are cranking out over 10,000 plants. While I don't agree with the Styrofoam containers or the cost of starting a hydroponics system (not really practical for your average food-desert resident), I was impressed with the amount of food being produced right there in an old auto yard in South Florida.

WWOOF: World Wide Opportunities on Organic Farms; a nonprofit organization that links organic farms with potential volunteers and works to support the organic food movement worldwide.

Legacy of Injustice

It's actually fitting that the end of my farming and food justice journey for this season has brought me to Florida. It is where I grew up and is home to my family, and it's also home to many farmers of color who have emigrated here from the Caribbean and Central and South America.

Neighborhoods like Little Haiti and Little Havana in Miami are home to many such immigrants, but the rural areas that make up the majority of the state have also drawn large populations of Haitian and Latino immigrants with the promise of work.

The only problem is that some of the employers in these agricultural areas of Florida apparently think they're the Spanish colonizers of 1565 . . . meaning slavery is OK in their book. Over the past decade, 12-plus employers in the state of Florida have been federally prosecuted for the enslavement of over 1,000 farmworkers.

Yes, I said enslavement. Workers have been chained and held captive in produce trucks, beaten, and shot, among other atrocities that are reminiscent of this nation's past. 15

> The reality is that the issues within our food system are rooted in historical racial and economic injustice.

Immokalee, Florida, once home to the Calusa and Seminole Native American nations, is now the largest farmworker community in the state. Immokalee has become infamous for the violation of human rights taking place on the tomato fields in the area, and the Coalition of Immokalee Workers has fought hard and in some cases successfully for improved wages and working conditions for the tomato pickers. But farmworkers here in Florida, and around the world, have been suffering from these injustices for years, and although some effort has gone into changing that, we still have a long way to go. The Coalition of Immokalee Workers continues to fight for the rights of its majority Latino, Haitian, and Mayan Indian farmworkers, and continues to investigate slavery in the fields today.

I just wonder if we will ever get past such blatant disregard for human rights as seen in Immokalee and erase the negative legacy that agriculture has seared into our minds for people of color.

While this trip has opened my eyes to some incredible and inspiring urban farming and food-justice projects being led by brown folks in under-served communities, the reality is that the issues within our food system are rooted in historical racial and economic injustice.

And unless we step together out of the shadow of denial and into the brutal light of honesty, we will only be repeating those patterns, and standing in the way of a truly just and healthy food revolution.

Understanding the Text

1. What is a permaculture farm?
2. What is a hydroponics farm?
3. What is a food desert?

Reflection and Response

4. One of Bowens's goals is to put farmers of color and food activists of color on the map. Why is this goal important to her? What role or roles might writing play in helping her achieve it?
5. According to Bowens, how does the legacy of racial and economic injustice affect the food system in the United States? What kinds of evidence does she give to support her assertions?
6. What would be required for us to step "out of the shadow of denial and into the brutal light of honesty" (para. 19)? Who would have to do what?

Making Connections

7. What concerns about worker rights does Bowens raise? Compare them to the concerns raised by Sally Kohn ("Do Foodies Care about Workers?" p. 214). What other authors in this reader might share their belief in the need for worker justice? Support your response with specific textual references.
8. Frances Moore Lappé argues that global hunger problems are "not caused by a scarcity of food but by a scarcity of democracy" ("Biotechnology Isn't the Key to Feeding the World," p. 249). What role does Bowens see for democracy in the fight for food justice? What values or beliefs do Lappé and Bowens share? What role does the political process play in their respective causes? What relationship do you think should exist between the future of food and the political process?

Chicago: The Vertical Farm

Jennifer Cockrall-King

Jennifer Cockrall-King is an award-winning Canadian journalist whose writings have appeared in many prominent Canadian and U.S. publications. She writes the food blog foodgirl.ca; she cowrote and copublished the cooking journal *The Edible Prairie Journal*; and she runs the annual Okanagan Food & Wine Writers Workshop. In *Food and the City* (2012), her first book, she explores various urban agriculture projects and movements across the globe and examines the role of urban agriculture in relation to food security and the global, industrial food system. The chapter included here documents the complexities and realities of a vertical farming project in Chicago.

> The line of the buildings stood clear-cut and black against the sky; here and there out of the mass rose the great chimneys, with the river of smoke streaming away to the end of the world.
>
> —UPTON SINCLAIR, *THE JUNGLE* (1906)

Dickson Despommier's *The Vertical Farm: Feeding the World in the 21st Century* arrived in late 2010 to as much promotion and anticipation as a book gets these days.[1] Well before the book's publication, Despommier appeared as a guest on the *Colbert Report*, the culturally influential satirical news program on U.S. specialty channel Comedy Central. Musician and activist Sting blurbed the book's cover. Majora Carter, a MacArthur "genius" fellow, contributed the foreword. And the *Economist* appointed Despommier "the father of vertical farming" in its magazine pages. Articles about vertical farming were seemingly everywhere at once. According to the media, the year 2010 was the year of the vertical farm—essentially a skyscraper layered with pigs, fish, arugula, tomatoes, and lettuce. There was just one problem. No one had yet built one.

Sure, there were a number of architectural renderings on paper just waiting for a visionary developer or a wealthy billionaire looking for a legacy project. Despommier's book features images of the 30-story verdant spiraling staircase that American architect Blake Kurasek envisioned as his 2008 graduate thesis project at the University of Illinois at Urbana-Champaign.[2] It also includes the drawing for the Dragonfly vertical farm concept, an elaborate 132-floor wing-shaped "metabolic farm for urban agriculture" designed for the New York City skyline by Belgian architect Vincent Callebaut.[3] These visions were (and still are) undeniably intellectually interesting and aesthetically impressive, as are those of Despommier and fellow professor Eric Ellingsen's own glass pyramidal farm.[4] Ellingsen's work was designed with Abu Dhabi in mind, as it is likely the only city with the money to build such structures for food production. These vertical farms, however, would likely come with a $100 million price tag or more—perhaps just one of the reasons they remain more science fiction than food-growing reality.

A few years ago, not many outside academia had heard the term "vertical farm," but the concept has been around since the Hanging Gardens of Babylon, with its mythical living walls of cascading greenery. With traditional farming being so land-, water-, labor-, and fuel-intensive, it was a logical leap to transform the two-dimensional nature of farming by shrinking its footprint radically and adding a third dimension: height. A farm built as a high-rise, with different crops or livestock layered on every floor, could conceivably allow large-scale food production right into the middle of any space-starved urban setting.

> A farm built as a high-rise, with different crops or livestock layered on every floor, could conceivably allow large-scale food production right into the middle of any space-starved urban setting.

The vertical farming school of thought has led to some provocative designs. MVRDV, a Dutch design firm, proposed Pig City in 2001, an open-air 40-story farm that would house 15 million pigs and produce enough organic pork for half a million people and endless amounts of manure for biogas.[5] It earned the vertical farm an early nickname of "sky-scraper." Other open-air vertical-farming concepts emerged soon after on architects' drawing boards in Toronto, Vancouver, Paris, and Chicago, but none were actually built.

The most recent wave of vertical-farming ideas is especially focused on "closed-loop systems." (Think a traditional mixed farm, sliced into layers, stacked vertically, and hermetically sealed under glass.) Livestock waste is intensively recycled as plant fertilizer; freshwater fish grow in tanks and produce nutrient-rich water for salad crops; water loss due to evaporation is minimized; and the whims of Mother Nature no longer interrupt the 24/7, 365-day-a-year indoor growing system. Hungry deer, grasshoppers, and other pests wouldn't devastate crops. Climate wouldn't matter—nor would climate change, droughts, or mid-crop hailstorms.

For some, this will be the only way to feed our growing cities in scenarios of nine billion people living in the megacities of the very near future. For others, it's putting the cart before the horse. Vertical-farm designers and architects talk about aeroponics (soilless growing where roots are merely misted with nutrient-dense water), hydroponics (growing plants in nutrient-rich water but without the need for soil), and aquaponics (indoor fish farming tied in with hydroponic techniques to form a self-cleansing and self-fertilizing water-recycling loop) as if we've perfected these techniques. We've been experimenting with them on rather small scales, but large-scale farming is another matter. The technology isn't there yet. Then again, Leonardo da Vinci drew models for helicopters in the fifteenth century.

What will push the technology forward? Maybe a combination of factors that are currently upon us: Climate change, rapid urbanization, the rise in fuel costs of conventional farming and transportation, and population growth may finally stretch our current food resources to the limits.

Time will tell if these models, or versions of them, will become viable as the technology catches up to the visions of the future of urban farming. For that to happen, however, a lot of ground will have to be covered. Specifically, there will have to be a significant leap in construction and indoor growing technology, especially for the fanciful vertical-farm skyscrapers in Despommier's book to leap from page into being.

Just when I thought the vertical farm was decades away from becoming a reality and that we'd continue to imagine elaborate futuristic scenarios that seemed to completely ignore that agriculture is a marginal business, I learned of Chicago industrial developer John Edel and the new urban reuse project he's calling The Plant. It lacked the ego-driven designs of the other vertical farms that were languishing on paper, and its modesty and practicality made the idea of an indoor multistory farm seem feasible. It was enough to make me want to take a look for myself. After all, if Edel could accomplish even a modest version of a vertical farm, it would be urban-agriculture history in the making. I made plans to visit Chicago to see The Plant in its early stages of becoming the world's first, albeit four-story, vertical farm.[6]

The Plant, Chicago

As Blake Davis took off his dust mask and slapped puffs of concrete 10 off his hands, he joked, "Clearly, as you can see, I'm a college professor."[7] Davis, a burly Chicagoan with a crew cut and a constant grin, teaches urban agriculture at the Illinois Institute of Technology. The day I met him, however, he was putting some skills to use from his preprofessorial days. His worn Carhartt work jacket and overalls were covered in fine concrete dust from jackhammering concrete floors rotten with moisture. By afternoon, he'd be wielding a plasma torch— like a welding torch, but it cuts through stainless steel, slicing panels of it out of meat smokers for food-safe countertops and other novel reuses. Chicago had "literally, millions of square feet" of vacant, often abandoned, industrial space "right in the city," Davis said. "It costs too much to tear down."

Davis was just one of several members of Edel's team of highly skilled, sustainability-minded volunteers determined to strip the former 1925-built, 93,500-square-foot (8,700-square-meter) meatpacking plant back to its outer red-brick shell and put as much of the recycled materials back into use to create a working model for a vertical farm.

While other entrepreneurs might be tight-lipped about their prototype projects—vertical farms are the current holy grail of urban agriculture, and there will likely be significant amounts of money for those who can deliver workable models—Edel instead cleared a few hours to show me around his "fixer-upper." He let me roam at will to chat with people like Davis, Alex Poltorak (another volunteer with engineering credentials), and Audrey Thibault (an industrial designer who, as her jobs kept leaving for China, figured that she "just wanted to be part of something awesome" like The Plant).[8]

It's an experiment in motion with two rather ambitious purposes. If Edel and his team can figure out the right models and mix of elements that actually work synergistically,° they will have built a viable physical and economic model for a vertical farm. Edel also intends that The Plant will serve as an open-source laboratory and catalyst for industrial reuse in a city that has no shortage of ready-built shells just waiting for a reason to remain standing.

Chicago's Stockyards

In 1878, Gustavus Swift built the first refrigerated railcar, which quickly allowed the meatpacking industry to concentrate in Chicago, scale up to incredible efficiencies, and go on to dominate the national market. By the turn of the 1900s, the Union Stockyards covered 435 acres (176 hectares) and became known as "the hog butcher to the world." If that was a slight exaggeration, it was at least the butcher that fed America. Eighty-two percent of the meat consumed in the

synergistically: In a cooperative, mutually beneficial way.

United States at the time came from the Union Stockyards. It achieved huge efficiencies of scale that had never been attempted in livestock agriculture before. Historic photos show aerial views of the 40 acres (16 hectares) of cattle and hog pens; what would now be referred to as a Concentrated Animal Feedlot Operation (CAFO).

The industrialized meat trade came with significant hidden costs 15 then as it does now. The poverty, squalor, and brutal working (and living) conditions experienced by workers in the meatpacking industry were immortalized in Upton Sinclair's 1906 novel *The Jungle.* Waves of cheap, nonunionized immigrant and "underclass" labor allowed for the innovation of assembly-line slaughtering, butchering, and processing of the carcasses.[9]

The Back of the Yards neighborhood came to life as a bedroom community, if you will, for the waves of immigrants who cut and packed meat, and for the various businesses—tanneries, soap manufacturers, and instrument-string makers, for example—that surrounded the meatpacking industry on the south and west boundary of the Union Stockyards. By the 1950s, however, meatpacking was headed west, closer to the herds and where land was cheaper. The stockyards officially closed in 1971, and the only relic from that era is a giant limestone entrance arch. Back of the Yards transitioned somewhat into an industrial park. But over the years, the massive infrastructure had a dwindling reason to exist. And when industry leaves, as it did in this part of Chicago, infrastructure is left to crumble and decay. The scale of the surplus in Chicago has generally led to blight.

Much of what I saw as I left Chicago's vibrant skyscrapers and downtown core known as the Loop and made my way to the city's historic stockyards and Back of the Yards' district was heading in the direction of decay and blight. There were too many gaps in the residential streets where houses should otherwise be standing together. There were too many rusted padlocks on gates and chain-link fences encircling trucking depots, warehouses, and factories of indeterminate purposes. The businesses that remained were the signposts of a neighborhood in decline: fast-food joints, liquor stores, and convenience stores with bars on the windows.

The red-brick Peer Foods building, built in 1925 and added to over the years, was a holdout; the family-owned specialty smoked- and cured-meat company had stayed in business in the Back of the Yards until 2007.

At the time, Edel was in negotiations with the city to buy a six-hundred-thousand-square-foot World War I armory turned vacant

Chicago Board of Education building. Faced with a $12 million demolition price tag, the city seemed prepared to sell it for $1.[10]

Edel already had a bit of local reputation for industrial building 20 rehab. He had left a lucrative broadcast television design job that involved too much computer-assisted drawing and modeling to instead scratch an itch for preserving historic buildings by finding low-cost creative uses for them and reusing the materials that were simply lying around inside most of them.

In 2002, he bought a 1910 paint factory that had been officially unoccupied since the 1960s and had since become a derelict, bike-gang-ridden building with shot-out windows. (The building, in Edel's words, had been colonized by "lots of tough guys" with names like Googs, Mack, Santa Claus, the Boob, and Cowboy. There were "lots of guns, lots of knives," involved in the "informal economy" that had taken over the building.) Edel completely reformed the 24,000-square-foot (2,230-square-meter) building, putting his industrial design training, a tremendous amount of personal and volunteer sweat equity, and innate scavenger mentality into play. Useful industrial machines, like a giant, old air compressor that was left behind, were put back into service to run the air chisels used to poke holes in brick walls and the jackhammer used to remove unwanted concrete. Scrap sheet metal was refashioned to create such items as a new entrance awning, and former machine-tool parts and pipes found lying around became an art-school-esque stairway banister. Edel planted a living green roof with thousands of heat- and drought-tolerant sedum (a succulent plant that needs little irrigation) to mitigate storm water runoff and installed cisterns to catch rainwater for reuse in the building. (Seen from above, or on Google Earth, the thousands of sedum create a red-and-green pattern of Edel's daughter's smiling face.)

Edel did it all on a shoestring budget, and 95 percent of the existing derelict structure was repurposed. The building is now home to Bubbly Dynamics, though its official name is the Chicago Sustainable Manufacturing Center.[11] Bubbly Dynamics now runs at 100 percent occupancy and is a magnet for the niche boutique manufacturing and sustainable technologies entrepreneurs in Chicago. It is home to 35 permanent salaried jobs, which include a co-op of five custom-bicycle-frame builders, a fabric-print-screening outfit, and a tutoring program for at-risk children. It's full and extremely efficient, and it turns a profit for Edel, the landlord. It was all the proof he needed to confirm his gut feeling that no building is so derelict that it can't be saved and made profitable.

After the success of Bubbly Dynamics, Edel's next idea was to turn another hopeless case of a building into a zero-waste organic food-producing building in Chicago. He thought he'd found it with the Board of Education building. Edel wanted to create a net-zero building that combined some select food-manufacturing processes with the growing of food.

"Everybody in city government, except one alderman, was in support of it. Instead, he wanted to tear down the 'orange-rated' historical building we were trying to acquire and have a Walmart. That was *his* dream," Edel recounted.[12] (Orange-rated is a Chicago urban-planning term that means that the building was one step below landmark protection status.)

One alderman's Walmart dream was enough to stall the process 25 for two years, but during that time, Edel continued to plan an ambitious new life for the 600,000-square-foot (55,741-square-meter) space, using his team and networks of like-minded, hands-on experts who had gravitated to Edel and Bubbly Dynamics. That's when and how Davis fell into Edel's orbit. Davis was looking for urban-agriculture projects for his students, and Edel's business models included lots of volunteer hours and "open-source expertise." While Edel worked on acquiring space, Davis and his students began working on a symbiotic aquaponics/hydroponics system integrating fish production with a plant-growing system in the basement of Bubbly Dynamics.

Though the one-dollar price tag of the Board of Education building was attractive, the negotiations with the city were dragging on. Edel decided that ultimately it wasn't worth the wait, given all the existing inventory of available buildings in Chicago. He found a former meat slaughtering, smoking, and processing plant that was in relatively good shape. It had been built in 1925 but over the years had been upgraded and expanded. And it had sat empty for only four years, so there hadn't been time for too much to deteriorate. Most importantly, it was built for food production, which would save Edel an enormous amount of time and money because it was already up to code for many food-related commercial purposes.

Edel closed on the old Peer Foods Building on July 1, 2010, for $5.50 per square foot. What sounds like a real estate bargain, however, amounted to a $525,000 purchase that would test even Edel's resourcefulness. But Edel seems just as capable of attracting paying tenants as he is overqualified volunteers. There's already a list of entrepreneurs who have signed up for space at The Plant, which will move businesses in as its space is completed.

Touring The Plant

I wasn't prepared for how shockingly cold (and dark) it would be in-side The Plant on the early January day I had arranged to visit.[13] It certainly wasn't the natural-light-flooded ethereal skyscraper that the academic vertical-farming camp was known for; it wasn't even the conventional greenhouse structure one associates with a covered growing space. There were high ceilings, which on that particular day actually seemed to trap the chill, making it a few degrees cooler on the inside than it was outdoors.

I had somewhat naively assumed that Edel would have to "work around" the lack of natural light, that it was a problem to be solved. Instead, Edel explained that the thick brick walls and lack of win-dows was a major benefit of The Plant. What currently functioned as windows—antique glass block—would, however, have to be replaced. ("Glass block neither lets light in, nor does it keep heat in or out," said Edel. As windows, they were useless.) One of the few outside pur-chases that the building would get was some new windows with high-efficiency glass.

However, high-efficiency glass is very limiting as well, explained Edel, holding up a sample of a high-efficiency window product he had been considering. "See how dark the glass is?" It was a smoky-gray color. High-efficiency glass, by its very nature, blocks those parts of the light spectrum that plants need for growing. And clear glass, which lets more of the light spectrum pass through, allows too much heat transfer. Edel then explained the problem of light units in north-ern latitudes during the Chicago winter. "In the upper Midwest on a day like today," he snorted, "you'll get no usable light. In an ideal [summer] day, you might get light penetration of about 15 feet.

"That means you'll be growing under artificial lights anyway. And the last thing you want is huge amounts of glass for that heat energy to escape through." Any gains made by electrical savings on using natural light would be negated or completely irrelevant compared to the heating costs escaping out through glass. Besides, a well-insulated brick building such as The Plant will be very effective at trapping heat inside in the winter (the heat from the lights can go a long way toward heating a building if it's well enough insulated, Edel believes) and keeping it cooler in the summer. Heat, as I would learn that day, is as valuable an asset in an ultra-efficient vertical farm in a cold cli-mate as anything else.

But the great advantage, Edel explained, to the cavernous nature of the building is that "you can control the time of day." This gives

Edel the ability to "grow at night" when electricity costs are a fraction of what they are during the day when the demand is high. And plants need a period of darkness just like they need a period of light, so you can create night during the day, when energy costs are high. Edel figures he can cut the energy expenses in half by growing during nonpeak hours.

The other advantage, continued Edel, is that "you can create different time zones in various parts of the indoor system. You can flatten your nominal load so that you don't have demand spikes." Electrical utility companies like to charge you at the rate when you are at your peak daily energy consumption rate. By "moving the time of day around" between a few growing zones, again, you can achieve a "flatter," more consistent pattern of consumption and therefore save on utilities. Flattening the demand for electrical consumption will play a huge role in regulating the metabolism of the building as the building starts to produce its own electrical power and heating when the anaerobic digester is built and takes over the energy needs of the tenants and the food-growing spaces.

The one concession Edel has made to a tiny bit of inefficiency will be the "growing lobby." Large windows along the front of the building will let in lots of natural light. "We'll have things like hops and lavender, and probably the finishing tanks for the tilapia where the water is really clean and the fish look pretty."

Heat and light were not the only valuable commodities in the building's equation; oxygen and carbon dioxide also needed to be considered. Nathan Wyse, a fresh-faced twenty-something, came by The Plant that day to talk to Edel. Wyse was a potential tenant who was looking to take his Thrive label of kombucha—a fermented medicinal tea hitting the lucrative mainstream specialty-beverage market these days—to the next business level.

The yeasts used to ferment the sugars in kombucha require oxygen and produce excess carbon dioxide in the fermentation process. Growing plants, handily, love carbon dioxide. According to Edel, plants "do quite well on six times the normal atmospheric carbon dioxide." Wyse asked if Edel could think about how these two gases could be exchanged efficiently between the brewing space and the growing spaces at The Plant.[14] If they could be exchanged, Wyse's aeration of his batches of kombucha would be greatly enhanced. Edel suggested that they could likely pipe excess carbon dioxide into growing areas, while drawing oxygen out (one being a heavier gas than the other) to recirculate it between the kombucha fermentation beds and the growing beds.

"So you've already thought about this?" Wyse asked.

"I just did," said Edel, matter-of-factly.

"OK, well, I'd gladly exchange carbon dioxide for oxygen for better fermentation."

I felt like I'd stepped into the future, where resources like oxygen 40 and carbon dioxide are valued on an open-market trading system. Clearly, a closed-loop system, such as a vertical farm, as Edel conceived it, was so much more than providing artificial light to a few plants and recycling fish waste as plant fertilizer. It was about striking a delicate balance in the building to create a zero-waste ecosystem where "the only thing that will go out is food."

As we climbed the stairs to the second floor, the unmistakable greasy aroma of bacon wrapped itself around me. "The smokers were in use twenty-four-seven right up until the day Peer Foods moved out," confirmed Edel.

Some of the smokers were new: huge stainless steel tanks with what looked like ships' portholes at about five feet high. The stainless steel was valuable, and Edel and crew had already started to hack it into panels for food-grade countertops and tables. Other panels would become the new bathroom stalls.

There were also older cavernous smokers that smelled like they had been used continuously for a century, which was likely not far off. Smoke stains had left huge black licks up the beautiful 1920s glazed-tile walls. I remarked that it was a shame to think that buildings like this were decaying and being torn down due to a lack of knowledge of how to resuscitate existing construction. And yet, city aldermen had dreams of demolition and replacement with Walmarts.

"Building a new building is a really inefficient thing to do!" Edel fired back. "Plants don't care about columns, or taking a freight elevator to get out to a market. Really an existing structure is the best possible situation."[15]

The stainless steel smoke tanks were in the area designated to be the 45 bakery, one of the food-based business incubator areas. Start-ups will be able to rent the space by the hour and still be in a completely 2,000-square-foot (185-square-meter) food-grade shared commercial kitchen, a major economic hurdle for most people getting into the food-production business, given the overhead on commercial space. Tenants can also rent garden plots on the rooftop garden and source other items, like mushrooms, that will be grown in other parts of the building. "There'll be a wood-fired oven in here," enthused Edel. The heat from the bakery will be important to heat the other parts of the building. Because of the original function of the building as a food facility, the floors undulate every few feet where floor drains exist. "How expensive would that have been to put in?"

"All of these rooms were great forests of electrical wires, pipes, and everything else. There was meat-cutting equipment everywhere. We are keeping bits of it and reusing almost everything. The oldest wiring is only 15 years old, fortunately." There was even a beauty to the age-blackened iron rails formerly used to move the carcasses along from one worker to the next. Edel was planning to keep them suspended from the timber supports as a historical memento of the building's past.

"This is the one mess I'm going to keep because it's so out of control," he laughed, pointing toward one particularly absurd tangle of meters, pipes, wiring, gauges, and switches. Edel quipped that this is where his art school education will come into play. A floor-to-ceiling glass wall will be installed and dramatic lighting will be focused on the "industrial found art"—a ready-made point of interest that will be a central art piece on the third floor, visible from the conference room and the incubator office space that will be rented out to small businesses that will use The Plant's commercial baking, brewing, and food-preparation facilities.

The New Chicago Brewing Company has signed on to be a major keystone tenant, and there will even be a homebrew co-op that operates out of The Plant. Not only will brewing produce a lot of heat; it will supply vast amounts of spent brewing mash to compost for the gardens and greenhouse or for the biodigester.

We descended into a dark, cavernous basement for the grand finale. We cautiously picked our way around scrap metal, spools of wiring, and over curbs that were scheduled to be sledge-hammered like we were climbing through the innards of a submarine. Edel pointed out rooms that would soon be filled with mushroom beds. He had secured a former military fighter jet engine that would be put into use for electrical generation once the biodigester was built.

Edel yanked on a solid steel door, and we passed from the subma- 50 rine scenario into a laboratory-white immense room bathed in a fuchsia light on one side, with gurgling vats of tilapia-filled water on the other. The Plant Vertical Farm wasn't just demolition and future scenarios; there was actual food growing in test systems in this basement room.

"This is Growing System Number One," said Edel as we walked toward the four square plastic 275-gallon (1,000-liter) tubs that were the fish tanks. This was the project that Davis's students were working on, tweaking and perfecting, so that it could be implemented on a larger scale when The Plant ramped up its food ecosystem.

Slivers of fingerling tilapia flashed around the tank, and as soon as they saw us looming over, they made for the surface. "They would eat twenty-four hours a day," said Edel, as the fish poked at the water's surface. There were two more tanks attached to this chain of plastic vats and white plastic PVC pipes, and the nearby pump was noisily forcing water around through the tanks. Sixty market-weight tilapia swirled in the final tank. "You want to control how much you feed them or they'll get too big, too fast. And you also have to balance the amount of food with the amount of plants you are growing." Edel explained that the fish were "on a diet" until they got more plants into the system.

The water from the fish pens flowed into another water-filled tank with run-of-the-mill hardware-store black plastic garden netting for filtering. Edel explained that the netting caused "the richer stuff" to fall to the bottom of the filter tank. When The Plant's biodigester is ready, this solid fish waste will be used to produce methane gas, which will be turned back into heat and electrical energy.

The next tank after the netting had a black plastic honeycomb-like panel—"a $400 mistake," whined Edel. The tank is simply a place to harbor the bacteria that turns the ammonia of the fish waste into the nitrites and nitrates (the nitrogen compounds) that make fantastic plant fertilizer. Instead of the special, expensive plastic comb, Edel proposed that "rocks or old chopped-up plastic bottles" would do just as good a job for a fraction of the price.

The pump then sent the water from the filters into shallow pans 55 where foam rafts studded with tiny plant plugs floated on clear but nitrogen-rich water. Each hole in the raft contained a small plastic basket filled with coconut husk to stabilize the roots of each little seedling of arugula, red lettuce, or whatever the team wants to grow. The coconut husk fiber is nearly indestructible yet is porous enough to not restrict the rooting systems that dangle through the gaps in the baskets and into the water. As the plants take up the nitrogen, they effectively clean the water—as they do in ecosystems in nature—allowing the water to be recycled back into the fish tanks for the waste-fertilizer loop to begin again.

The plants looked very happy and healthy bathed in the fuchsia light of the state-of-the-art LED grow lights. "Plants can't see green," Edel explained, so you only need the red and blue lights. Edel, Davis, and students are testing the LED lights, as they are relative newcomers to the market; but if they work, they'll be much more efficient than other grow lights commonly used. A computer engineer is working out the open-source software and hardware that will move the lights along a variable-height track suspended above the seedlings. The lights move slowly from one end of the beds to the other "so they don't end up growing like this," explained Edel, listing sharply to one side.

I finally asked the big question that seems to be a sticking point where new ideas tend to hit the proverbial brick wall of city bylaws. "And you're allowed to do all of this?"

Overall, the city has just let Edel and company continue without too much concern. The brewing permit was a hassle, but they got it. "The only other resistance we'd had is from the zoning department that didn't like the idea of fish and aquaculture," said Edel. "Not for any *good* reason, because under the same zoning, you can crush cars, smelt iron, and slaughter cattle. But raising organic fish for some reason is bad. Go figure."

The fish were not yet a particular concern anyhow, as they were part of Davis's students' course work. They were working out the details of this aquaponics-agricultural loop as part of the student curriculum, which involved the microgreens, sprouts, and mushrooms that would soon be tested out at The Plant.

Part of this course work also included marketing plans and economic feasibility studies by students at the Illinois Institute of Technology. When I asked Davis how strong the demand was in Chicago for locally grown food, he replied that even drawing from a radius of 500 miles around the city, there aren't enough farms for the markets and the demand that already exists. And being right in the city will be a huge advantage for restaurants willing to pay a premium for ultra-fresh product. "We're about the only people who can say, 'We'll pick this for you at nine a.m., have it to you by ten, and you can serve it for lunch.'"[16]

The other factor that favors the viability of vertical farming in the city, according to Davis, is that Chicago's public school system now sets aside 20 percent of its school lunch budget for local foods. "Even keeping in mind that they don't actually go to school in the summer when most of the food is produced, it still creates opportunity for us."

Food wholesale produce suppliers have also told Davis that they'll take everything The Plant can produce. So whether it is Chicago's sustainable and premium restaurants willing to pay top dollar for The Plant's fresh, local, organic food, or local produce wholesalers, or the Chicago Public School System (though clearly the school board wouldn't be able to out-compete the other two on price), finding markets for the food will be the easy part.

In Davis's opinion, however, Edel's plan of having manufacturing tenants subsidize the food-growing spaces was a key element to turning The Plant into reality while the other more ambitious "food-only" skyscrapers are lingering on paper at this point. "We've been to almost every other urban agriculture site within 500 miles, and we noticed that almost all of them are being run on job-training grants from foundations. We thought that this was probably not a good way to run this. That's why I really jumped on to this project. It's technically interesting, but it has a commitment to creating a business model that can be replicated. The problem with social services and 40-story urban farms is that you train a bunch of people, but there are no businesses out there to hire them."[17]

When I remarked that it's somewhat surprising that the world's first vertical farm won't be nestled in among skyscrapers in uptown Manhattan, or in the anything-is-possible cities like Shanghai and Dubai; that it will happen on a very modest scale, on a very modest budget, in Chicago, Davis just smiled. "That's kind of the tension between New York and the Midwest. All the actual urban agriculture is happening within 500 miles of Chicago, and all the press is about these 40-story buildings."

"When Sam Walton [founder of Walmart] started, he didn't try to build a 400,000-square-foot superstore. He took an old Kresge's and said, 'I'm going to figure out this business model in this relatively small space. If it's successful, I'll make another one.' And at some point, you can afford to build a single-purpose building for a Walmart. I think if you get good at urban agriculture, and have a few technological breakthroughs, at some point you'll need an architect to design an 80-story urban farm. Maybe your business model will be sound to do that. It's just a bit premature right now."

I asked if the city was therefore giving The Plant any breaks or help in any way. "They're not subsidizing it," answered Davis. "But the most important thing in Chicago is that they're letting us do it."

Edel's concept of industrial reuse seems like a reasonable solution to the very sticky wicket that has so far kept urban vertical farms confined to academic presentations and scrolls of architectural plans. And, as Edel put it, "You've got to sell a lot of rutabagas to pay for a $100 million building." Edel's ability to reinvigorate unwanted commercial space, make it beautiful, and, perhaps most importantly, make it productive and profitable once again, might just be a catalyst that will serve post-industrial Chicago well. And it might be vertical farming's Sputnik moment, launching a vertical-farm race, so to speak, that will leave those ego-driven skyscrapers on the drawing board for the time being.

Notes

1. Dickson Despommier, *The Vertical Farm: Feeding the World in the 21st Century* (New York: Thomas Dunne Books, 2010).
2. Blake Kurasek's Living Skyscraper can be viewed at http://blakekurasek.com /thelivingskyscraper.html.
3. Vincent Callebaut's Dragonfly vertical farm can be viewed at http://vincent.call ebaut.org/page1-img-dragonfly.html.
4. Despommier and Ellingsen's pyramidal vertical farm can be viewed at http:// www.verticalfarm.com/designs?folder=b9aa20a4-9c6a-4983-b3ad-390c4f1fa562.
5. MVRDV's website is at http://www.mvrdv.nl.
6. The Plant's website is at http://www.plantchicago.com/.
7. Blake Davis (adjunct professor of urban agriculture at Illinois Institute of Technology), personal interview with the author, The Plant, Chicago, Illinois, January 29, 2011.
8. Personal interviews were conducted on-site at The Plant with John Edel (owner/ developer/director, The Plant), Blake Davis (adjunct professor of urban agriculture, IIT), Alex Poltorak (volunteer, The Plant), and Audrey Thibault (volunteer, The Plant), Chicago, Illinois, January 29, 2011.
9. I found several sources that reference the influence of the Chicago Stockyard's "disassembly line" on Henry Ford's idea for the automobile assembly line. He saw the efficiencies gained by giving one worker one specific task and then moving the carcasses on to the next worker. Ford reversed the process to put cars together, but the idea of worker specialization was born on the blood-soaked floors of stockyard slaughterhouses. One source, among many online, that states this is http://www.pbs.org/wgbh/amex/chicago/peopleevents/p_armour.html.
10. The backstory of how John Edel came to purchase the Peer Foods building and information on The Plant came from a personal interview with John Edel, January 29, 2011.
11. Bubbly Dynamics draws its nickname from nearby Bubbly Creek, a waterway named during the days of the stockyards and the attendant business that sprung up around the century-long livestock and slaughter industry in Chicago, where boiled waste and decaying matter made the creek appear to bubble.
12. John Edel, personal interview with the author, The Plant, Chicago, Illinois, January 29, 2011.
13. Ibid.
14. John Edel and Nathan Wyse in conversation with the author, The Plant, Chicago, Illinois, January 29, 2011.
15. John Edel, personal interview with the author, The Plant, Chicago, Illinois, January 29, 2011.
16. Blake Davis, in-person interview with the author, The Plant, Chicago, Illinois, January 29, 2011.
17. Ibid.

Understanding the Text

1. What is urban agriculture?
2. What is a vertical farm?
3. How is a vertical farm different from a traditional mixed farm?

4. What are some of the reasons Cockrall-King and those she interviews give for why this project is becoming a reality in Chicago?

Reflection and Response

5. What stress factors on our current food system might help make vertical farming a reality, according to Cockrall-King? Does she make a good case?

6. Why do you think Cockrall-King compares theoretically attractive vertical farming visions to Leonardo da Vinci's fifteenth-century drawings of models for helicopters? How realistic is the comparison? What does the comparison imply about vertical farming?

Making Connections

7. Compare the vertical farm described by Cockrall-King to other depictions of farms in this collection. (Refer to the essays by Barbara Kingsolver ["You Can't Run Away on Harvest Day," p. 184], Blake Hurst ["The Omnivore's Delusion," p. 204], and Natasha Bowens ["Brightening Up the Dark Farming History of the Sunshine State," p. 252], for instance.) What essential features do they share? What important differences do you notice? How do these depictions of farms compare to your conception and/or knowledge of a "typical" farm? Explain your answers with textual evidence.

8. What role might urban agriculture play in the future of food? How realistic is the claim that urban agriculture is the beginning of a new food revolution? Select several authors to help support your position on the place of urban agriculture—in its various forms—in the future of food.

Acknowledgments (*continued from page iv*)

Text Credits

Donald L. Barlett and James B. Steele. Excerpts from "Monsanto's Harvest of Fear" by Donald L. Barlett and James B. Steele, originally published in *Vanity Fair*. Copyright © 2008 by Donald L. Barlett and James B. Steele. Used by permission of The Wylie Agency LLC.

Wendell Berry. "The Pleasures of Eating" from *What Are People For?: Essays* by Wendell Berry. Copyright © 2010 Wendell Berry. Reprinted by permission of Counterpoint.

David Biello. "Will Organic Food Fail to Feed the World?" from *Scientific American*, April 25, 2012. Reproduced with permission. Copyright © 2012 Scientific American, a division of Nature America, Inc. All rights reserved.

Natasha Bowens. "Brightening Up the Dark Farming History of the Sunshine State" from *Grist* magazine, January 4, 2011. Reprinted by permission of the author.

Jennifer Cockrall-King. "Chicago: The Vertical Farm" from *Food and the City: Urban Agriculture and the New Food Revolution* (Amherst, NY: Prometheus Books, 2012), pp. 263–282. Copyright © 2012 Jennifer Cockrall-King. All rights reserved. Used with permission of the publisher; www.prometheusbooks.com.

Eliot Coleman. "Real Food, Real Farming," September 2001. Reprinted by permission of Eliot Coleman.

Masanobu Fukuoka. "Living by Bread Alone" (pp. 139–141) from *The One-Straw Revolution*. Copyright © 1978 Masanobu Fukuoka. Reprinted by arrangement with the Fukuoka Estate.

Blake Hurst. "The Omnivore's Delusion: Against the Agri-intellectuals" from the *American*, the online magazine of The American Enterprise Institute, July 30, 2009. This article reprinted from The American magazine, a publication of the American Enterprise Institute, www.american.com. Reprinted by permission of American Enterprise Institute.

Michael Idov. "When Did Young People Start Spending 25% of Their Paychecks on Pickled Lamb's Tongues?" by Michael Idov, originally published in the April 2, 2012, issue of *New York* magazine. Reprinted by permission of New York Media.

Dhruv Khullar. "Why Shame Won't Stop Obesity" from *Bioethics Forum*, the blog of *The Hastings Center Report*, first published March 28, 2012. Reprinted from *Bioethics Forum*, the blog of The Hastings Center Report.

Barbara Kingsolver. Excerpt from "You Can't Run Away on Harvest Day" (pp. 219–235) from *Animal, Vegetable, Miracle* by Barbara Kingsolver, Steven L. Hopp, and Camille Kingsolver. Copyright © 2007 Barbara Kingsolver, Steven L. Hopp and Camille Kingsolver. Reprinted by permission of HarperCollins Publishers.

Camille Kingsolver. "Taking Local On the Road" by Camille Kingsolver (pp. 332–333) from *Animal, Vegetable, Miracle* by Barbara Kingsolver, Steven L. Hopp, and Camille Kingsolver. Copyright © 2007 Barbara Kingsolver, Steven L. Hopp, and Camille Kingsolver. Reprinted by permission of HarperCollins Publishers.

Sally Kohn. "Do Foodies Care about Workers?" from *Salon.com*, July 19, 2012. Copyright © 2013 Salon Media Group, Inc. This article first appeared in *Salon.com* at http://www.Salon.com. An online version remains in the Salon archives. Reprinted with permission.

Frances Moore Lappé. "Biotechnology Isn't the Key to Feeding the World" from the *International Herald Tribune*, July 5, 2001. Copyright © 2001 Frances Moore Lappé. Reprinted by permission of Frances Moore Lappé on behalf of Small Planet Institute.

Jill McCorkle. "Her Chee-to Heart" by Jill McCorkle, originally published in *Allure*, August 1996. Copyright © 1996 by Jill McCorkle. All rights reserved. Reprinted by permission.

Bill McKibben. "The Only Way to Have a Cow" from *Orion* magazine, April 2, 2010. Copyright © 2010 Bill McKibben. Reprinted by permission of the author.

Lily Wong. "Eating the Hyphen" from *Gastronomica: The Journal of Food and Culture,* August 1, 2012. Copyright © 2012 University of California Press Journals. Reprinted by permission of University of California Press Journals.

Image Credits

Pages 91–94, © Peter Menzel / menzelphoto.com.
Pages 112–13, U.S. Department of Agriculture.

Index of Authors and Titles